GIRTON COLLEGE STUDIES

EDITED BY LILIAN KNOWLES, LITT.D., READER IN ECONOMIC HISTORY
IN THE UNIVERSITY OF LONDON

No. 3

SIDELIGHTS ON TEUTONIC HISTORY

DURING

THE MIGRATION PERIOD

SIDELIGHTS ON TEUTONIC HISTORY

DURING

THE MIGRATION PERIOD

BEING

STUDIES FROM BEOWULF AND OTHER
OLD ENGLISH POEMS

BY

M. G. CLARKE, M.A.

Cambridge :
at the University Press
1911

CAMBRIDGE UNIVERSITY PRESS
Cambridge, New York, Melbourne, Madrid, Cape Town,
Singapore, São Paulo, Delhi, Mexico City

Cambridge University Press
The Edinburgh Building, Cambridge CB2 8RU, UK

Published in the United States of America by Cambridge University Press, New York

www.cambridge.org
Information on this title: www.cambridge.org/9781107696327

First published 1911
First paperback edition 2013

A catalogue record for this publication is available from the British Library

ISBN 978-1-107-69632-7 Paperback

PREFACE

THE following chapters are the outcome of two periods of study undertaken during the tenure of research scholarships awarded by Girton College, and form an attempt to discover the amount of historical truth underlying the allusions to persons and events in the Old English heroic poems.

The essay deals with an aspect of these poems, which has not, so far as I know, been treated systematically by anyone who has previously written on the subject. Thus, in the absence of any model, I have had to work on independent lines, especially as regards the grouping and arrangement of different traditions, and the method of discussion followed in the several chapters. The actual arrangement has been adopted for convenience of discussion, according to the nationality of the persons concerned, except in cases where a particular section forms a complete epic narrative with a personal (as opposed to a national) interest of its own: in these cases the tradition has been discussed under the heading of the poem in which it is contained, or that of the character round whom the narrative centres.

Each chapter is arranged thus:—

I. An account of the tradition respecting the nation or hero in question, pieced together from the scattered allusions in the poems.

II. The evidence of other authorities dealing with the same traditions or with the same characters.

III. A comparative view of the evidence of these authorities in its relation to the substance of the Old English poems.

IV. A summary of the inferences as to historical truth which may justifiably be deduced from the allusions in the poems.

The positive results obtained are often extremely meagre, and in no case do they make any claim to finality. Though much work has been done in this direction, much still remains: and any value which this study may possess lies chiefly in exploring new possibilities and in indicating the paths along which further research may in time lead to more definite conclusions.

NOTE. In the first three chapters a certain amount of repetition has been inevitable owing to the close relations existing between Swedes, Gautar and Danes, and the frequent necessity of citing the same facts in connection with each.

Some explanation must be added regarding the use of proper names, which may at times appear somewhat inconsistent: each name has, as far as possible, been given in the form in which it occurs in the particular authority under discussion at the moment, e.g. in dealing with English evidence the English form has been given, as 'Beowulf,' 'Offa,' while in citing Scandinavian evidence, the Scandinavian forms have been employed, as 'Boðvar,' 'Uffo,' and so on. (The exceptions to this are well established English forms such as 'Swanhild,' 'Walther.' I have used these wherever possible, usually giving in brackets the particular forms employed by different authorities.) On more neutral ground, viz. sections III and IV of each chapter containing the comparison of evidence and probable historical value of the tradition in question, the most generally accepted form of the name—where possible its English equivalent—has been adopted.

In Scandinavian personal names, it may be added, the final inflexional consonant has been discarded, except in the case of names ending in a vowel.

The subject of the study was originally suggested to me by Mr H. M. Chadwick, Fellow of Clare College, Cambridge: I have been under constant obligation to Mr Chadwick for the help he has given me in the course of my work, and many valuable ideas, which I owe to him, are incorporated in the essay. My thanks are equally due to Professor Napier of Oxford University for assistance especially in the latter stages of the work, including many useful criticisms and suggestions. Many facts regarding Icelandic literature and sociology have been brought to my notice by Miss B. S. Phillpotts, lately Librarian of Girton College. I have also to acknowledge the assistance which I have received from Miss Bentinck Smith, Headmistress of St Leonard's School, St Andrews, formerly Lecturer and Director of Studies in Mediaeval and Modern Languages at Girton College: Mr Eiríkr Magnússon, late Assistant Librarian, Cambridge University Library; Sir W. M. Ramsay, Professor of Humanity in the University of Aberdeen; Mr H. J. C. Grierson, Professor of English Literature in the University of

Aberdeen; my father, Mr John Clarke, Lecturer in Education in the University of Aberdeen, and others: as also the facilities for study and the courtesy and kindness extended to me by the Librarian and Assistants of the Cambridge University Library.

M. G. CLARKE

St Andrews
28 *January* 1911

CONTENTS

LIST OF CHIEF ABBREVIATIONS

Aarb. f. nord. Oldkynd.	*Aarbøger for nordiske Oldkyndighed.*
Abh. d. Berl. Akad.	*Abhandlungen der Berliner Akademie.*
Acad.	*Academy.*
A.f.d.A.	*Anzeiger für deutsches Altertum.*
Alp.	*Alphart's Tod.*
Ammian.	*Ammianus Marcellinus.*
Angl.	*Anglia.*
Ann. Quedl.	*Annals of Quedlinburg.*
Archiv	*Archiv für das Studium der neueren Sprachen und Litteratur.*
Ark. f. nord. Fil.	*Arkiv for nordisk Filologi.*
A. S. Chr.	*Anglo-Saxon Chronicle.*
B.B.z.A.	*Bonner Beiträge zur Anglistik.*
Beo.	*Beowulf.*
Bit.	*Biterolf.*
Bjr.	*Bjarkarímur.*
Dfl.	*Dietrich's Flucht.*
D.H.D.	*Danmarks Heltedigtning.*
D.H.S.	*Deutsche Heldensage.*
E.E.T.S.	*Early English Text Society.*
E.W.S.	*Early West Saxon.*
Eng. St.	*Englische Studien.*
Fas.	*Fornaldar Sǫgur.*
Finn.	*Finn Fragment.*
Gen. Vip.	*Genealogia Viperti (XIIth century).*
Germ.	*Pfeiffer's Germania.*
Get.	*De rebus Getarum (Jordanes).*
Gr.	*Greek.*
Goth.	*De bello Gothico (Procopius).*
Greg. Tur.	*Gregory of Tours.*
Grottas.	*Grottasǫngr.*
H. B. Anh.	*Anhang zum Heldenbuch.*
Hsg.	*Heldensage.*
Hskr. (Heimskr.)	*Heimskringla.*
Hrolfss. (Hrss.)	*Hrolfssaga Kraka.*
Hyndl.	*Hyndluljóð.*
Icel.	*Icelandic.*
Kl. Schr.	*Kleinere Schriften.*

L.W.S.	*Late West Saxon.*
Ld.	*Lied.*
Lex Burg.	*Lex Burgundionum.*
L.G.	*Low German.*
Lgfđg.	*Langfeđgatal.*
Ltg.	*Litteraturgeschichte.*
Mhg.	*Middle High German.*
M.L.N.	*Modern Language Notes.*
Mon. Germ. Hist.	*Monumenta Germaniae Historica (Pertz).*
Nib.	*Nibelungenlied.*
N.R.	*Neue Reihe.*
O.E.	*Old English.*
O.E.T.	*Oldest English Texts.*
Ohg.	*Old High German.*
O.N.	*Old Norse.*
Paul Grdr.	*Paul's Grundriss der germanischen Philologie.*
P.B.B.	*Paul und Braune's Beiträge zur Geschichte der Sprache und Litteratur.*
Procop.	*Procopius.*
Q.F.	*Quellen und Forschungen.*
Rab.	*Rabenschlacht.*
Scand.	*Scandinavian.*
Skáldsk.	*Skáldskapermál.*
Sn. Ed.	*Snorra Edda.*
S.R.D.	*Scriptores Rerum Danicarum.*
Sv. Aag.	*Sven Aagesen.*
Thđs.	*Thiđrekssaga.*
Verhandl. d. Wien. Phil. Vers.	*Verhandlungen des Wiener Philosophischen Vereins.*
Vǫlss.	*Vǫlsungasaga.*
Wald.	*Waldere.*
Wids.	*Widsith.*
Wiener S. B.	*Wiener Sitzungsberichte der königlichen Akademie der Wissenschaften.*
Yngls.	*Ynglingasaga.*
Z.f.d.A.	*Zeitschrift für deutsches Altertum.*
Z.P.H.	*Zeitschrift für deutsche Philologie.*

INTRODUCTORY CHAPTER

About the middle of the fifth century, bands of Teutonic invaders began to land on the south-east coasts of Britain. The flow of immigration, once started, continued steadily for the next hundred years, and by the end of the sixth century the new-comers had conquered and colonized a great part of the southern half of Britain, pushing the Celtic population westward into the mountainous recesses of Cornwall, Wales and Cumberland. These Teutonic invaders appear, according to the latest authority*, to have been of two distinct nationalities, viz. Anglo-Saxon and Jutish, who migrated across the sea to Britain from Jutland and Schleswig-Holstein. The Jutes, who were numerically in the minority, seem very soon to have lost their national identity and to have become incorporated with the Anglo-Saxon tribes; for their name does not long survive, and in the end of the ninth century we find King Alfred writing—presumably with reference to the whole population—of the nation as *Angelcynn* and their language as *Englisc*. At the time of the migration the English were still heathen, but Christianity was introduced in 597, the date of Pope Gregory the Great's first mission

* Cf. Mr H. M. Chadwick, *The Origin of the English Nation*, pp. 88 ff.

to Kent, after which the new faith spread steadily through-out the country.

The settlement of Teutonic tribes in Britain was one of the products of the Great Age of National Migrations, which corresponds roughly to the fourth, fifth and sixth centuries. These stirring times, when life meant warfare and every man was a warrior, gave birth to " hero saga," —the record of the lives and exploits of great kings or other national heroes—usually in the form of song. Our Teutonic ancestors, like other nations, delighted in such songs, which were probably performed before them at banquets and on similar occasions. These—still of course in an unwritten state—were carried in the mouths and memories of the people from the continent to their new home, where they very soon attained literary form. Thus, during the first centuries of our forefathers' occupation of England, signs are found of the existence of an heroic, national poetry—essentially heathen in tone—which has its roots in the Migration Period, and therefore goes back to a time previous to the Teutonic Invasion of Britain. There is considerable ground for believing that the poems, as they stand, are the work of professional court minstrels rather than of regular literary men, and in the case of two of them—*Widsith* and *Deor*—we have indeed definite statements to this effect. But in no event are the poems to be regarded as popular; that is, in their present form they do not represent merely the transmission of a common stock of oral tradition amongst the untaught masses of the people; they are the highly-finished productions of men trained to their art, and are probably, in almost every case, to all practical intents the work of single poets. Judging from the—for the most part fragmentary—

survival of our early heroic national poetry, it seems likely that only a small part of it has been preserved, but notwithstanding this, our literature is richer in this respect than that of any other Teutonic nation, and is unique in the possession of one complete great epic poem dating from this period, viz. the *Beowulf*.

The Old English heroic poems possess then more than a purely literary interest: they are full of allusions to persons, events and traditions of a distant, almost prehistoric age. These allusions are, however, for the most part, of such an obscure and fragmentary nature as to be at times unintelligible, while their interpretation presents in every case a considerable amount of difficulty.

The names of some of the characters which occur in the poems are known to us in history, and for one or two of the events alluded to or described we have also a sure background of historical fact; but the majority of the persons referred to, with the deeds ascribed to them, are known to us only from the popular traditions and sagas of other nations, while some again are unknown from any other source whatever.

The *Beowulf*, which is by far the most important specimen of early English national poetry, is an epic poem of 3183 lines. The MS., which is preserved in the British Museum, dates from the tenth century. In view of the many excellent descriptions of the *Beowulf* which already exist it is not proposed to give here more than the briefest outline of the argument of the poem : those who have the misfortune to be unacquainted with its contents are referred to any good history of English literature, where a full account of it will be found.

The scene of the poem is laid entirely in Baltic

lands: the hero Beowulf belonged to the people of the Geatas (i.e. Götar), who occupied the southern part of Sweden*, but the action of the most important part of the poem takes place in Denmark, at the court of the Danish king, Hrothgar. Lines 1–63 trace the descent of the Danish kings from their earliest ancestor, Scyld Scêfing, down to Hrothgar, who was then on the throne. Lines 64–2199 relate how Beowulf, a noble warrior and the nephew of King Hygelac of the Geatas, freed King Hrothgar's court from the ravages of two monsters of the fens—Grendel and his mother—by killing them both, and how he returned home from the Danish court, covered with glory and laden with rich gifts. This section of the poem contains several important episodes dealing with persons and events not directly concerned in the story. The chief of these are: the so-called Finn episode (ll. 1068–1159), containing the story of Hnaef and Finn (cf. Ch. v), the passage referring to Thrytho, the wife of Offa (ll. 1931–1962), and an account of the relations between the Danish kings Hrothgar and Hrothulf (Hrothgar's nephew and joint occupant of the throne with him) and the princes of the Heathobeardan Froda and Ingeld (ll. 2020–2069).

Some years after the events recorded in the first part of the *Beowulf*, Hygelac fell in battle—as we hear later on, he was killed in the land of the Frisians, while Beowulf escaped by swimming (ll. 2354–2372). He was succeeded by his son Heardred, who, however, was slain by the Swedish king Onela, for having given sanctuary

---

* I.e. with the exception of Skåne and, probably, Halland, which belonged to Denmark. Blekinge belonged to Denmark in the eleventh century and later, but at the time of Wulfstan's voyage (Alfred's *Orosius*) it seems to have belonged to Sweden.

and showed kindness to Onela's nephews Eanmund and Eadgils. Beowulf then became king of Geatland. He assisted Eadgils to take vengeance on his uncle Onela, and reigned gloriously over his people for fifty years. At the end of that time he was killed, as the result of a fight with a fiery dragon, whose ravages had reduced the whole land to a state of misery. Beowulf was successful in slaying the monster, and in setting free the hoards of hidden treasure over which it kept guard, but he was mortally wounded in the combat. His body was burnt on a huge funeral pyre, and over his ashes a large barrow was erected, in which was placed all the treasure found in the dragon's den. The poem ends with a panegyric on the dead king, spoken by twelve warriors who rode round his barrow (ll. 2373–3183). The chief digression from the direct course of the narrative in the last section of the poem deals with the past history of the royal family of the Geatas.

Of equal importance with the *Beowulf*, though very much shorter, is *Widsith**, a poem of 143 lines, chiefly of a narrative character, though it cannot, like the *Beowulf*, claim the name of epic. The poem is an account of the fortunes of a professional minstrel (such minstrels, as we have seen, flourished during the Migration Period), told by himself under the figurative name of Widsith ("the Far-Travelled"). In the prologue of the poem, the singer tells that he belonged to the people of the Myrgingas, and that, in company with a princess named Ealhhild, he visited the court of the Gothic king Eormenric. From l. 10 onwards he gives a list of the chief nations and kings known to him, with special reference to any deeds of note

* MS. *Exeter Book.*

which are associated with their names*. In l. 50 the poet resumes the thread of his narrative, and gives a further account of his travels, again enumerating the nations whom he has visited. He also tells of his own skill in song, and of the gifts which he received from Guthhere, king of the Burgundians, from Alboin in Italy, from Eormenric, king of the Goths, and from Eadgils, his own patron, the prince of the Myrgingas. Then follows a list of the chief Gothic heroes whom the poet visited, most of whom are known to us from other sources: two of these, Wudga and Hama, are treated at somewhat greater length than the rest, on account of their great prowess. The poem closes with a short epilogue containing reflections on the lives and fortunes of travelling singers.

The great importance of *Widsith* for the history of the Migration Period lies in the catalogues of kings and nations incorporated in the poem, which in many cases confirm the evidence of other authorities. The poet has apparently gone on the principle of naming in every case the *most famous* king of the nation or tribe in question, irrespective of time considerations ; for many of the persons mentioned side by side with one another are, as we shall see, separated from each other in history by large spaces of time.

The remainder of Old English heroic poetry consists but of three fragments, *Finn*†, *Waldere*‡ and *Deor*§, of which the first two are also epic. The *Finn* fragment is apparently part of a lost epic, which—if we can make any

---

* Many of these are already familiar figures, while others are quite unknown.

† MS. lost.   ‡ MS. in Royal Library, Copenhagen.

§ MS. *Exeter Book.*

surmises from the *Beowulf*—was probably of considerable length. It deals with the same story as that referred to in the so-called Finn episode of the *Beowulf* (ll. 1068–1159). (Cf. Ch. v, pp. 177 ff.)

The other two poems, *Waldere* and *Deor*, go off into quite a new field for their subject-matter. The two *Waldere* fragments—presumably like *Finn*, part of an epic poem—deal with the Walthari saga, of which several continental (chiefly German) versions exist: this saga was a very favourite theme of song and story on the continent all through the Middle Ages. (Cf. Ch. vii, B.)

Deor's Lament is a short elegy and the only Old English poem in strophic form which has survived: like *Widsith* it purports to be the work of a court minstrel, but, in marked contrast to that poem, is an outburst of grief, describing the troubles attending a singer's career, and the misfortunes which have fallen in his later life on the minstrel himself, who has been ousted from his office as bard of the Heodeningas by a rival singer. The value of the poem for us lies in the references made by the poet to well-known characters of the Heroic Age, whose misfortunes he cites in order to illustrate his own unhappy state. The poem consists of six strophes of unequal length, each of which ends with the refrain *Thaes ofereode, thisses swâ maeg!* ("That came to an end, this may likewise").

Old English, like other early northern poetry, is written in alliterative metre, and it is generally supposed that all old Teutonic poetry, in addition to being alliterative, was strophic. The extant Old Norse heroic poems are without exception in this form, and there are distinct traces of a similar structure in *Widsith*, while in *Deor* the division into strophes is made quite clear by the recurrence —unique in Old English poetry—of a lyrical refrain at the end of each.   Strenuous attempts have been made to reconstruct the *Beowulf* in strophic form, but so far without success*.

We have evidence for only the most general conclusions with regard to the age of the Old English heroic poems. None of the MSS. date from before the tenth century, but the poems themselves belong without doubt to a very much earlier period, for the subject-matter of all of them, as we have seen, relates to the continental period of our nation's history.

The *Beowulf*, as will be seen more clearly at a later stage, contains no reference to any event known to have taken place after the middle of the sixth century, and there is, further, no evidence of communication between England and the Baltic lands for about two hundred years onward from that time.   It is a reasonable presumption, therefore, that all the information regarding the persons and events celebrated in the *Beowulf* had reached England by the middle of the sixth century, and that the materials for the poem and even songs on the subject were already in circulation within the next fifty years, that is, before the close of the century.

Yet another circumstance has to be taken into account in determining the probable age of the *Beowulf*.   All the ceremonies described in the poem are heathen, and the poet is perfectly conversant with heathen rites. An instance in point is the practice of cremation, which is described in detail (ll. 3110–3183).   Now this practice must have died out early in England, for we nowhere hear of the

* Cf. also *Cambridge History of English Literature*, p. 219.

Christian missionaries forbidding it, as they did elsewhere, and as they certainly would have done in England, had the occasion arisen. As missionary activity spread very quickly over England after the introduction of Christianity in 597, it is therefore difficult, taking this and other circumstances into account, to place the composition of the *Beowulf*, as a whole, later than the earlier part of the seventh century (c. 630)*. The Christian invocations and other passages were probably added when objection began to be made to the heathen background of the poem. There are difficulties in the way of assigning the composition of the *Beowulf* to any one part of England, but the language of the poem seems on the whole to indicate that the first MS. was of Anglian origin.

The *Widsith* can make perhaps a claim to even greater antiquity than the *Beowulf*. The poet represents himself as contemporary with Ermanric, the great king of the Ostrogoths, who is known to have died c. 375 (Amm. Marc. XXXI. 3, 1), and characters belonging to the same period predominate in the poem. But there are also references of a later date, and the latest-known historical character alluded to (in the poem) is Alboin (O.E. Aelfwine), king of Lombardy, who died c. 572 (cf. Paulus Diac. *Hist. Langob.* I, 27). The most recent hypothesis with regard to the composition of *Widsith*† is that it is based on the work of an unknown fourth-century minstrel: this existing nucleus was at a later time added to and enlarged, with the idea of following out the earlier poet's

---

* For a different view, cf. L. Morsbach, " Zur Datierung des Beowulf Epos " (aus den *Nachrichten der k. Gesellschaft der Wissenschaften zu Göttingen*, 1906).

† Cf. *Cambridge History of English Literature*, I, p. 36.

apparent intention, and making the poem a kind of encyclopaedia of national heroes and their deeds. As such, in fact, it is invaluable to us, for no poem goes further back in its description of persons and events of the Heroic Age than *Widsith.*

Little positive evidence can be adduced regarding the date of composition of *Finn, Waldere* and *Deor.* There is nothing to prevent us assigning them to the same period as *Beowulf* and *Widsith*, for they contain very few allusions to events which took place even as late as the first half of the sixth century, and if the account of the authorship of *Deor* which we possess is reliable, the poem must be of very great age indeed. In any case it seems improbable that the composition of any of the Old English heroic poems is to be placed later than the first part of the seventh century. The Christian element present in the poems is quite foreign to their main structure and tendency, and may probably be attributed to monastic revision at a later date, which revision did not, however, otherwise affect their form or contents to any appreciable extent.

It may be thought that too much space has been devoted to a consideration of the age of these poems, but the question is an important one, inasmuch as it is just their age which determines their value as historical evidence. What we have learned so far on this point only increases our regard for the poems as amongst the most reliable documentary evidence which we possess regarding the events of the Migration Period, and the circumstantial nature of the facts which they relate tends to show, further, that their contents were not regarded in any way as accounts of legendary or mythical exploits, but as records of the most recent history, which had a claim on the attention and interest of the nation as a whole.

About a hundred years ago the scholastic world awoke to the existence of the Old English heroic poems, which have proved themselves a most fruitful subject of study and discussion ever since. It is difficult to estimate the amount of erudition and industry which has been lavished on these poems—on their every line and almost every word—chiefly by foreign authors. The pioneers in this study were Thorkelin and Grundtvig, Danish scholars, and Kemble, an Englishman, to whom we owe the first really critical edition of the *Beowulf* and *Widsith* in 1833. Kemble's edition was only superseded in 1857 by Grein's, which included all the heroic poems in addition to many others, and which—revised by R. P. Wülcker, 1881–3— has remained the standard edition up to the present time notwithstanding the presence of many rivals in the field *.

It is impossible here to do more than very briefly touch on the work of one or two of the principal writers on this subject. Besides those already mentioned, the names of Grimm, H. Möller, Ten Brink, Sarrazin, Bugge, Olrik, and above all, Müllenhoff, stand out from amongst a host of scholars who have made these poems, and in particular the *Beowulf*, the subject of special study. The first impulse towards the systematic historical investigation of the *Beowulf* was given at an early stage, for by 1820 Grundtvig had discovered the identity of Hygelac, king of the Geatas, who figures in the poem, with Chochilaicus, whom the historian Gregory of Tours reports to

* For chief *Beowulf* editions, cf. Bibliography at end of book.

have been killed by the Franks c. 520[*]. Thus one time-point in the story was fixed, and interest in this aspect of the poems having been once aroused, soon developed in the works of Kemble, Grein, Müllenhoff and many others. Curious, hitherto-unnoticed coincidences of names and of descriptions and events between the Old English poems and continental—chiefly Scandinavian—poems, sagas, and historical works of a later date began to be discovered, and when attention had been called to these, the clues were followed up—and are still being followed—with great zeal and with excellent results throughout the whole of early Teutonic literature.   Much information valuable for the interpretation of the Old English poems has also been obtained from the works of early historians (cf. *inf.* p. 23).

The poems, owing to the extremely meagre data which exist concerning them, offer a wide field for conjecture, of which in some cases full advantage has certainly been taken ; for Grundtvig, Sarrazin, Bugge and others go even the length of attributing a Scandinavian origin to the *Beowulf*! As a rule too, great weight has been laid on the mythological aspect of the *Beowulf*, which has sometimes indeed been allowed to overshadow its historical significance[†]. Of all those who have approached the poem from this side the greatest is probably Müllenhoff. His view, which has been shared by many others, but which in the light of subsequent study it is very difficult to accept, is that Beowulf's exploits against Grendel and his mother are of purely mythical interest, although Beowulf

* Grundtvig, *Bjowulf's Drape*, Copenhagen, 1820.
† This remark is specially applicable to the works of Kemble, Leo and Ettmüller.

in his relation to Hygelac, Hrothgar, etc. is probably to be regarded as an historical figure.   There is still a tendency amongst many scholars to emphasize the mythical element in the poems, and though there can be no doubt that such an element is present in them, it is equally certain that its importance has been much over-rated in the past. Although much has been done along the lines of the historical investigation of the English heroic poems, much still remains to do : but the good results already obtained give promise of a not too far distant time when research shall have firmly established their position as historical documents, as well as the actual value of the characters and events which they describe.

NOTE.—In the following chapters there will be frequent occasion to quote, and otherwise refer to, works of Scandinavian origin.   It has therefore been thought desirable to add to this chapter a brief survey of Old Norse literature.   This section can make, however, no claim to completeness, as it only professes to deal with those works of Old Norwegian and Old Icelandic literature which contribute in some way towards the elucidation of the Old English heroic poems.

OUTLINE SKETCH OF OLD NORSE LITERATURE*.

The expression "Old Norse" is commonly used as a generic term to cover both Old Norwegian and Old Icelandic literature : for the latter, as it were, grew out of and inherited the greatness of the former.   Iceland

* The materials for this section have been drawn from F. Jonsson, *Den oldnorske Litteraturs Historie*, 2 Bd. Copenhagen, 1898–1902, and E. Mogk, in Paul's *Grundriss*, Vol. II, pp. 71—142.

was politically an offspring of Norway, and was founded in the last quarter of the ninth century (870), by those Norwegian chiefs who were dissatisfied with the newly assumed supremacy of Harold Fair-Hair, and who left their country in order to obtain freedom in voluntary exile.   The new democratic state founded on the western shores of Iceland enjoyed complete political independence for four centuries: but during that time, although they refused to acknowledge Norwegian supremacy, the Icelanders never lost their "national Norwegian self-consciousness," but preserved throughout a close bond of union with the mother-country.   Movements, begun in Norway, developed and came to fruition in Iceland.   The history of culture and literature in the two countries during these centuries cannot be separated, for it really forms one continuous growth, towards which the existence up to the twelfth century of a common language was a powerful contributory factor.

The literary, like the political history of Norway, does not really begin until the ninth century, and in O.N. literature three periods are clearly distinguishable, the outstanding features of which may be tabulated as follows:

I.   Scaldic Period.

> From the beginning of historical times, i.e. c. 850–1100.
>
> *Edda* and scaldic poems.

II.   Saga Period.

> c. 1100–c. 1300.
> Original prose works, viz. sagas and laws.
> Translations: revisions of sagas.

III. Copying and Collecting Period.
    c. 1300–c. 1450.
        (1) Copying and collecting of older works.
        (2) Writing of annals and rhyming poems.

I. The *Edda* Poems are anonymous poems in simple metre, the subjects of which were first drawn from the ancient northern mythological system, and later on—like O.E. heroic poetry—from hero saga. In view of their language and metre these poems are assigned by the best authority to various dates between c. 850 and c. 1050. The great majority are probably of Norwegian origin, and they appear—once more like the O.E. heroic poems—to have been the work of professional minstrels. Closely allied to, and a secondary development of Eddic poetry, was scaldic song, which was, however, of a much more formal and elaborate nature. The scaldic poems also made use of oral tradition, mythology and hero saga, but unlike those of the *Edda*, which were of general import, they always celebrated the person or deeds of a king or prince, and thus had a special significance.

The scalds, in fact, probably cultivated their art fully as much from a practical as from a poetic point of view, as a young warrior immediately made a name and procured himself advancement by the composition of songs in praise of his master.

We are here directly concerned with only a few of the Eddic poems. Undoubtedly one of the oldest of them is *Skírnismál*[1], dating probably from c. 900. It is an ardent love poem and relates how the God Frey passionately loved a maiden named Gerda, and how he at last won her love in return.

Vǫlundarqviða[1] belongs to almost the same period as *Skirnismál*. It dates, according to Finnur Jonsson, from the first quarter of the tenth century, and deals with one aspect of the well-known Wêland saga. Of later date, from the second half of the tenth century, is *Grottasǫngr*[1], the mill-song sung by two giant handmaidens, who grind out, first wealth and peace but then death and destruction, to the tyrant king their master who will grant them no rest from their labours (cf. p. 75). The poem unites myth with hero saga, and the story of the mill seems to symbolize the Golden Age of peace and security, before the entrance of discord.

Hyndluljóð[1], which in contents forms a transition from myth to hero saga, belongs to approximately the same date as *Grottas*. It is the account of a conversation between the Goddess Freyja and the giantess Hyndla, and its importance for us lies in the genealogies of various families which Hyndla recites at the request of the Goddess.

A number of the Eddic poems deal with the exploits of Sigurð, the dragon-slayer—the famous Siegfried of German hero saga. Sigurð, although of little importance in the present connection, was one of the chief heroic figures of the Migration Period, and as such necessarily enters to some extent into any attempt to reconstruct the history of that period.

We must finally note the fragmentary *Bjarkamál*[2] which appears to have been originally a poem celebrating the death of Bǫðvar-Bjarki, the famous warrior of the Danish king Hrolf Kraki, but of which only a few lines have been preserved.

The only two specimens of scaldic poetry to which we shall have to refer are *Eíríksmál* and *Hákonarmál*, both of which have, in theme and treatment, much in common with the heroic poems of the *Edda*. The former is an anonymous poem on the death of King Eric Blood-Axe (A.D. 950), composed by order of his widow. *Hákonarmál* is a similar poem—in fact an imitation of *Eíríksmál*—in honour of King Hákon the Good (A.D. 961), written by the scald Eyvind Fimsson, the devoted follower of Hákon and himself of royal blood. Both poems follow the device common to scaldic poetry of deriving the genealogy of the prince in question from the Gods, and of connecting him with the life in Valhalla. Eyvind was one of the last great Norwegian scalds, for by the end of the tenth century, scaldic poetry had emigrated to the new settlement in Iceland, which was henceforth regarded as its home *. Up to this time, i.e. for about a hundred years after the first settlers landed in Iceland, the process of colonization and settling of the land had continued. It was only now, when a period of comparative peace succeeded that of internal dissension, that the age of Iceland's literary greatness began, culminating at the end of the twelfth and the first half of the thirteenth century in the works of Snorri and Sturla.

II. The Saga Period, c. 1100–c. 1300, is the Golden Age of Northern literature. The historical prose saga was a distinctively Icelandic growth, and arose from the Icelanders' love of recording their genealogies, and from the weight which they laid on a good pedigree. These narratives of individuals or of families were told first as a

---

* In *Brávallakvad*, the song of the Battle of Brávalla, which is contained in Saxo's history (see beginning of Book VIII) and there attributed to Starkad, Dr Olrik sees the remains of a Norwegian scaldic poem, dating probably from about the middle of the eleventh century.

means of entertainment (*at skemta*) round the fire on
the long winter evenings, but they are of enormous
historical and sociological importance, for almost all we
know of northern family and intellectual life, culture,
architecture, and heathen religion is derived from them.

The climax of the period was reached in the work of
Snorri Sturlason, perhaps the greatest figure in the whole
history of O.N. literature.   Snorri lived from 1178–1241.
To his great literary ability he added civic distinction,
and was well known both as a politician and diplomatist.
Snorri was greatest as a prose writer and pre-eminently
as an historian, for not only did he test all his sources
most carefully, but he possessed the power—invaluable
to the writing of good history—of discriminating between
true and false, between good authority and bad.   His
greatest work is *Heimskringla*[3], which belongs to the
period 1220–1230.   The title of the work means "the
Globe," and it is a history of the kings of Norway from
the earliest times up to the year 1177, based partly on
tradition, partly on scaldic verses and partly on previous
written works.   *Heimskringla* is composed of a series of
single sagas, but these Snorri has skilfully linked up to
form one complete whole.   The first of them is *Ynglingasaga*, being an account of the earliest kings of south
Norway and their Swedish ancestors, and forming a kind
of introduction to the work.   It is based on the *Ynglinga-
tal* of the scaldic poet Thjodolf, who lived about the end
of the ninth century.   The only other section of *Hskr.* to
which we shall have to refer is *St Ólafssaga*, containing
the history of the reign of St Olaf (1016–1029).

Snorri, in addition to his other claims to fame, was a
poet of some note, but he lived at a time when scaldic

poetry had become highly artificial, and his own verses owe more to art than to inspiration : they are remarkable for their technical skill, and the author's intimate knowledge of prosody and the laws of versification is further manifested in the prose *Edda*. The *Edda* is a treatise in three parts illustrative of the art of poetry. The first part—*Gylfaginning*—contains a survey of northern mythology, and a description of the courses of the world and of nature. The second and third parts—*Skáldskaparmál* and *Háttatal*—are concerned with the nature of poetry, and deal, as their names imply*, with language and metre respectively. *Skáldskaparmál* ("poetical diction") illustrates, by examples drawn from myth and hero saga, the peculiar figures of speech, and in particular the "kennings," i.e. artificial circumlocutions, commonly used by the scalds. *Háttatal* is a poem illustrating by example every known kind of metre. The *Edda*, which was completed about 1222, still holds its own as an excellent handbook on the language and technique of the verse of that time. It is systematic and well arranged, and Snorri has brought to bear on his materials great knowledge, a love of his subject, and much critical insight.

In *Hskr.* and the prose *Edda* Snorri refers to one of his authorities as the *Skjǫldungasaga*. The greater part of this work is lost ; a sixteenth-century scholar, Arngrim Jonsson, has, however, preserved some fragments of it which he published in 1597 under the title *Rerum Danicarum Fragmenta* (repr. *Aarb. f. nord. Oldk.* 1894). *Skjǫlds.* was probably composed about 1200; it is believed to have contained an account of the earliest kings of Den-

* *Skáldskapr*—scaldship ; *mál*—speech, i.e. the speech of poetry. *Háttr*—metre ; *tal*—list, i.e. a list of metres.

mark, and may very possibly have been intended as a prologue to a history of the kings of Denmark. It would thus form a parallel to *Ynglingasaga,* which stands as a prologue to *Heimskringla* the history of the kings of Norway. This work, could it be recovered, would be of very great value to us, for it seems likely that the relations between Denmark and Sweden during the period covered by the action of the *Beowulf,* as represented not only by Snorri but by all works subsequent to c. 1200, were derived from this source.

By the thirteenth century the decay of the saga had already set in in Iceland, largely on account of (*a*) a prevalent literary tendency to compile and add to already existing materials, and (*b*) a growing taste for the French mediaeval romances. This led to the introduction of all sorts of extraneous matter into the sagas, often of an extravagant nature, and the historical sense, the sincerity and truthfulness, which had hitherto been their outstanding characteristic, became in great part lost. *Grettissaga*[5] and *Ormsþáttr Stórólfsson*[6], both composed about the year 1300, are examples of this tendency. The groundwork of both sagas is historical, but many folk-tales and legendary traits are introduced, which gives them a romantic and altogether post-classical tone.

The chief product of the post-classical saga period in Iceland consists of the so-called *Fornaldar Sǫgur*[7], i.e. Old-Time Sagas. These dealt with historical, pseudo-historical or purely fictitious characters, and were usually compiled from a number of single episodes: *sat sammen* was the phrase employed to describe their composition. The *Fornaldar Sǫgur* cannot, like the historical sagas, be considered reliable, for they were designed merely to amuse, and drew largely on myth and fairy lore for their contents. Many of them also took their materials from foreign sources. There is some evidence for the existence of the *Fornaldar Sǫgur* as early as the twelfth century, but they were probably first committed to paper in the latter half of the thirteenth, as for long they were not considered worthy of being written down. We shall have to take account of several of these in our present survey.

The *Thiðrekssaga*[8] deals with the life and deeds of Thiðrek, i.e. Dietrich of Bern, the great figure of German hero saga. The chief sources of this saga were probably songs and stories which were carried to Scandinavian lands by North German traders at the end of the twelfth and beginning of the thirteenth century. These materials were collected and worked up into a complete saga probably before the middle of the thirteenth century. The composition of the *Thiðrekssaga* may have been due in part to the love of chivalry and of the saga of chivalry which prevailed in the north during the reign of Hákon the Old (1217–1263); on the other hand, it reacted en current taste by increasing a love of foreign literature, and thus affected indirectly both literary language and style.

One of the best of the *Fornaldar Sǫgur (Fas.)* in style and composition is the *Hervarar oc Heiðrekssaga*[7], which in the trenchant simplicity of its language and characterisation recalls the poems of the older *Edda*. A good deal of the action of the story takes place amongst the Huns and Goths, and the saga is unique amongst the *Fas.* in the information which it gives about these peoples.

Hrolfssaga Kraka[7] is a compilation of several detached episodes dating in its present form probably from the later fourteenth century. The work is lacking in unity, and several of its episodes have little direct connection with the king from whom it takes its name. The saga must without doubt at one time have existed in an earlier and better form.

Sǫrlaþáttr[7], which is in some MSS. more rightly entitled "Sagas about Heðin and Hǫgni," is peculiar on account of its mythical framework, which, although corrupt, is doubtless derived from old tradition. It cannot date from before the first half of the fourteenth century.

III. *Bjarkarímur*[9] ("The Rhymes of Bjarki") deals with the same set of events as those which form the subject matter of the *Hrolfss.*, and is the only rhyming poem which falls under our consideration. It belongs to c. 1400, and, judging from its language and metre, belongs to the oldest group of rhymes. The form of tradition contained in *Bjr.* is nearly related to that of *Skjǫlds.*, and the authority of the poem is, therefore, valuable.

The *Flateyjarbók*[10], which takes its name from the island of Flatey to the north of Iceland, is a great collection of sagas about Norwegian kings, written, or rather compiled, from older sources by two Icelandic priests between the years 1387 and 1395. It also contains annals up to the year 1394. The *Flateyjarbók*, in spite of many defects, still remains a most valuable authority for the history of Norwegian politics and culture.

Landnámabók. *Landnámabók* is really an inventory of Iceland from the time of its first colonization, but contains many anecdotes and tales in addition to the names and genealogies of the settlers. The book exists in three texts, by different authors, all from the twelfth century, and the original compilation of the work underlying these must have been made about the beginning of that century.

There is still another class of authorities from whose works has been obtained much information valuable for the interpretation of the Old English poems, viz. professed historical writers, but these are difficult to characterise collectively, as they belong to a variety of ages and nationalities. The earliest of them are Tacitus and Pliny in the end of the first century, while the latest to whom we shall have occasion to refer are a little group of mediaeval Danish historians who flourished about 1200, and the chief of whom was Saxo Grammaticus. All these early chroniclers, being learned men, wrote in the learned tongues, viz. Greek or Latin. For our subject Saxo far surpasses any of the others in importance. His great work *Historia Danica*[12] carries back the history of Denmark to the very earliest times. The first books are probably chiefly based on oral tradition, and form a history of northern myth and saga the importance of which it is difficult to over-estimate.

N.B.—The German poems and sagas, to which reference may be made in the following pages, are generally known, and it has, therefore, not been considered necessary to add here any description of them.

1. *Edda Saemundar*, ed. Th. Möbius. Leipzig, 1860.
2. *Corpus Poeticum Boreale*, ed. Vigfússon and Powell. Oxford, 1883. Vol. I, p. 188.
3. *Heimskringla, Noregs Konunga Sǫgur*, ed. F. Jonsson. Copenhagen, 1893–1900.

4. *Snorra Edda*, ed. Thorleifr Jonsson.   Copenhagen, 1875.
5. *Altnordische Saga-Bibliothek*, vols. VIII and IX, ed. Boer.   Halle, 1900.
6. *Flateyjarbók*, vol. I, pp. 521–532, see below.
7. *Fornaldar Sǫgur Nordrlanda*, ed. Rafn.   Copenhagen, 1829.
   Hervarar oc Heiðrekssaga, vol. I, pp. 409 ff.
   Hrolfssaga Kraka, vol. I, pp. 1 ff.
   Sǫrla þáttr, vol. I, pp. 389 ff.
   Vǫlssungasaga, vol. I, pp. 113 ff.
8. *Saga Thiðreks konungs af Bern*, ed. C. R. Unger.   Christiania, 1853.
9. *Hrolfssaga Kraka* and *Bjarkarímur*, ed. F. Jonsson.   Copenhagen, 1904.
10. *Flateyjarbók*, ed. C. R. Unger.   Christiania, 1868.
11. *Landnámabók*, ed. F. Jonsson.   Copenhagen, 1900.
12. *Saxonis Grammatici Gesta Danorum*, ed. A. Holder.   Strassburg, 1886.   Books I–IX, translated into English by O. Elton.   Nutt.   London, 1894.

CHAPTER I

THE GEATAS.

I. THE GEATAS IN BEOWULF AND WIDSITH.

A prominent part is played in *Beowulf* by the Geatas. Beowulf himself, whose exploits form the subject of the poem, belonged to the royal family of the Geatas on his mother's side, and other members of the same family occur frequently throughout the poem.

The scattered references to the Geatas when collected and arranged yield a fairly connected, although meagre, account of the history of this people during the period with which the poem deals. The account of Beowulf's expedition against Grendel forms a complete epic narrative, which is quite independent of the fortunes of the royal family of the Geatas, and will, therefore, be discussed separately.

The Geatas are merely mentioned in passing by the Widsith poet: the traveller speaks of having visited them in the course of his travels (*Wids.* ll. 57 f.).

The genealogy of the royal family of the Geatas appears from *Beowulf* to have been as follows:

```
            Hrethel                        Hæreth
     ┌────────┴──────────────────┐   ┌───────┴──────┐
  daughter  Herebeald  Haethcyn  Hygelac=Hygd  Hereric?  Wonrêd
 =Ecgtheow                       └──┬──┘       └───┬────────┘
     │                       Heardred  daughter=Eofor
  Beowulf
```

The first king of the Geatas of whom there is explicit mention is Hrethel. Hrethel's son Hygelac is described as *nefa Swertings* (l. 1203), but as the meaning of the word *nefa* varies in A.S. this expression is too vague for us to draw any definite conclusions as to the relationship between Hrethel and Swerting.

King Hrethel had three sons, Herebeald, Haethcyn, and Hygelac, and one daughter who was married to Ecgtheow and became the mother of Beowulf (ll. 373–5). At the age of seven Beowulf was adopted by his grandfather, Hrethel, and brought up with the royal princes his young uncles (ll. 2428 ff.). Hrethel's eldest son, Herebeald, was accidentally killed by an arrow shot by his brother, Haethcyn, and this occurrence preyed upon the mind of King Hrethel to such an extent that he died of a broken heart (ll. 2435–2471). He was succeeded by Haethcyn, whose reign does not, however, seem to have been of long duration. It appears that shortly after Hrethel's death, strife broke out between the Geatas and the Swedes (*Svear*), but the course of the campaign is obscure. The sons of Ongentheow, king of Sweden, made a series of raids on the territory of the Geatas in the neighbourhood of Hreosna-beorh (ll. 2472–2478), and Haethcyn apparently retaliated by carrying war into the heart of the enemy's country, in the course of which he succeeded in taking prisoner Ongentheow's queen. Ongentheow then appears to have sallied out against the Geatas before they had time to get away with their spoil. In a great battle near Hrefnesholt he regained his queen and killed Haethcyn. Haethcyn's younger brother, Hygelac, then assumed chief command of the Geatas, and showed conspicuous bravery by marching into the wood and rescuing Haethcyn's troops, which had been surrounded there by Ongentheow after the fall of their leader. This exploit turned the tide of events, and, the army of the Geatas having been relieved, a second battle immediately took place, in which the Swedes began to get the worst of it, and fell back, pursued by the Geatas, Ongentheow being singled out for attack by the brothers Wulf and Eofor. Wulf and Ongentheow met first and Ongentheow felled his opponent with a blow; this was, however, quickly avenged by Eofor, who, with one mighty stroke, clove the skull of the Swedish king. After the victorious home-coming of the Geatas, Hygelac rewarded Wulf and Eofor for their services with gifts of treasure and land, while to Eofor he also gave his only daughter in marriage (ll. 2479–2489, 2922–3007).

Hygelac's wife was Hygd, the daughter of Hæreth (l. 1929): but as, after Beowulf's return from Heorot, she is spoken of as "the very young Hygd" (l. 1926), it seems impossible that she should have had a daughter of marriageable age at the beginning of her husband's reign. The question, therefore, arises, whether Hygd was not the second wife of Hygelac, and the latter had not a previous wife, of whom we hear nothing in the *Beowulf*.

There is no further reference in the poem to any events of Hygelac's reign previous to his fatal expedition against the Franks, Frisians, and Hugas, but Beowulf's visit to the court of Hrothgar, and his exploit in killing the monster Grendel, must, of course, belong to this interval.

Various scattered and fragmentary references are made in the poem to Hygelac's ill-starred expedition against the

Frisians and Franks. Hygelac himself was slain in Fries-
land by the combined forces of Franks and Frisians
(sometimes designated by the poet as Hetware and Hugas
(ll. 2914 ff. Cf. Appendix I, p. 268), while Beowulf escaped
by swimming; he is reported to have carried away with
him thirty* coats of mail.

On his return home Beowulf was offered the throne
by the widowed Hygd, Hygelac's son Heardred being as
yet only a boy. Beowulf would not accept the throne,
but he offered to act as Heardred's guide and adviser till
the young king should reach mature years. Heardred
was, however, killed shortly afterwards by an attack made
on the Geatas by Onela, king of Sweden. (For a fuller
treatment of this incident, cf. Chap. III on Swedish traditions.) (ll. 2354–2390.)

Beowulf was then chosen king of the Geatas, and is
reported to have reigned gloriously for fifty years, but the
history of his reign is a blank, except for a mention of the
assistance which he rendered Eadgils, an exiled prince, in
what proved a successful endeavour to obtain the Swedish
throne. As Onela was killed by the combined forces of
Eadgils and Beowulf, the expedition also served from the
point of view of the latter as a revenge for the death of
Heardred (ll. 2208 f., 2390–2396).

Beowulf was killed in an attempt to free his people
from the ravages of a dragon which devastated the land;
he slew the dragon, and obtained the stores of hoarded
treasure over which it kept guard, but was mortally
wounded in the fight, and died immediately after achieving his triumph over the monster. At the end of the

* We may notice in passing that the strength in Beowulf's arm is
elsewhere said to equal that of thirty men (cf. l. 380).

first bout in the long struggle Beowulf's warriors, panic-stricken at the terrible appearance of the fire-spewing dragon, all deserted him with the exception of the faithful Wîglaf, the son of Weohstan, a Swedish knight (cf. *inf.* p. 153), who stayed with him to the end and in whose arms he expired. The body of Beowulf was burned on a huge funeral pyre raised by his sorrowing people (ll. 2496–3183).

The account of Beowulf's expedition to the court of Hrothgar, king of the Danes, and of the exploits which he there performed, is briefly as follows :

Hrothgar, king of the Danes, had built for himself and his court a great hall which he called Heorot; this hall was rendered uninhabitable by the ravages of Grendel, a gigantic monster, half beast, half man, who had his home in the marshy fen-lands near at hand. At night, after court had been held in Heorot, Grendel would steal up from the fens, and snatch away for his prey as many as thirty of Hrothgar's sleeping thanes. These ravages had continued for twelve years.

Beowulf, son of Ecgtheow, thane of Hygelac, and a warrior of great strength, had heard of Grendel's inroads, and resolved to undertake an expedition to Denmark in hopes of being able to free the land from this scourge.

With fourteen companions, Beowulf sailed across the sea to Denmark : on their arrival, the warriors were warmly received by King Hrothgar, to whom Beowulf was already well known both by name and reputation.

Beowulf, having stated his name and errand, gave, after the fashion of these times, a long account of all his previous exploits, the most important of which was his swimming-match with Breca. Hrothgar, in his turn, told of Grendel's inroads, and of the reign of terror under which he and his men had lived at Heorot for so long. At nightfall, Hrothgar and all his household retired to rest, leaving Beowulf and his men to guard the hall, but Beowulf alone remained awake keeping watch for Grendel.

When all was still, up from the fen-land stalked Grendel on his nightly visitation to the hall Heorot; breaking into the hall, he seized and devoured one of the sleeping thanes, but before he had time to snatch a second, Beowulf (who was unarmed) closed with him in a desperate hand-to-hand struggle. They struggled and strained for a long space, until at last, with a mighty effort, the monster succeeded in breaking away; but he left his hand and arm in Beowulf's grip, and got back to the fen only to die.

In the morning there was great rejoicing at Heorot over Beowulf's victory. The day was passed in feasting, and Hrothgar bestowed many rich gifts on Beowulf and his followers in recognition of the service they had rendered him. Next evening the warriors went to rest in light-hearted assurance of safety, which was rudely disturbed by the avenging entrance of Grendel's mother: Beowulf being absent, she snatched away, unhindered, Aeschere, the most beloved of Hrothgar's thanes. Joy was thus again turned to sorrow. In the morning Hrothgar appealed to Beowulf to avenge the outrage, and gave him a description of the water-fiend and her haunts in the fens. Beowulf expressed himself willing to undertake the adventure, and attended by the blessings of his companions he pursued the monster to her home at the bottom of a lake; with him he took the sword Hrunting which had been lent by Unferth, the *thyle* or "spokesman" of Hrothgar's court, but it proved of no avail against the troll. He then tried to overpower his opponent in a wrestling-bout, but in spite of his immense strength she had almost overpowered him, when Beowulf, laying hold of an old sword which he found amongst the war-gear lying in the den, succeeded in killing the monster.

On rising to the surface of the lake, Beowulf was received with great joy by his companions, who had almost given him up for lost; together, they returned to Heorot, where rejoicing and feasting were renewed. Beowulf had brought back with him various trophies of his victory, amongst them Grendel's head, which four men had to carry back across the fens to Heorot.

In recognition of his great services Hrothgar again gave Beowulf many rich gifts. The Geatas then took their leave, and with many regrets set sail from Denmark. On their return Beowulf related his adventures to Hygelac, and presented him with a helmet, sword, and coat of mail, which were among the gifts which he had received from Hrothgar: Hygelac, on his side, rewarded Beowulf richly for the valour which he had displayed, and for the honour which his deed reflected on the whole nation of the Geatas (ll. 53–2199).

II. (*a*) EVIDENCE DERIVED FROM SCANDINAVIAN LITERATURE REGARDING THE PERSON OF BEOWULF.

The person of Beowulf and the story of his struggle with Grendel have usually been taken as possessing a purely mythical interest—as, for example, that of the culture-hero bringing deliverance to a nation harassed by the ravages of the North Sea. This so-called myth, it is argued or assumed, has been furnished with an historical setting and attached to the person of Hygelac, king of the Geatas, an historical character who lived and reigned at the beginning of the sixth century. It is, however, surely somewhat rash to dismiss the character of Beowulf as purely mythical, and in so doing to ignore an important fact which has been pointed out by various scholars, namely that there is another character within the range of ancient Teutonic tradition whose personal traits and the events of whose career correspond in a very striking way to those of our hero.

Our knowledge of the early history of the Scandinavian peoples rests in large measure upon the materials to which we have access in the great wealth of saga and folk-tale of Old Norwegian and Old Icelandic literature; we are indebted to a slightly less extent to Saxo Grammaticus and other early Danish historians, who, in addition to sagas of a somewhat earlier date but of similar character to those which we possess, were also able to draw from certain old Danish traditions which have not been otherwise preserved; but the evidence furnished by these authorities although of great value must be carefully tested, as the liberties which the writers have taken with their materials, in many cases, detract considerably from the value of their work.

In our poem, the scene of Beowulf's exploits is laid at the court of Hrothgar, king of the Danes, who is represented as the ideal monarch—wise, brave, gentle, and generous. All Scandinavian sources agree as to the existence of a Danish prince, Ro or Hroar (Hrothgar), the son of Halfdan (Healfdene) and the brother of Helgi

(Halga). But Ro is a very shadowy character: he has none of those characteristics which mark a man out as a leader among his fellows. The figure of his nephew, Hrolf Kraki (Hrothulf in *Beowulf*), the hero of Scandinavian song and story, corresponds much more closely to that of Hrothgar in *Beowulf*. King Hrolf Kraki was the national hero, the king admired, beloved, and feared by all.

Amongst the many stories and traditions which centre round Hrolf Kraki, our attention is arrested by one concerning a certain Bǫdvar-Bjarki, a warrior in Hrolf's service, on account of its remarkable resemblance to the story of the life and exploits of Beowulf; this story is most fully contained in the Icelandic *Hrolfssaga Kraka*.

According to *Hrss.* (Chs. 24–36) Bǫdvar was the son of Bjǫrn, the son by a first marriage of Hring, a king of the Norwegian Uplands. Bjǫrn's mother died, and Hring took as his second wife Hvit, the daughter of the king of the Finns.

On one occasion when King Hring was away, Hvit made professions of love to Bjǫrn, but because he would not fall in with her wishes, she, through her magic powers *, turned him into a bear, and laid on him a curse that he should ever be forced to prey upon his father's cattle. When Hring returned home, his son had disappeared, but on all sides he was met with reports of a devastating bear which worked havoc on his flocks.

Now Bjǫrn had before loved a peasant maiden named Bera; Bera recognised the eyes of the bear as those of her

---

* "Throughout O.N. literature as well as in Saxo, Olavus Magnus, and others, the Finns are held in high repute as magicians"; cf. Handbooks on the History of Religions—*The Religion of the Teutons*, by de la Saussaye, p. 95.

lover, Bjǫrn, and she followed him to his cave, where every
night he was able to lay aside his bear's mask, and become
a man until the morning. For some time, Bera and Bjǫrn
thus spent every night together, until eventually, the bear
was killed by the King's men. After his death Bera bore
three sons—Elgfróði, who was half a man and half an
elk ; Thorirhundsfót, who was a man except for his dog's
feet, and Bǫdvar. (Bǫdvar appears occasionally in *Hrolfss.*
as Bǫdvar-Bjarki.) It is with the last alone that we are
here concerned.

When Bǫdvar grew up, he avenged his father by
killing the queen Hvit. Soon after this King Hring died,
and Bǫdvar ruled the kingdom for a short time. He
then started on his travels and first sought out his brothers,
Elgfrodi and Thorir. With the latter, who had become
king of Gautland, he remained some time, but finally left
him in order to join the service of Hrolf Kraki*.

On his way to Hrolf's court at Hleidrgardr (Leire),
Bǫdvar came to the house of some people who were in
great trouble on account of their son Hǫtt; this Hǫtt
was in Hrolf's service, but as he was somewhat of a weak-
ling, the king's men took advantage of this, and tormented
him by throwing bones at him. Bǫdvar promised to do
what he could to help Hǫtt, and on his arrival at Hleidrgardr, he found the unfortunate man in the corner of the
hall entirely hidden by a heap of bones. He succeeded in
rescuing him from this plight, but when the king's men

---

* In ancient times, the determining factor in the choice of an over-
lord or warrior entering upon military service appears to have been not
patriotism, but the personal qualities of individual leaders, e.g. Weohstan
was in the service of Onela, king of Sweden, while his son Wíglaf served
under Beowulf, king of Geatland.

saw it, they attacked both of them, and again with bones: Hǫtt was so frightened that he could do nothing, but Bǫdvar retorted, killing some of the assailants by one or two well-aimed shots, and the strife was soon at an end. Hrolf Kraki, learning of the incident, commended Bǫdvar's bravery, and took him into his service. Bǫdvar took Hǫtt henceforth under his own protection.

With the approach of Christmas, gloom and sadness became visible on the faces of Hrolf's warriors. Bǫdvar, enquiring the cause of the depression, was told by Hǫtt that for the last two years, at the same season, a great winged beast (*dyr*) had appeared in the land, working great havoc and causing much loss of life; weapons availed naught against it. Bǫdvar expressed wonder that in the domain of such a king as Hrolf Kraki a thing like this could come to pass, but Hǫtt explained to him that the creature was a troll rather than an animal, and that more than ordinary bravery was necessary in order to vanquish it.

When Christmas Eve came, the king gave orders for silence in the hall and forbade any of his warriors to attack the monster when it appeared. Bǫdvar, however, determined to be beforehand, and went outside to await its coming, with Hǫtt, who was in such a state of terror that Bǫdvar had to carry him. When the troll appeared, Hǫtt screamed; Bǫdvar dropped him and attacked the beast, killing it by a sword-thrust through the belly. He then made Hǫtt eat of its heart and drink of its blood, saying that he would thereby become strong and fearless. Together they propped up the monster as though it were still alive, and stole back to the hall, where their absence had not been noticed.

In the morning, the king asked if anything had been seen of the animal : he sent out messengers who returned saying that it was outside the hall. Thereupon Hǫtt, encouraged by Bǫđvar, offered to go out and slay it with the sword of Gullinhjalti, which he asked for this purpose from the king. This request was somewhat reluctantly granted, as Hrolf was well acquainted with Hǫtt's reputation for cowardice.

Armed with Gullinhjalti, Hǫtt sallied forth and attacked the monster, which at once fell dead from the blow ! The king congratulated Bǫđvar on all that he had done for his protégé, and decreed that Hǫtt should henceforth be called Hjalti, after the sword with which he had performed his exploit.

After these events, Bǫđvar remained in the service of Hrolf Kraki : he took part in many expeditions with the king, married his daughter, and finally fell in battle while fighting at his side (cf. *inf.* p. 49 f.)   (Chs. 47–52.)

Even the casual observer cannot fail to note the striking similarity between the account of the exploits of Beowulf at the court of Hrothgar, and those of Bǫđvar at the court of Hrolf Kraki.   In either case a warrior arrives at the court of a Danish king, and earns the lasting gratitude of the king by slaying a monster which has been the scourge of the country.

Saxo Grammaticus, the Danish historian of the twelfth century, relates a story (Bk II, pp. 56–68, ed. Holder) concerning one Biarco a warrior of Rolvo "Krake": this Biarco clearly corresponds to the Bǫđvar-Bjarki of *Hrolfss.* as, in addition to the evidence of the name Biarco, which is obviously a Latinised form of "bjarki," the two accounts are practically identical.

According to Saxo (II, 56, ed. Holder), as in *Hrolfss.*, Biarco and Hjalti were companions in arms: the monster which devastated the country each Yule-tide has been replaced by a huge bear, which Biarco slays in the forest, but Saxo does not lay nearly so much stress on the incident as does the writer of the *Hrolfss.* On the other hand, the story of Rolvo Krake's last battle, and the part played in it by Biarco and Hjalti, is treated in greater detail than in *Hrolfss.* (II, pp. 58–68, ed. Holder). Both accounts are based on the O.N. *Bjarkamál*, but while Saxo's version is apparently a complete translation of the poem, that of *Hrolfss.* is very corrupt.

Although strictly speaking outside the scope of this treatise, we may notice the striking parallel to the story of Beowulf and Grendel with which we are confronted in the Icelandic *Grettissaga* (chs. 64–67).

The *Grettissaga* dates from about the end of the thirteenth century, and deals with the adventures of an outlaw Grettir, who was an historical character, and who died about the year 1031. The story of Grettir's encounter with two water-demons corresponds so remarkably to the account of Beowulf's fight with Grendel and his mother that it is impossible to look upon the resemblance between the two as merely accidental. The *Grettissaga* contains no sign of having been influenced by the *Beowulf*, and it is in itself almost inconceivable that the O.E. poem should have exercised any such direct influence as would be necessary to account for the similarity of the two narratives. It has been suggested by Mr H. M. Chadwick (*Cambridge Hist. of Eng. Lit.* vol. I, p. 27) that there may have existed some old folk-tale of a fight with water-demons on which the portions of the

Beowulf and of *Grettissaga* in question may both have been based, the adventure being in the one case attributed to an historical prince of the Götar—Beowulf—and in the other to an historical Icelandic outlaw—Grettir. This explanation certainly seems more satisfactory than any other, and, if it were proved correct, would remove one of the chief difficulties at present brought forward against regarding Beowulf as an historical character, namely, the alleged mythical nature of his contest with Grendel and Grendel's mother.

For a fuller treatment of this subject, the reader is referred to an article by Hugo Gering entitled "Der Beowulf und die isländische Grettissaga," which is to be found in *Anglia* III, pp. 74 ff. Bugge (*PBB.* XII, pp. 57 ff.) has pointed out that the saga of Orm Stórólfsson has, like the *Grettiss.*, marked affinity with the account of Beowulf's struggle with Grendel and that reminiscences of the same legend of a life and death struggle with a monster are also contained in several Faroëse and Swedish ballads.

The question of the apparent confusion between the Hrothgar (Ro Hroar) of *Beowulf*, and the Hrolf Kraki (Hrothulf) of Northern tradition, will be discussed in the following chapter on Danish traditions. A further account of the Hall Heorot, the palace of King Hrothgar, and the scene of Beowulf's struggle with Grendel, is also reserved for the next chapter.

b. Evidence derived from Scandinavian Literature regarding the Geatas.

We are now in a position to consider the actual identity of the people who are called in *Beowulf* the Geatas; regarding this question, controversy has been rife. Some scholars. (Bugge) would identify the Geatas with the O.N. Jótar—Jutes, who inhabited Jutland. The other and more generally accepted theory (Müllenhoff) is that the Geatas represent the O.N. Gautar (which is quite a different word from O.N. Jótar), and, therefore, correspond to the modern Götar who occupy the southern part of Sweden (with the exception of the southern extremity Skaane which was formerly Danish). In *Heimskr. St Ólafss.* ch. 76, there is given a geographical description of the divisions of Sweden, which are arranged thus:

1. Swíthjóð, with its provinces.
2. Vestrgautland. Vermaland. Markir.
3. Eystrgautland, with Gottland, and Eyland.

The chief reasons for identifying the Geatas with the modern Götar are these:

1. As regards phonology Geatas corresponds exactly to O.N. Gautar, whereas it does not correspond to O.N. Jótar, in which *jo* represents an earlier *eu**.

2. What is said regarding the relations between the Geatas and the Svear (Swedes) in *Beowulf* indicates that the lands respectively occupied by the two peoples lay in close proximity to one another. Hostilities were constantly going on between Geatas and Svear; e.g. there was the campaign of Haethcyn and Onela (*Beo.* ll. 2472 ff. 2922 ff.), and again, when Eadgils undertook an expedition against Onela, he was assisted by Beowulf and an army of the Geatas, the combined forces eventually defeating Onela, who fell in the battle, and was succeeded by Eadgils (*Beo.* ll. 2391 ff.). It is most unlikely that such close relations should have existed between Swedes and Geatas, had they not been near neighbours as the Svear and Gautar were: we know, too, that there was

---

* Cf. also p. 183.

constant friction between the Svear and Gautar throughout the Middle Ages, although by that time both peoples
were nominally united under a common ruler.

3. In the *Skáldsk.* (ch. 44) Bǫđvar who, according to
Hrss., came from Gautland, is found in alliance with or
assisting Ađils (Eadgils), king of Sweden, in the campaign
which is, as we shall see, identical with that described
in *Beowulf* as undertaken by Eadgils and Beowulf, king of
the Geatas. According to *Skáldsk.* and *Yngls.* the battle
in which Bǫđvar assisted Ađils took place on Lake Wener,
which lies between Götland and Sweden on the one side,
and Norway on the other. The passage is as follows :

"Another instance of the bravery of Hrolf Kraki is
related, that a king ruled over Upsala whose name was
Ađils ; he married Yrsa the mother of Hrolf Kraki. He
was engaged in war with the king who ruled over Norway
whose name was Áli. They agreed to fight each other on
the frozen lake Vaenir ("on the ice of the lake which is
called Vaenir "). King Ađils sent word to Hrolf Kraki,
his kinsman, to come to his assistance, and promised
payment to all of his army who took part in the expedition ; and the king himself should possess three treasures
which he might choose from Swíthjóđ. King Hrolf was
not able to go, because of his strife with the Saxons, but
he sent to Ađils his twelve berserks ; there was Bǫđvarr
Bjarki and Hjálti Hugprúđi, Hvitserkr Hvati, Vǫttr
Véseti, the brothers Svipdagr and Beigađr. In that
battle King Áli fell, and a great portion of his army."

It may be objected that the value of this evidence
is conditional on our acceptance of the characters of
Beowulf and Bǫđvar as identical. This is true, but it is,
at the same time, also true, that both sets of facts act

and re-act upon one another to such an extent, that the evidence which we have just been discussing is in itself an additional and almost a convincing proof of that identity.

4. The Gautar were as a people much more important than the Jótar at the time when the events described in the poem were gradually becoming crystallised in literary form. Procopius mentions the Gautoi as one of the most populous races of Northern Europe (*vide inf.* p. 42); and they are certainly the only Northern people powerful enough to have fought the Swedes on equal terms as the Geatas undoubtedly did.

The sum total of this evidence seems to show satisfactorily and conclusively that the Geatas of *Beowulf* represent the people known in modern times as the Götar (O.N. Gautar) and not the O.N. Jótar, O.F. Jutae—the inhabitants of Jutland. The mistake appears to have been due in the first instance to a passage in the O.E. translation of Bede (*Eccles. Hist.* I, 15) where the Jutae of Bede has, on one occasion, been translated as Geatas.

The following are the chief classical and Scandinavian authorities from which we obtain information about the Geatas in early times:

Ptolemy. *Geographia Claudii Ptolemaei.* Part I. (Müller, Paris, 1901.)

Procopius.

Jordanes. (J. P. Migne, *Patrologiae cursus completus.* Ser. I. Vol. LXIX.)

Gregory of Tours. (*Recueil des Historiens des Gaules et de la France.* Vol. I.) Bouquet, 1739.

Gesta Regum Francorum. Pertz, *Mon. Germ. Hist. Script. Rer. Merov.* Vol. I.

Liber Monstrorum. (*Traditions Tératologiques.* Berger de Xivrey.)

Sagas.

Historical References to the Geatas (Götar) in Foreign Authorities.

Ptolemy, writing in the second century, mentions the Goutai as one of the peoples inhabiting the southern part of the island of Scandia*.

Procopius†, writing in 550, mentions the Gautoi as the chief people inhabiting the island of Thule.

Jordanes‡ mentions the Visigauti as a keen, fierce race, ready for war.

In Northern Sagas dealing with the events of the fourth and fifth centuries, we find mention of kings of the Gautar, but in historical times Gautland (Götland) was no longer an independent kingdom. It was governed by an earl and had its own laws, but was subject to the kingdom of Sweden of which it formed a part. At the time of the events recorded in *Beowulf*, the Geatas were still an independent people, but their kingdom may have —and probably did—come to an end comparatively soon afterwards. Gregory of Tours (III, 3) and the *Gesta Regum Francorum* give an account of Hygelac's expedition to the Lower Rhine between the years 512 and 520. In both records, however, the expedition is described as a

* ἀπ' ἀνατολῶν δὲ τῆς Χερσονήσους τέσσαρες αἱ καλούμεναι Σκανδίαι, τρεῖς μὲν μικραὶ ὧν ἡ μέση ἐπέχει μοίρας μα λ' ν̄η, μία δὲ μεγίστη καὶ ἀνατολικωτάτη κατὰ τὰς ἐκβολὰς Οὐιστούλα ποταμοῦ ἧς τὸ μὲν δυτικώτατον ἐπέχει μοίρας μ̄γ ν̄η τὸ δ' ἀνατολικώτατον μ̄ϛ ν̄η τὸ δ' ἀρκτιτώτατον μδ λ' ν̄η λ' τὸ δὲ μεσημβρινὸν με ν ϛγο'. καλεῖται δὲ ἰδίως καὶ αὐτὴ Σκανδία καὶ κατέχουσιν αὐτῆς τὰ μὲν ἀρκτικὰ Κυεύωνες, τὰ δὲ δυτικὰ Χαιδεινοί, τὰ δ' ἀνατολικὰ Φαυόναι καὶ Φιραῖσοι, τὰ δὲ μεσημβρινὰ Γοῦται καὶ Δαυκίωνες, τὰ δὲ μέσα Λευῶνοι.

† *Goth.* II, 15. οὕτω μὲν Θουλῖται βιοῦσιν ὧν ἔθνος ἕν πολυάνθρωπον οἱ Γαυτοί εἰσι, παρ' οὓς δὴ Ἐρούλων τότε οἱ ἐπηλύται ἱδρύσαντο.

‡ *Get.* III, 22. Post hos Athelnii, Finnaithae feri, Visigautigoth, acre hominum genus et ad bellum promptissimum.

Danish one, and Hygelac is spoken of as king of the Danes. The passages are as follows :

Greg. Tur. III, 3.

*His ita gestis, Dani cum rege suo, nomine Chlochilaicho, evectu navali per mare Gallias appetunt. Egressique ad terras, pagum unum de regno Theuderici devastant atque captivant : oneratisque navibus tam de captivis quam de reliquiis spoliis, reverti ad patriam cupiunt. Sed rex eorum in litus residebat, donec naves altum mare comprehenderent, ipse deinceps secuturus. Quod cum Theuderico nuntiatum fuisset, quod scilicet regio ejus fuerit ab extraneis devastata, Theudebertum filium suum in illas partes cum valido exercitu ac magno armorum apparatu direxit. Qui, interfecto Rege, hostes navali praelio superatos opprimit, omnemque rapinam terrae restituit.

Gesta Regum Francorum, ch. XIX.

†In illo tempore Dani, cum rege suo nomine Chochilago, cum navale hoste per altum mare Gallices appetunt,

---

* After this, the Danes, with their king by name Chlochilaichus, took ship and made an attack upon the Gauls by sea. Having disembarked, they devastated a part of the kingdom of Theuderic, and took captives. They then loaded their ships with spoil and prisoners, and prepared to return home. But their king remained on shore, until the ships had reached the open sea, intending then to follow himself. When the news was brought to Theuderic that his land had been laid waste by a foreign army he sent his son Theudebert with a strong force and ample equipment for war into those regions. He first killed the king, after which he defeated the army in a naval battle, afterwards recapturing the whole of the booty.

† About this time the Danes, under their king Chochilagus, crossed the ocean with a fleet to attack the Gauls. They laid waste a part of the kingdom of Theuderic inhabited by the Attoarii and others, taking many prisoners. Having filled their ships with captives they made for the ocean, while their king remained on shore. However, when news of this was brought to Theuderic, he despatched his son Theudobert with a

Theuderico pagum, Attoarios vel alios devastantes atque captivantes, plenas naves de captivis habentes, alto mare intrantes Rex eorum ad litus maris resedit. Quod cum Theuderico nuntiatum fuisset, Theudobertum filium suum cum magno exercitu in illis partibus dirigens. Qui consequens eos, pugnavit cum eis caede maxima, atque ipsis prostratis, Regem eorum interfecit, praedam tulit, et in terram suam restituit.

In addition to these historical references, there is in the *Liber Monstrorum* a collection of mediaeval texts edited by Berger de Xivrey, a passage which bears on Hygelac of the Geatas. The allusion is as follows:

*" Of tremendous stature was king Huiglaucus (var. lect. Huncglacus) who ruled over the Getae, and was slain by the Franks. At the age of twelve years, no horse could carry him. His bones rest on an island at the mouth of the Rhine, and are shown as a wonder to visitors from afar."

III and IV. Comparison of Evidence, and Summary of Historical Facts underlying the reference to the Geatas (Götar) in Beowulf and Widsith.

Amongst the references of Latin historians to the Götar, the only two which make definite mention of any event connected with this people are the *Gesta Francorum* and Gregory of Tours.

great army into those regions. The latter pursued them, fought with and overcame them with great slaughter, put their king to death, and having recovered all the booty departed with it to his own country.

* Et sunt mirae magnitudinis: ut rex Huiglaucus qui imperavit Getis et a Francis occisus est. Quem equus a duodecimo anno portare non potuit. Cujus ossa in Rheni fluminis insula, ubi in Oceanum prorumpit, reservata sunt, et de longinquo venientibus pro miraculo ostenduntur.

In both of these sources there is explicit reference to a marauding expedition made by a Danish king, Chochilaichus, on the territory of the Franks, between the years 512 and 520, which terminated in the defeat and slaughter of Chochilaichus by a Frankish army under Theoderic and Theodobert. This account coincides so exactly with that of Hygelac's fatal expedition against the Franks and Frisians as related in *Beowulf*, that they may be taken without doubt as referring to one and the same event. Scholars have accepted the date given by Gregory of Tours and the *Gesta Francorum*, as a starting-point on which to base time calculations with regard to the whole subject matter of the poem.

The results gained from an investigation of the historical value of the part played by the Götar in *Beowulf* are but meagre. They can be expressed in very few words: there was in South Sweden at the time of the events recorded in *Beowulf* a people called the Gautar, who had been there, as we learn from Ptolemy, at any rate since the second century, and who were a large tribe of considerable importance. At the beginning of the sixth century they were ruled by a king named Hygelac*, who was killed

* The only discrepancy which occurs between the historical references to the Götar, and those contained in *Beowulf*, is in connection with Hygelac. Gregory of Tours refers to Chochilaichus-Hygelac as king of the Danes. In the document quoted by Berger de Xivrey, Huiglaucus is described as ruling over the Getae (Götar) ("qui imperavit Getis"), which would agree with *Beowulf* where Hygelac is king of the Geatas.

We may venture to assume that Gregory of Tours is inaccurate in his description as regards this point. There is no reason to suppose that the Franks had very minute knowledge of the geography of the Northern kingdoms at this time, and as the Danes who were notorious marauders lay comparatively near to them, it was natural that they should describe other Northern invaders as Danes also.

probably about 520 (cf. note p. 185) by the combined
forces of Franks and Frisians in a raid which he made on
their territory.

It is strange that historical sources should make no
mention whatever of Beowulf the great warrior of the
Geatas, whose figure completely overshadows that of
Hygelac in the poem, and the question arises: what
grounds have we for believing in Beowulf's actual existence as an historical character?

All the evidence which we have considered tends to
establish as fairly certain the identity of the Bǫdvar-Bjarki,
whose name occurs in so many Scandinavian sources, as
one of the most valiant champions of Hrolf Kraki, with
the English Beowulf. These two were contemporaries
and both were famous warriors; both came to the court of
the Danish king, whom by their prowess they freed from an
ever-recurring source of danger, thus earning his deepest
gratitude; both were involved in the contemporary war
of succession in Sweden; both assisted Eadgils-Adils to
gain the Swedish throne; lastly, supernatural traits of a
similar kind appear in the character of each. In view of
the striking agreement of the facts related of these two
men, and in the absence of any important negative
evidence, it is difficult to resist the conclusion that they
were not two, but indeed one and the same person.

The belief here expressed in the identity of the O.E.
Beowulf and the Scandinavian Bǫdvar-Bjarki may perhaps be considered unjustified, in view of the very different
attitude adopted with regard to this point by such an
authority as Dr Axel Olrik in his recent book *Danmarks
Heltedigtning* (Copenhagen 1903). Dr Olrik denies most
emphatically the identity of Beowulf and Bǫdvar-Bjarki

on the ground of the different nature of the struggles ascribed to the two warriors. Beowulf fights against a monster Grendel—neither human being nor animal— while Bǫdvar-Bjarki simply kills a beast of prey—most probably a bear. It is true that in the Icel. *Hrolfss.* of the fourteenth century the bear of Saxo has become a winged monster (*Fas.* I, 69), but this is merely one of the many exaggerations and embellishments of the old stories which mark the compositions of the period; late Icelandic tradition shows everywhere a tendency to degenerate into the fantastic. Thus Dr Olrik concludes that the two cases are essentially different, and can have nothing in common with one another. He even goes the length of discrediting the truth of the Scandinavian bear-story, which he regards merely as an invention to account for the transformation of Hjalti from a coward to a warrior ! Surely, however, in consideration of the many other points of similarity in the two stories, the minor difficulty of identifying the Beowulf, who killed a demon monster, with the Bǫdvar-Bjarki, who killed a great bear, may be overlooked, if it is not altogether removed, by the time that we have made allowances for the imaginative treat-ment and the liberty of thought and expression, which are of the essence of every great poem such as the *Beowulf.* From a devastating beast of prey the transition to a monster or even a demon is an easy one, especially if we have to take into account in the *Beowulf* the influence of some old folk-tale, as the striking parallel version of a fight with water-demons in the Icel. *Grettissaga* would seem to suggest (cf. *supra* p. 37).

The acceptance of the identity of Beowulf and Bǫdvar-Bjarki makes it a degree easier to tackle the question of the historical validity of this character—Beowulf-Bǫðvar (as for convenience sake we may style him). The fact that English and Scandinavian traditions, which are quite distinct, which have developed independently of one another, and which belong to altogether different periods, both testify to his existence with abundance of circumstantial detail, although not conclusive, certainly goes a long way towards proving that he was an actual historical character, and not, as has been suggested, a mythical or legendary one. It further makes some facts concerning him so highly probable as to be almost certain. Beowulf-Bǫðvar was a warrior of notable strength and valour, and probably belonged to the people of the Götar* (O.N. Gautar, O.E. Geatas): he was at some time during his life, though perhaps only temporarily, a thegn of the Danish kings, and apparently rendered them some signal service, the exact nature of which cannot be determined. Beowulf-Bǫðvar took part in the Swedish dynastic struggle and assisted Eadgils-Aðils to gain the Swedish throne, notably in a decisive battle which was fought on the frozen Lake Wener. There is also no reason why he should not have taken part in the expedition of Hygelac (Chochilaicus) to the Lower Rhine, as the *Beowulf* reports him to have done.

Even apart from the question of his identity with Beowulf, Dr Olrik believes firmly in the historical existence of Bǫðvar-Bjarki; he bases his conclusions mainly on the evidence of *Bjarkamál*, in which Bjarki, though serving as

* Dr Olrik points out (*DHD.*, pp. 215 ff.) that Bǫðvar-Bjarki appears for the first time as a Norwegian in the *Bravǻllakvad* written in 1066, and later in the *Hrolfss.* and *Bjarkarímur*, where a further account of his upbringing has been added.

the personification of a type—that of stern, warlike valour
in contrast to the mildness and geniality of Hrolf Kraki—
is, notwithstanding, a purely individual figure ; Bǫdvar-
Bjarki takes part further in the campaigns between the
Danes and Heathobeardan, which we have reason to
regard as historical, and the names with which he is associated go back to old tradition, and, therefore, presumably
to historical characters and events (*D. H. D.* p. 66).

An objection has been raised that the figure of Beowulf in the poem is not that of a normal human being,
and that the elements of the supernatural which appear
in his character are incompatible with its historical truth.
But this objection can easily be met on the ground that
amongst primitive peoples there was no clear line of
division between the natural and the supernatural ; as a
matter of fact, the figures of almost all early heroes unite
elements of both, as for example, Dietrich of Bern, in
whose case mediaeval German tradition has interwoven
history and myth in the most extraordinary way.

An examination of the Scandinavian authorities will
help to make clear the significance of the supernatural
traits in the character of Beowulf-Bǫdvar.

As we have seen, Bǫdvar was, according to *Hrolfss.*,
the son of Björn, who was turned into a bear, and of Bera
(O.N. *bera* = she-bear). When Bǫdvar first came to
Hrolf's court, he earned his reputation by slaying a great
troll, which came every Yule-tide and carried off warriors,
doing great havoc throughout the country (cf. *sup.* p. 35).

In Saxo, Biarco (Beowulf-Bǫdvar) first became
famous through slaying a bear. In the last great battle
in which Hrolf Kraki was defeated and slain, Biarco had
to be roused three times before he came out to the fight

(Saxo, ed. Holder, pp. 59 ff.). Saxo makes no comment on this curious fact, but some light is thrown on it by the parallel account in the *Hrss*.

In Hrolf's last fight, as in Saxo, so too in the saga, Bǫđvar at first did not come out to fight: but a huge bear fought in front of Hrolf, and killed as many of the enemy as any five of his warriors. When Bǫđvar was at last roused and came out, the bear disappeared (*Fas.* I, pp. 102 ff.).

From this tradition it appears that the conception of Bǫđvar in the minds of the people was so intimately associated with the figure of a bear, that finally the one came to be regarded as the metamorphosis of the other.

In the O.E. *Beowulf* this same metamorphosis may be traced, although its existence is nowhere explicitly stated. Beowulf generally fought in the dark, or where no man could see him, and he very seldom fought with weapons. Cf. the whole passage on the killing of Grendel, ll. 745–818, especially such expressions as:

l. 764.   Wiste his fingra geweald on grames grâpum *.

ll. 788—90.   *Heóld hine tô faeste*
se the manna waes maegene strengest
on thaem daege thysses lîfest †.

l. 813 f.   Ac hine se môdega maeg Hygelaces
haefde be honda ‡.

ll. 963—6.   "Ic hine hraedlîce *heardan clammum*
on wael bedde *wrîthan thôhte*.
thaet he *for mund-gripe* mînum scolde
licgean lîf-bysig, bûtan his lîc swice §."

* He knew that the power of his fingers was in the grip of the enemy.

† He, who was of men the mightiest in strength, in the day of this life, held him too fast.

‡ But the bold kinsman of Hygelac had him by the hands.

§ "Quickly I thought to pin him down on the bed of slaughter with hard grip, that he should lie struggling for life, by reason of my hand-clasp, unless his body escape."

and again such passages as these :

ll. 2506—8.   Ne waes ecg bona
     ac him *hilde-grâp* heortan wylmas
     bân-hûs gebraec*.

ll. 2682—4.   Him thaet gifethe ne waes
     thaet him îrenna ecge mihton
     helpan aet hilde ; waes sió hond tô strong
     se the mêca gehwane mîne gefraege
     swenge ofersôhte †.

These passages, with others which might be quoted, seem to show plainly that Beowulf fought like a wild animal, not killing his enemies by sword and spear, but squeezing them in a fierce embrace—thus more like a bear than any other animal‡.

This exactly corresponds to the figure of Bǫdvar in *Hrolfss.* Thus the entering in of the spirit of Beowulf-Bǫdvar into a bear in times of battle seems to be an essential part of the legend concerning him, occurring in all its versions, and we have here an instance of metamorphosis, the idea of which was not only possible, but common amongst early Teutonic peoples. Beowulf-Bǫdvar was

---

* Nor was the sword the slayer, but the battle-grip crushed his "bone-house" (i.e. body), the surgings of his heart.

† That was not granted him, that iron blades might help him in battle : too strong was the hand which, as I have heard, surpassed every sword in its stroke.

‡ It is true that Beowulf did, on two occasions, fight with a sword, viz., against Grendel's mother, and in his last fight against the dragon. But this second struggle may be, as is thought by many writers, a later addition made by the poet to the original story of Beowulf. When Beowulf attacked Grendel's mother, the main part of the combat consisted of a deadly wrestling-match, which is quite consistent with what we know of his methods of fighting at other times : it was only as a last resource that he used a sword, and that not his own, but an old one which he found hanging on the wall of the den.

the bear, and the bear was a metamorphosis of him. The force of this is brought out by the name Bǫðvar-Bjarki, by which Bǫðvar is usually known in Scandinavian tradition; indeed, in earliest Scandinavian tradition, preserved in Saxo's Latin version of the Icel. *Bjarkamál*, he appears merely as Bjarki, and this, according to Dr Olrik, was probably originally his real name *. Thus the fact that supernatural elements are traceable in the character of Beowulf is no argument against his historical existence. Dr Olrik believes that the bear-like qualities or the "bear-nature" was first attributed to Bǫðvar-Bjarki in the twelfth century, owing to the influence of a similar story told of Siward the Fat, a Danish earl who settled in Northumbria in the time of Canute (1017–1042). He asserts that in the case of Siward we have the story of a man appearing in the shape of a bear for the first time. (*D. H. D.* pp. 215 ff.) But this belief in the possibility of the metamorphosis of men and animals is an ancient one, and dates as we have seen from very much earlier than the eleventh century: in the particular instance of Bǫðvar-Bjarki there is no proof—nor on the surface at any rate does there seem any probability—that the story owes anything to the similar one told of Siward the Fat.

* Bjarki is merely a hypocoristic formed from *björn* = bear. It was well known as a personal name, and is also found in Danish place-names from early times. The name Bǫðvar is apparently derived from *bǫð* = battle (perhaps the genitive) and was most probably given to Bjarki on account of his prowess. Dr Olrik supposes Bǫðvar to have been at first merely an epithet, namely, *bǫðvar Bjarki* = Bjarki of the battle, or, freely translated, "Fighting Bjarki," which in later records was misunderstood and reproduced as Bǫðvar bjarki, where Bǫðvar has become the real name, and "bjarki" is now merely an epithet or surname (cf. *D. H. D.* p. 139 f.). An alternative explanation of Bǫðvar is that it = O.E. *beaduhere*, i.e. battle-army.

There is, however, a serious difficulty with regard to the later history of Beowulf-Bǫðvar: Beowulf became king of the Geatas, and had a long and glorious reign, whereas Bǫðvar-Bjarki remained in the service of Hrolf Kraki until the end of his life, fell with him in battle and was buried in the same barrow. But Beowulf, as king of the Geatas, is a very shadowy character, as we have already seen; he is much more a type than an individual; even the killing of the dragon whereby he met his own death is a thoroughly typical exploit of the ideal king—cf. Sigmund in *Beowulf* (ll. 884–900), Sigurð in *Vǫlss.* (Ch. xviii), Frotho I in Saxo (ed. Holder, p. 38 f.)—and may well be a later accretion to the original story. This supposition is rendered more probable by the consideration that the reign of fifty years attributed to Beowulf would bring us up to near the end of the sixth century, and we have no evidence for believing that communication was maintained between England and northern countries as late as that time.

But even if we reject the story of Beowulf's fifty-year reign as given by the poet, it still seems probable that there was some foundation for representing him as ruling over the Gautar at some period following on Heardred's death.

The most probable theory seems to be that Beowulf-Bǫðvar ruled over the Gautar as a vassal or tributary king of Hrolf Kraki, and as such assisted Eadgils-Aðils in his struggle to obtain the Swedish throne. We have already accepted as historical the fact that he did take part in this struggle, and according to the *Beowulf* he did so as an independent sovereign. But we have seen that the evidence of the poem with regard to Beowulf's reign is probably untrustworthy; on the other hand, all Scandinavian sources represent Bǫðvar as a vassal of Hrolf Kraki, and according to *Skáldsk.* (Ch. 44), it was in this capacity, and at the command of Hrolf, that he and others went to the assistance of Aðils.

There are various further indications that the kingdom of Sweden (i.e. Svealand) was at this time subject to Denmark, and that the king of Sweden paid tribute to the king of the Danes. These will be dealt with when we come to speak of the relations between Aðils and Hrolf Kraki (cf. also *Yngls.* Ch. 31), but the matter may be referred to at this point, as it gives evidence of the widespread power of the Danish kings, and also because the fact that Svealand was under the sway of Denmark would increase the probability of the sister kingdom of Götland being in a similar position. Regarding the end of Beowulf's life, as English and Scandinavian traditions disagree, we have no certain ground to go upon. But the account of Beowulf's death in the *Beowulf* stands or falls with that of his fifty-years' reign over the Geatas; if we reject this story, there seems no reason why we should hesitate to accept the account given in Scandinavian authorities, viz., that Beowulf-Bǫðvar met his death in battle with Hrolf Kraki in the manner described by Saxo (pp. 57 ff.) and *Hrss.* (*Fas.* Vol. I, pp. 96 ff.)*

The question of the presence of mythical features in the *Beowulf* is, strictly speaking, beyond the scope of this study, but it is one which is so intimately bound up with the whole interpretation of the story of Beowulf and Grendel that a few words must be said about it.

* But cf. Ch. III, p. 153 f.

From the evidence which we have considered, we believe Beowulf to have been an historical character, who corresponds to the character of Bǫðvar-Bjarki in Scandinavian tradition, and who performed some exploit at the court of a Danish king through which he acquired great fame. The constant association of Bǫðvar-Bjarki with a bear, as also the name itself, would seem to indicate that it was from the ravages of some unusually fierce bear that he delivered the Danish court.

If this be true, the theory that the interest of the Grendel story is purely mythical must necessarily fall to the ground ; for while an historical narrative may easily develop some mythical traits, it cannot, as such, contain a fully-developed myth, except where the lapse of centuries has caused the historical interest, which attaches to persons, time and place, to become merged with, and lost in, the more general interest of the myth. In the case of the Grendel-story there was not time for this to take place, as the poem must have been composed comparatively soon—probably within two or three generations— after the events recorded in it took place, at any rate long before they could have lost their historical significance in order to become merely the vehicle of a myth.

The most we can say about this story is, that there are possibly some mythical features in the description of Grendel (cf. suggestion made on p. 37), who differs considerably from the bear, which we believe to have been the corresponding figure of the original story. Beowulf no longer fights against an animal, but against some monstrous being, more man than beast, whose outstanding feature is the malignance of his personality. This Grendel lurked in the fens and marshland surrounding Heorot which were evidently uninhabitable by any other creature, for in every reference to him stress is laid on his solitary existence, and the curse which his presence always carried with it; cf. *Beo.* ll. 102–6, l. 160, *deorc deáth-scúa*, l. 165, *atol án-gengea*, l. 712, *mán-scatha.* A further significant feature of the story is that Grendel's ravages only took place when court was being held at Heorot, and the great hall itself was actually in use. At other times, the monster does not appear to have left his home in the marshes.

It is possible that in this one instance the poet may have read into his very much elaborated description of the creature slain by Beowulf more than the actual facts warranted, in short that he may have taken this opportunity of representing in mythical form the encroachments of the sea on the low-lying fenland, or the ravages of the agues and fevers which lurked in the miasmic swamps of Zealand (cf. suggestion on p. 38).

Further than this it is, however, impossible to go, and even this is merely surmise, as the whole description of Grendel in *Beowulf* may merely be due to poetical exaggeration. In any case, the idea that Beowulf himself could have been conceived by the poet as a myth seems extremely improbable. In the first place the *Beowulf*, as already mentioned, appears to have been composed within about a century after Beowulf's death, when the memory of his personality and of his deeds must still have been fully alive in men's minds; and further, if the figure of Beowulf has mythical significance, it can only be that of representing in a general way the progress of civilisation and of the arts—for no one will, surely, attempt to prove that his victory over Grendel represents anything so concrete as the invention of a new system of sanitation or the building of a dyke, by one single man. It seems quite possible that the pictorial imagination of early peoples was sufficient to conceive of the ravages of sea or disease as those of some fierce monster; but there are no grounds for believing—nor is it in itself at all probable—that these same peoples were capable of rising to such heights of abstract thought as the general conception of a culture-hero would imply.

CHAPTER II

THE DANES.

I. THE DANES IN BEOWULF.

THE Danish royal family is traced in *Beowulf* from its first founder, Scyld Scêfing, whose mythical coming and departure are described (ll. 1–52). Scyld was succeeded, as king of Denmark, by his son Beowulf the Dane, who in his turn was followed by his son Healfdene (ll. 56–57). Healfdene had three sons, Heorogar, Hrothgar, Halga, and one daughter, who apparently became the wife of Onela of Sweden (l. 62), although the text of the poem is unfortunately corrupt at this point. Heorogar died young, but he may have reigned for a short time (cf. l. 2158 f.); the story of his early death was told by King Hrothgar to Beowulf on his arrival at the Danish court (ll. 467 ff.).

Hrothgar reigned in Heorot, the beloved and venerated king of the Danes, but owing to Grendel's ravages gloom hung over his court for many years, until, through Beowulf's victory, joy was restored in Heorot. Hrothgar's wife was Wealhtheow of the Helmingas (ll. 612 f.); he had by her two sons, Hrethric and Hrothmund (l. 1189), and a daughter Freawaru (ll. 2020 ff.). He had also a nephew Hrothulf (ll. 1017, 1163 f.), who was held in high favour at his uncle's court; Wealhtheow showed great

The Danes (Dene), also called in *Beowulf* Scyldingas (ll. 30, 53, &c.), in O.N. Sagas, Skjǫldungar.

The relationships of the Danish royal family were according to *Beowulf* as follows:

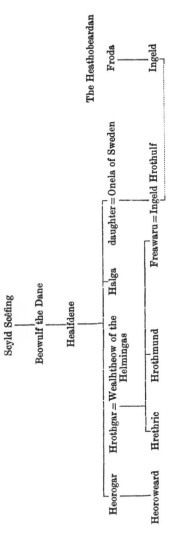

Scyld Scēfing

Beowulf the Dane

Healfdene

Heorogar   Hrothgar = Wealhtheow of the Helmingas   Halga   daughter = Onela of Sweden

Heoroweard   Hrethric   Hrothmund   Freawaru = Ingeld   Hrothulf

The Heathobeardan

Froda

Ingeld

confidence in Hrothulf, and said that he would make a good guardian for her sons in the event of Hrothgar's death (ll. 1180 ff.). The poem hints surprise (cf. also *Widsith*, ll. 45–49) that such friendly relations should have existed between Hrothgar and Hrothulf (l. 1164).

The subsequent history of Freawaru, Hrothgar's daughter, introduces a new set of characters. Froda, the king of the Heathobeardan, had fallen in battle against the Danes. The strife was ended by the promise of Freawaru in marriage to Froda's son Ingeld. Hrothgar was glad to settle the dispute in this way, but the marriage ended unhappily. Freawaru took with her as esquire a young Dane, who boasted to the Heathobeardan of Froda's defeat, and Ingeld, at last roused from apathy by the repeated admonitions of an old warrior, took terrible vengeance on the Danes for his father's death (ll. 2022–2069).

THE DANES IN WIDSITH.

The allusions made to the Danes in *Widsith* consist merely of isolated references.

Lines 45–49. "Hrothwulf and Hrothgar, the nephew and uncle, maintained their friendship for a very long time, after they had expelled the 'Wicinga cyn' and brought Ingeld's spear low, cutting down at Heorot the host of the Heathobeardan*."

Line 58. The singer also visited the South Danes.

> * Hrothwulf and Hrothgar heoldon lengest
> sibbe aetsomne suhtorfaedran
> siththan hie forwraecon Wicinga cynn
> and Ingeldes ord forbigdan
> forheowan aet Heorote Heatho-Beardna thrym.

II. Other References to the Danes.

The chief authorities which contain evidence about the Danes in general, and about the period of their history in particular with which the *Beowulf* deals, are the following:

Historians and Records.

Tacitus.

Saxo Grammaticus' *Danish History.*

Sven Aagesen (genealogies) (Langebek, *S. R. D.* Vol. I, pp. 42–64).

Jordanes (Migne, *Patrologia*, Vol. I, p. 69).

Procopius.

Gregory of Tours (Pertz, *Mon. Germ. Hist. Script. Rer. Meroving.* Vol. I).

Venantius Fortunatus (Pertz, *Mon. Germ. Auct. Antiquiss.* Vol. IV).

Chronicle of King Eric (Langebek, *S. R. D.* Vol. I, pp. 148–170).

Peter Olavus (*S. R. D.* Vol. II, pp. 68–148).

Landnámabók.

William of Malmesbury, ed. W. Stubbs. *Gesta Regum Anglorum*, Bk. II, p. 121. Rolls Series, No. 90.

Aethelweard (Sir Henry Savile. *Rerum Anglicarum Scriptores*).

Scandinavian Sagas, &c.

Hrolfssagakraka (Fas. I).

Ynglingasaga (Hskr.).

Skáldskapermál (Sn. Edd.).

Arngrim Jonsson's Epitome of *Skjǫldungasaga (Aarb. f. n. Oldkynd.* 1894).

Bjarkarímur, ed. Finnur Jonsson. Copenhagen, 1904.

Flateyjarbók.

HISTORICAL REFERENCES TO THE DANES.

We do not find the Danes mentioned by name earlier than in works of the sixth century.

Tacitus, *Germania*, Ch. 40, mentions a confederation of tribes who worshipped the Goddess Nerthus on an island in the ocean, the most probable identification of which is Zealand, but the name Dane does not occur*.

Jordanes, Ch. III, refers to the Danes, but the passage is obscure and corrupt.

The Danes, he says, had dispossessed the Heruli of their (the latter's) country, but we do not know where the country of the Heruli was†.

Procopius (A.D. 513?), *Goth*. II, 14, says that the tribe of the Heruli on their migration northwards ran past the tribes of the Dani‡.

Gregory of Tours (*Hist. Franc.* III, 3), writing late in the sixth century, gives an account of the raid of Chochilaichus in which *Rex Danorum* is used wrongly. But the reference shows that the name of the Danes was known at that time.

Venantius Fortunatus (VII, 7, 50 and IX, 1, 73)§,

---

* Tacitus, *Germania*, Ch. 40: "Reudigni deinde et Aviones et Anglii et Varini et Eudoses et Suardones et Nuithones fluminibus aut silvis muniuntur—nec quicquam notabile in singulis, nisi quod in commune Nerthum, id est, Terram matrem colunt, eamque intervenire rebus hominum, invehi populis arbitrantur. Est in insula Oceani castum nemus dicatumque in eo vehiculum, veste contectum; attingere uni sacerdoti concessum."

† "Dani......Herulos propriis sedibus expulerunt."

‡ μεθ' οὓς δὴ καὶ Δανῶν τὰ ἔθνη παρέδραμον.

§ Venantius Fortunatus, VII, 7, 50: "Quae tibi sit virtus cum prosperitate superna, Saxonis et Dani gens cito victo probat"

IX, 1, 73: "Ne ruat armatus per Gallica rura rebellis, nomine victoris hic est et ampla tegis;

writing about A.D. 580, speaks of Saxons, Danes and Jutes as the enemies of the Franks.

A Danish tradition which is preserved in several mediaeval chronicles is that King Dan (the eponymous ancestor of the Danes) reigned over Zealand, Moen, Falster and Laaland; this kingdom was called Vihtesleth.

Peter Olavus, who belongs to the late Middle Ages, writes that the Germans attacked the Jutes, who called in King Dan to help them ; they afterwards offered Dan the kingdom so that he thus acquired Jutland as a possession. He also made subject Frisia, Fyn, Scania and other Danish islands (S. R. D. Vol. I, p. 68).

In the Chronicle of King Eric, we are told that Dan came from Sweden and ruled over four islands ; he was afterwards called in by the Jutes (S. R. D. Vol. I, p. 148).

HROLFSSAGA KRAKA.

There were two brothers named Hálfdan and Fróði who were both kings; Hálfdan had two sons, Hroar and Helgi, and a daughter, Signy, who was married to Earl Saevil. Fróði was jealous of his brother, who was king of Denmark ; he surprised and killed Hálfdan, after which he ruled Denmark in his stead. He would also have killed Hroar and Helgi, but they were rescued by their foster-father Regin, and taken by him for protection to the court of Vifill, who had been Hálfdan's best friend. Frodi, however, traced the boys and followed them to their hiding-place, and Vifill only succeeded in saving

quem Geta, Vasco tremunt, Danus Euthio, Saxo, Britannus,
cum patre quos acie te domitasse patet."

their lives by disguising them as his two dogs, Hopp and Ho, until the king had gone away again; but he saw that they were no longer safe with him, so Hroar and Helgi, now aged twelve and ten respectively, left Vifill and went in disguise to the home of their brother-in-law Saevil, where they were kindly received. After three years, when accompanying Signy and Saevil on a visit to King Fróði, they were accidentally recognised by their sister, but in spite of all warning and persuasion to turn back, they insisted upon completing their journey. Their presence was revealed to Fróði by a sibyl, and they were in imminent danger of their lives, had not the faithful Regin helped them a second time to escape. Shortly afterwards, with the assistance of Regin and Saevil, the brothers succeeded in killing Fróði by burning him in his hall.

Fróði was succeeded as king of Denmark by his nephew Helgi, while Hroar went to England, and settled with the king of Northumberland, whose daughter Ögn he afterwards married.

King Helgi was a rover, and on one occasion when on a sea-raid he sought the hand of Ólof, the queen of Saxland, in marriage, but was repulsed with scorn. In revenge for the treatment he had received, Helgi returned after some time to Saxland, and forced Ólof to be his mistress. In due time Ólof bore a daughter, Yrsa. Some years afterwards, while on another raid, Helgi met Yrsa, and without recognising her, took her home as his wife; he had by her a son, Hrolf Kraki. Helgi and Yrsa remained unconscious of their relationship to one another, until Ólof, who had known how matters stood from the first, came and told him the truth. When Yrsa heard that her husband was her own father she went back to Saxland with Ólof. There she was wooed by King Adils, whom she married and accompanied to Sweden.

Helgi, in the meantime, having lost his wife, was left disconsolate. One night a woman arrived at his house, and stayed with him until the morning. This woman was ᴧᴧ elf. Three years later she sent Helgi a child named Skuld, who, she said, was his daughter. Skuld was herself half an elf, and grew to be a woman of a very strange disposition. She practised magic, and was, later on, the means of bringing destruction to many.

After a time Helgi discovered that Yrsa was living at Upsala as the wife of King Adils, and he followed her there. Yrsa received her former husband with great joy; but Adils surprised Helgi and treacherously killed him.

Hrolf Kraki succeeded his father as king; he built a castle, Hleiðrgarðr (Leire), where he lived surrounded by his thanes—*kappar* and *berserkir*—and his fame soon spread, so that other warriors came from foreign courts in order to join his service. (This was apparently a very common practice in ancient times, and one which lasted indeed into the Middle Ages.)

Hrolf's sister, Skuld, the elf-maiden, married King Hiǫrvarð. Hrolf had two daughters, Scur and Drifa, the latter of whom was married to his warrior, Bǫðvar. Some insight into the court-life of Hleiðrgarðr is given in the story of Bǫðvar and Hjalti or Hǫtt (cf. *supra*, pp. 34 ff.).

Hrolfss. dwells at length on an expedition made by Hrolf to the court of King Adils; to this Hrolf was incited by Bǫðvar, who urged him to go and regain his father's inheritance—consisting of the money which Helgi had had with him when he was killed—which had been appropriated by Aðils. Hrolf consented to the plan somewhat reluctantly, and set out for Sweden with a retinue consisting of his twelve chosen warriors (*kappar*), twelve berserks, and a hundred fighting men.

In the course of their journey the Danes halted at the house of a man named Hrani, who, after testing their powers of endurance, advised Hrolf to take with him to Sweden only his twelve champions (*kappar*) and to send all his other men home again, as they would be of no use to him. Hrolf followed this advice; he despatched his whole retinue back to Hleiðrgarðr, with the exception of the twelve champions, in whose company he continued his journey.

Once at Aðils' court, Hrolf and his warriors had a series of hairbreadth escapes, and finally only succeeded in getting away with their lives.

Aðils, who was determined to kill his stepson, tried various ruses in order to achieve his purpose. He caused warriors to be concealed under the benches where the Danes were to sit, but they, fearing treachery, had persuaded their master not to reveal himself to Aðils; so this scheme failed, as the Swedish soldiers did not know which of the strangers was King Hrolf. Aðils gave orders for a great fire to be kindled in the hall, hoping thus to make an end of his enemies; but the Danes threw their shields on the fire, leapt over it, and almost succeeded in killing Aðils. Queen Yrsa was, however, favourably disposed towards her son; she tended him and his followers hospitably, and assigned to him as faithful servant a man named Vǫgg. It was Vǫgg who first gave Hrolf the name of " Kraki," * on account of his lean stature, and who at the

---

* Icel. *kraki*, Dan. *krage* = pale, stake.

same time promised solemnly to avenge his master, if, when Hrolf should be killed, he himself should remain alive. Vǫgg also warned Hrolf of the danger which threatened him from Aðils.

Aðils made a final attempt against his enemy's life by setting fire to the house in which the Danes were, and surrounding it with an army. Hrolf and his men succeeded, however, in escaping, and having been furnished by Yrsa with much treasure—including Aðils' prized ring Sviagris —and fresh horses, for their own had been maimed by the Swedes, they got away as far as Fyrisvellir, but were pursued and overtaken there by Aðils and an army. The Danes flung down the treasure they were carrying, in hope of checking the pursuit. But while his soldiers grovelled on the earth for the gold, Aðils himself pressed on, and only when Hrolf threw down the ring Sviagris did avarice triumph over hatred; as he stooped to pick up the precious gem, Hrolf lamed him with his sword Skǫfnung, at the same time revealing his identity to his baffled enemy. Aðils gave up the chase and returned to Upsala, while Hrolf was left in possession of Sviagris; after this the Danes had no difficulty in getting away.

On the return journey they again fell in with Hrani, who offered to give Hrolf a sword, shield and coat of mail. Hrolf refused these gifts although warned by Hrani that he would suffer for doing so. Only after they had parted, and the Danes had gone some way, did they realise that the man with whom they had been speaking, and who called himself Hrani, was in reality the all-powerful Odin. King Hrolf turned back quickly, hoping to make good his mistake, but found that both Hrani and his house had vanished. Having thus incurred the wrath of the great

God of war, the Danes went home filled with presentiments of impending misfortune.

Their fears were realised, for after an interval of peace, a conspiracy was formed against Hrolf by Skuld and her husband Hiǫrvarð. Hiǫrvarð was bound to pay Hrolf a yearly tribute, and this vexed the soul of Skuld, who felt it as a deep humiliation, and, therefore, incited her husband to revolt against Hrolf. The payment of the tribute was postponed for three years, at the end of which time Hiǫrvarð arrived at Hleiðrgarðr with great piles of what purported to be tribute-money, but which consisted in reality of weapons for his followers. A great battle took place in which Hrolf was defeated and his army annihilated. Hiǫrvarð himself was also killed on the same day. Skuld took the kingdom and governed very badly for a short time. But Vǫgg (who had taken a vow to avenge Hrolf's death) led against her an army which had been gathered by Thorir and Elgfroði (the brothers of Bǫðvar) with the assistance of Yrsa. In the battle which ensued Skuld's army was defeated, and she herself was killed.

A barrow was made for Hrolf Kraki, and his sword was buried with him.

LANDNÁMABÓK (Twelfth century).

An entry in the *Landnámabók*, Ch. 140, relates that a pirate merchant, named Miðfiarðar-Skeggi, who was journeying in the Baltic, landed in Zealand and harried the barrow of Hrolf Kraki. He seized Hrolf's sword and Hjalte's axe, but was prevented from further plunder by

the shade of Bǫdvar which fell on him and would have
done him great hurt, but for the intervention of Hrolf
Kraki *.

YNGLINGASAGA.

Ch. xxv.   "Aun or Áni was the name of Jǫrund's son,
who was king of the Swedes after his father : he was a
wise man and offered many sacrifices : he was not a
warrior, but stayed at home and ruled his kingdom.
During the time that these kings reigned at Upsala, of
whom we have now spoken, there reigned over Denmark,
first Dan the great (*hinn mikillati*); he lived to be very
old : then his son Froði the great, or the peaceful (*hinn
mikillate eda hinn frithsami*) : then his sons Halfdan and
Fridleif, who were great warriors.   Halfdan was the elder
and took the lead in everything.   He went with his army
to Swidjoð against King Aun, and they fought some
battles, and Halfdan was always victorious.   And in the
end King Aun fled to West Gautland : he had then been
king of Upsala for twenty-five years.   He was also in
Gautland for twenty-five years, while King Halfdan was
at Upsala.   King Halfdan died of a sickness at Upsala,
and he is buried there."

Ch. xxvi.   At the beginning of the chapter it is
related how, after the death of Aun, when Egil his son
had ascended the throne, Tunni, the former herdsman of
Aun, formed an insurrection and was successful over Egil
in several battles.

* *Lándnámabók Hauksbók*, c. 140 : "hans svn var Midfiarðar-Skeggi
Garpr mikill, hann heriadi i Austrveg ok la i Danmork vid Sioland, hann
var lutadr til at briota haug Rolfs konungs kraka ok tok hann thar or
Skǫfnung sverd Rolfs ok exi Hiallta ok mikit fe annat, enn hann nadi ei
Laufa thvi at Bodvarr villdi at hanum enn Rolfr konung vardi."

"After that King Egil fled from the land away to Sjaelland in Denmark to Froði the Bold (*hinn frøkni*); he promised tribute from the Swedes to King Froði in order to obtain his help: thereupon Froði gave him an army and his chosen warriors (*kappa*). So Egil journeyed to Sweden. But when Tunni heard that he went out against him with his army. Then there was a great battle, in which Tunni fell, so Egil took his kingdom, and the Danes went home. King Egil sent King Froði many large and valuable presents every season, but paid no tribute to the Danes; however his friendship with King Froði still continued. After Tunni's fall, King Egil ruled over the kingdom for three years."

Ch. XXVII. "The son of Egil was named Óttar: he took the sceptre and the kingdom after his father: he did not enter into friendly relations with King Froði. Then King Frodi sent men to King Óttar to demand the tribute which Egil had promised him. Óttar answered saying that the Swedes had never paid tribute to the Danes, nor would he. The ambassadors returned. Frodi was a great warrior. During one summer Frodi went with his army to Swiðjoð, made raids, harried, killed many, and took some away as prisoners. He took from there a great deal of booty: he also burned houses far and wide, and did a great deal of damage. Another summer Froði went on a raid to the Baltic: King Óttar heard that King Froði was not at home. So he got into his galley, sailed away to Denmark and harried there without encountering any resistance. He heard that a host was being gathered in Sjaelland, so he sailed westwards to Eyrarsund, then sailed south to Jutland, ran into Limfjorth, and harried in Vendill, burning and devastating the land. Vǫtt and

Fasti were the names of Froði's earls, whom he had set to protect Denmark during his absence. But when the earls heard that the king of the Svear was raiding in Denmark they collected an army, took ships and sailed south to Limfjorth. There they came upon Óttar quite at unawares, and at once engaged him in battle; the Swedes responded manfully and soldiers fell on both sides. But as fast as men fell on the Danish side other large contingents from the surrounding districts came to take their place, and thus all the ships in the neighbourhood were engaged in the combat. The end of the battle was, that King Óttar fell and the greater part of his army. The Danes took his body to land, and laid it on a mound and let the beasts and birds devour his flesh. Then they made a wooden trunk and sent it to Swiðjoð, and said that their King Óttar was not worth any more than that. And after that they called him Óttar the Vendil-crow."

Ch. xxviii is included in the discussion of Swedish traditions.

Ch. xxix contains an account of the relations of Helgi, Aðils and Yrsa of Saxland, three figures with whom we are already familiar. *Yngls.* differs from all other sources in representing Yrsa as the wife of Aðils previous to her marriage with Helgi.

Ch. xxix. "At that time King Helgi the son of Halfdan was ruling at Hleiðra: he came to Swiðjoð with such a large army that Aðils saw no alternative but flight. King Helgi landed with his army, harrying and taking much booty. He captured Queen Yrsa, and took her with him to Hleiðra, where he married her: their son was Hrolf Kraki. But when Hrolf was three years old, Queen Álof came to Denmark: she told Yrsa

that her husband, King Helgi, was her father, and that
she was her mother. Then Yrsa went back to Sweden to
King Aðils, and was queen there as long as she lived.
King Helgi fell while on a raid: Hrolf Kraki was eight
years old at that time, and was made king at Hleiðra.
King Aðils had a great strife with King Áli of Uppland
(*hinn Upplenzki*): he was from Norway. They fought a
battle on the ice of Lake Wener: King Áli fell there,
while Adils was victorious. Much is said concerning
this battle in the Skjǫldungasaga, and also concerning
Hrolf Kraki's coming to Upsala to Aðils; it was then
Hrolf Kraki sowed gold in Fyrisvellir."

Ch. xxx. The Fall of Hrolf Kraki. "The son of
Aðils who reigned next over Svealand was called Eystein;
in his days Hrolf Kraki fell at Hleiðra. In these times
many kings harried in Sweden, both Danes and Northmen.
There were many sea-kings who had many men but no
land. He alone was thought to have a right to the name
of sea-king, who never slept under sooty rafter, and never
drank at the chimney corner."

SAXO*.

(Ed. Holder, pp. 57–68.) Saxo's account of Hrolf Kraki
(Rolvo Krake) is in its essentials the same as that contained
in *Hrolfss.*, although the two vary in some points of detail.

Saxo differs from most other authorities in what he
says of Hrolf's predecessors. According to him, Frotho I
(Frodi) had three sons, Haldanus (Halfdan), Roe and
Scatus (Skat). Haldanus killed his two brothers and took

---

* It is impossible in this section to separate Danes from Swedes, as
the fortunes of the two peoples were so intimately connected during this
period.

the kingdom: he had two sons, Roe (Ro, Hroar) and Helgo
(Helgi), who reigned jointly in Denmark after their father's
death. Roe (Ro, Hroar) was the founder of Roeskilde :
he was killed by the Swedish king, Hothbroddus (Hoth-
brodd) the son of Regnerus (Ragnar). The sons of Hothbroddus were Athislus (Aðils) and Hotherus (Óttar).

Helgo (Helgi) avenged the death of Roe by killing
Hothbroddus and putting the Swedes into bondage, and
from this time onwards he reigned alone in Denmark.
The relations of Helgo (Helgi) to Ursa (Yrsa) and her
mother Thora (Ólof) are the same in Saxo as in all other
records. In later years Helgo became ashamed of the sins
of his youth, and of the wild life he had formerly led : he
left his kingdom and went to the East, where he died : it
was rumoured that in his despair he had committed suicide.

Helgo was succeeded by his son Rolvo Krake (Hrolf
Kraki) who, in the words of the historian, "was comely
with every gift of mind and body, and graced his mighty
stature with as high a courage *." In the meantime Hothbroddus had been followed on the Swedish throne by
Athislus (Aðils) who contrived to marry Ursa (Yrsa) the
mother of Rolvo Krake (Hrolf Kraki) in the hope that
by this stroke of diplomacy he might win his stepson's
friendship, and thus, ultimately, free Sweden from the
yoke of Denmark. But Aðils was of a miserly disposition,
and was thoroughly despised by Yrsa, who longed to get
rid of him. With this end in view, she invited her son Hrolf
to Sweden, and laid a plot to make her escape with him.

While Hrolf remained at the court of Aðils, appearances of friendship were carefully kept up between the
two kings : they vied with one another in giving proofs of

* Saxo, Books I—IX, trans. by O. Elton.

endurance and generosity respectively, and Aðils, much against his will, was constrained to present Hrolf with a beautiful necklace, one of his most prized possessions. On the third day after Hrolf's arrival, he and Yrsa succeeded in stealing away with much treasure. They were pursued by Aðils, and in order to make good their escape, had to throw down all that they carried with them. Aðils grovelled on the earth in order to re-obtain the necklace which he had been forced into giving Hrolf, and the fugitives succeeded in getting away*.

Various other isolated incidents of Rolvo Krake's reign are recorded by Saxo, amongst which may be noted the episode of Wiggo (Icel. Vǫgg) who, on entering Rolvo's service, bestowed on him the nickname of "Krake," and who, in return for the king's gifts, vowed to avenge his death. From this Saxo passes to the last scene of Rolvo's career, the attack on Leire made by the treacherous vassal Hiartuarius at the instigation of his wife Sculda (Rolvo's sister) and Rolvo's subsequent defeat and death. Saxo has incorporated in his narrative what is apparently a Latin version of the Old Icelandic *Bjarkamál*. This poem is a dramatic dialogue between Bjarki (Biarco) and his companion in arms Hjalti (Hjalto), in which the course of the battle is gradually unfolded.

SKÁLDSKAPERMÁL.

Skáldsk. Ch. XLIII gives the following account of the Danish kings :—

"The son of Odin was named Skjǫld, from whom sprang the Skjǫldungar: he lived in and ruled over the

* Cf. story of Atalanta in Gk mythology.

land which is now called Denmark, but which was then
called Gotland. Then Skjǫld had a son named Friðleif
who ruled over the land after him. The son of Friðleif
was named Froði, he took the kingdom after his father;
at this time Augustus Caesar ruled over the Roman
Empire, and brought about a universal peace: then
Christ was born. But because Froði was the most
powerful of all the kings in Scandinavian lands, therefore
the peace was ascribed to him in all Danish-speaking
countries, and the northmen call it the peace of Froði
(Froða-fri d)."

Skáldskapermál goes on to tell how Froði bought
from the Swedish king two giant handmaidens Fenja and
Menja to grind a huge wishing mill which he possessed.
He made them grind him out gold and prosperity without
ceasing: but, because he gave them no rest, they cursed
him by causing the mill to grind out destruction instead
of prosperity. As Fenja and Menja turned the mill, they
sang the Grottasǫng, in which these words occur, "the
son of Yrsa will avenge the death of Halfdan on Froði*."
In so far, this agrees with *Hrolfss.*, which also represents
Froði as killing Halfdan. But Frid-Froði was, according to *Skáldsk.*, a contemporary of Augustus Caesar, and
his name occurs very high in the genealogies, while
Halfdan, the father of Hroar, belongs to the fifth century!
The various Froðis have been confused with each other
throughout Scandinavian tradition; we shall have to

---

* This seems the most probable reading of the words:

" Mun Yrsa sonr
við Halfdani
hefna Frotha."

Some scholars read " vigs " for " við."

attempt later on the difficult, if not impossible, task of disentangling their respective identities (cf. *inf.* pp. 114 ff.).

Ch. XLIV, XLV. *Skáldsk.* relates the story of Hrolf Kraki's visit to Aðils with little variation from the other accounts. The visit was in this case a hostile one, and was caused by the failure of Aðils to pay certain of Hrolf's warriors rewards which he had promised them in return for their assistance in a campaign against King Áli of Norway.

The Danes were helped by Yrsa, who gave her son Hrolf treasure (namely the Sviagris, a bracelet or necklace (*baugr*) which was an heirloom in Aðils' family) and assisted him to escape. He was overtaken by Aðils at Fyrisvellir. In order to gain time for his flight, Hrolf threw down the necklace, and exulted when he saw Aðils bow to the ground to pick it up, for he was glad that the most powerful of the Swedes should bend before him.

ARNGRIM JONSSON'S EPITOME OF SKJQLDUNGASAGA.

The genealogy of Danish kings contained in *Skjǫld-ungasaga* will be found with the other genealogies in Appendix II. The figure of Frið-Froði (called by Arngrim, Frode fridgode) appears at the same point, and in the same connection as in *Skáldsk.*, Ch. XLIV (Arngr. Ch. III). Six generations later than this Frode fridgode (Frið-Froði) we find a certain Rigus, a chieftain of noble birth who won the hand of Dana, the daughter of Danprus of Danpsted. Rigus was the first who bore the title of king. His son Dan or Danus inherited the kingdom and it was called after him (Ch. VI). Dan II* was called *hin mikillâti*; he conquered Åleifus, the king of Selandia†, and married Olafa, the daughter of Vermundus, by whom he had a son Frodo (Ch. VII). Frodo, surnamed the peaceful (cf. *Froði hin friðsami*), married Inga, the daughter of Ingo, king of Sweden, and had two sons Fridleivus (Friðleif) and Halfdanus (Halfdan) (Ch. VII, 2). Fridleivus succeeded his father as king; he was a valiant and warlike prince, and was surrounded by a band of famous warriors of whom the greatest was Starcardus (Starkað). Fridleivus carried off Hilda, daughter of Alo (Ale), the king of the Norwegian Uppland. He had by her a son Alo (Áli) and by another wife a son Frodo (Froði) (Ch. VIII).

Frodo, having been born in lawful wedlock, took precedence of his brother and became king; he was surnamed *hin fraege* (the famous), while Alo, who was a sea-king, was called *hin froekni* (the bold). Alo was successful in warfare and had conquered Sweden, when Frodo bribed Starcardus to kill him, out of jealousy of his growing power. Starcardus performed the deed, but was afterwards disgusted at his own action, and left Frodo's service in order to go upon campaigns in Russia and Sweden. Frodo conquered Jorundus (Jǫrund) king of Sweden and exacted tribute both from him and from the Swedish earl Sverting; he also ravished Jorundus' daughter who bore him a son Halfdanus, while by his own wife he had a son Ingialldus (Ingjald). Ingialldus made good to Sverting the defeat which he had suffered, by marrying

---

* Arngrim believes several kings to have intervened between Dan I and Dan II, but is entirely ignorant of their names and histories.

† It is not clear whether Selandia is to be interpreted as Sjaelland, or as the district called by King Alfred Sillende.

his daughter. But Jorundus and Sverting conspired against Frodo's life, and the latter was murdered by Sverting and his sons (Ch. IX). Ingialldus took no vengeance on Sverting, but allowed him to expiate his crime by the payment of blood-money; his brother Halfdanus, however, avenged the death of their father Frodo by killing the sons of Sverting, while Ingialldus, at the instigation of Starcardus, put away his wife, Sverting's daughter, who had borne him a son Agnarus (Agnar). Ingialldus rewarded Halfdanus for killing Sverting's sons by giving him a third of the kingdom, whereupon Halfdanus married Sigrida, by whom he had two sons, Roas (Hroar) and Helgo (Helgi), and a daughter Signya (Signy). But Ingialldus became jealous of his brother; so he killed Halfdanus and married his widow; they had two sons, Raerecus (Hraerek) and Frodo. In the meantime Halfdanus' daughter Signya was married to Earl Sevillus (Saevil) in Selandia; his sons Roas and Helgo were brought up in secret on a certain island of Scania, and when they grew up, avenged the death of their father by killing their uncle, Ingialldus (Ch. X).

Helgo and Roas now became kings of Denmark; Roas was peacefully inclined and remained at home, while Helgo went on viking. The story of Helgo's adventure with Olava (Ólof), wife of Geirtiofius (Geirđjóf), earl of the Saxons, is practically the same as that of *Hrolfss*. It may be observed, however, that here, as in *Yngls.* (Ch. XXXII f.), Yrsa is represented as having been queen of Sweden before she married her father Helgo. Helgo was killed on viking five years after Yrsa had finally left him (Ch. XI).

When Helgo was killed, his son Rolfo Krake (Hrolf

Kraki) was eight years old : Rolfo reigned jointly with
his uncle Roas, until the latter was killed by Raerecus
and Frodo the sons of Ingialldus, after which Rolfo Krake
reigned alone. At this point Arngrim introduces the story
of Vǫgg (Woggerus) which it is unnecessary to repeat, as
his account does not differ from that of other sources.

Rolfo Krake's daughters were Driva and Skur ; the
former he married to his warrior Witserchus (Hvitserk)
while the hand of the latter was gained by Bodvarus
(Bǫðvar) who killed Agnarus the son of Ingialldus.
Rolfo's half-sister Scullda (Skuld) the daughter of Yrsa
and Adilsus (Aðils) had been taken in marriage by
Hiorvardus (Hiǫrvarð) a king of Eyland (Öland), without
Rolfo's consent : Rolfo therefore made war on Hiorvardus,
and having defeated him, forced him to pay tribute for his
kingdom.

The account of the relations between Rolfo (Hrolf) and
Adilsus (Aðils) as contained in Arngrim's *Skjǫlds.* is
much the same as that of *Skáldsk.* (Ch. 44), with one
important exception. The three treasures promised by
Aðils to Hrolf Kraki before the battle on Lake Wener,
and afterwards withheld by him, are mentioned, but are
not specified by name, and, as after events show, Arngrim
at least had not realised that Sviagris was one of them.
For when the Danes fled from Upsala (Arngr. Oppsala)
and had thrown down gold in a vain attempt to check
the Swedish pursuit, Rolfo Krake drew from his finger
" a ring of enormous value, which his ancestors had
brought back as booty from the vanquished kings of
Sweden," and threw it down before Aðilsus, with the
result which we already know (cf. p. 76). Rolfo Krake's
subsequent history as told by Arngrim, viz. Hiorvardus'

treachery, Rolfo's death (Ch. xɪɪ), and Woggerus' (Vǫgg's) revenge, corresponds to the narrative of *Hrolfss.*, except that the incident of the burning down of Leire during the attack of Hiorvardus is not referred to at all in *Skjǫldungasaga.*

III. Comparison of Evidence with regard to the Danes.

Now that we come to compare and sift all the evidence regarding the Danes, which has been collected, we shall find it a very difficult if not impossible task to separate genuine tradition from mere legend in the tangled web of saga, poem, and historical document presented to us. The allusions made by classical historians to the Danes are so bare, that they afford practically no foothold on which to base conclusions: the Scandinavian evidence, on the other hand, might be compared to the work of many artists, all of whom have attempted to make a memory sketch of some great picture: in the work of each the pictures are differently grouped, their expressions, attitudes, costumes are different, even the background is not always the same: each artist has drawn upon his imagination to fill up the gaps left by memory or by ignorance of the facts. By far the most important recent work on early Danish tradition seen through the medium of poem and saga is the *Danmark's Heltedigtning* of Dr Axel Olrik (Copenhagen, 1903), and in the course of the following pages an attempt has been made to embody his chief results, though it has not always been possible to accept his conclusions. Dr Olrik lays great stress on the evidence of the *Bjarkamál*, a poem of which the original (except for a couple of fragments in Old Norse) has been lost, but which has been preserved in an apparently complete form in a Latin translation by Saxo (ed. Holder, pp. 59–66). It is also partially preserved, although in a very corrupt form, in the last chapter of *Hrolfss.* According to Dr Olrik (*D. H. D.* pp. 42–61, 83–114) this poem is undoubtedly the oldest and most important piece of Scandinavian evidence which we possess regarding the events in question (viz. Rolf Kraki's defeat and death at the hands of Hiǫrvarð): he claims further that the poem is of Danish origin, and that it was composed about the middle of the tenth century. For these reasons its authority is a valuable criterion of genuineness in the investigation of early Danish tradition. There is no conflict of evidence among the early historical documents (Jordanes, Procopius, etc.) which mention the Danes, but, as already mentioned, these references, owing to their extreme meagreness, do not yield us results of any great value in the reconstruction of the early history of the nation.

Scandinavian sources which deal with the period of Danish history in question agree in their broad outlines, but vary in points of detail. All accounts agree as to the existence of a Danish king Halfdan, who is certainly identical with the Healfdene of the *Beowulf* (*vide inf.* pp. 130 ff.); but while according to the *Beowulf*, Halfdan had three sons, Heorogar, Hrothgar and Halga, and a daughter, who was probably the wife of Onela, king of Sweden, but whose name is not preserved in the MS. (cf. *Beo.*, l. 62), Scandinavian authorities allow Halfdan only two sons, Ro (Hrothgar) and Helgi (Halga). The Halga of the *Beowulf* is merely a lay figure, whereas

Helgi plays a most important part in Danish tradition, although different records do not always agree as to the facts of his career. Thus, according to Saxo (p. 51), King Helgi, overcome by the thought of his former sins, went to the East and died, or committed suicide. According to *Yngls.* (Ch. 33) Helgi met his death in battle, while according to *Hrolfss.* (Ch. 12) he was treacherously slain by Aðils, during a visit to the Swedish court at Upsala.

YRSA AND HROLF KRAKI.

The version of the story of Yrsa contained in *Yngls.* varies from that of Saxo and *Hrolfss.*, inasmuch as in the first mentioned authority the course of events has without doubt been confused (*vide inf.* p. 142); thus in *Yngls.* Yrsa is represented as the wife of Aðils, king of Sweden, before she married Helgi, and became the mother of Hrolf Kraki. In *Yngls.* and *Hrolfss.* the mother of Yrsa is called Ólof or Álof of Saxland: in Saxo she appears as Thora of the island of Thorey, and is not a queen, as she is said to be in *Yngls.*

Dr Olrik's theory about Yrsa, which is based on philological grounds, presents her whole story in a completely new light. By means of a lengthy enquiry into the origin of the name Yrsa, and of similar names, he shows (*a*) that the name Yrsa is otherwise unknown in Norse, and must, therefore, be of foreign origin, (*b*) that it is derived from the Lat. *ursus* = bear, (*c*) that although various names derived from this root are found amongst Teutonic peoples, they always occur in districts which either bordered on the Roman Empire, or had been otherwise subject to Roman influence. As a further proof that the name Yrsa was foreign to the North, he cites *Hrolfss.*, where it is said that Ólof called her daughter after her dog (cf. *Fas.* I, p. 22). Hence he arrives at the conclusion that if Yrsa is an historical character she must have belonged not to the Danes, but to some Southern people on the borders of the Roman Empire, probably the Franks —and that Helgi must have found and married her on one of his freebooting raids. Evidence of communication between the Danes and the Franks at this time is provided by Gregory of Tours' account of Hygelac's raid (Greg. Tur. III, 3). This supposition about Yrsa leads Olrik to discard the whole story of her birth as given in Scandinavian sources, and consequently also that of Hrolf Kraki's incestuous origin. The only point in the story which he allows to stand is that "Helgi, in the course of his voyages as a sea-king, landed on a foreign shore, whence he took away with him a fair maiden as his bride*." The whole account of Helgi's relations with Yrsa's mother, Ólof or Thora, he rejects as a modern accretion to the story.

The question of Hrolf's incestuous birth is discussed at length, and it is shown that there is no epic necessity for its truth, as it may have been first ascribed to him merely by analogy with other heroes. Almost all the greatest figures of hero-saga had this stain; Sinfjǫtli, Cuchullin, Gawain, Roland, all sprang from the union of brother and sister. The offspring of such a union was in most cases the greatest of his race—sometimes the chief figure within the range of the national poetry— inasmuch as he had in his veins the combined strength of two members of the same great family. But with him

* *D. H. D.* p. 154: "Helge, på sin faerd som søkonge, kom til en fremmed kyst, og bortførte den fagre jomfru som sin brud."

the whole stock usually came to a sudden and violent end ; from which our natural inference is that the guilt of the parents was visited on the child. It is thus possible, according to Olrik, that as Hrolf was the greatest and also the last of his race, an incestuous origin may have been attributed to him as a sort of necessity arising from the facts of his subsequent career. This necessity may even have been extended to include and consequently to account for the whole story of Helgi's life and of his early unhappy end (cf. *inf.* p. 141).

The important part played by Yrsa Dr Olrik attributes to the circumstance that Hrolf's father had died while he was still an infant, in consequence of which, according to ancient usage, Hrolf would be brought up by his mother and would be called by her name (*D. H. D.* pp. 144–159).

Closely connected with Yrsa is Hrolf Kraki's visit to Upsala. Saxo, *Hrolfss.* and *Skjǫlds.* (as repr. by *Skáldsk.* and Arngrim Jonsson) agree as to the fact of Hrolf's expedition to the court of Aðils, but differ in the reason which they assign for this expedition.

According to Saxo (ed. Holder, pp. 53–55) Yrsa hated her husband Aðils on account of his miserly disposition, and desired to be rid of him. She therefore invited Hrolf to come to Sweden, and together they stole away, taking with them much of Aðils' treasure.

In *Hrss.* (*Fas.* I, pp. 76–95) the motive assigned for Hrolf's expedition to Sweden is that he was desirous of regaining the money which his father Helgi had had with him in Sweden when he was treacherously killed by Aðils some years before.

In *Skáldsk.* (Ch. 44) the story differs yet again. Here Hrolf's expedition was in order to force Aðils to pay money which he refused to give up, and which he owed Hrolf and his berserks for the assistance they had given him against King Áli of Norway.

According to *Skáldsk.* then, Hrolf's expedition was avowedly a hostile one : according to Saxo and *Hrolfss.*, he went to Sweden on the pretext of paying Aðils a visit, but the relations between the two were no more amicable in the one case than in the other, and the details of Hrolf's stay correspond more or less exactly in all three accounts. The incident is not directly alluded to in the *Yngls.*

The absence of any sort of agreement amongst existing records regarding the motive of Hrolf's visit to Upsala makes us suspicious of all the explanations which they offer to account for it. It is also difficult to accept Dr Olrik's interpretation of the incident (*D. H. D.*, pp. 37 f., 179–184, 202–208) which is largely affected by his disbelief in the identity of Beowulf and Bǫðvar-Bjarki. He rejects, as of late Norwegian origin, the view which regards Hrolf's visit as a sequel to the battle of Lake Wener, and, in fact, repudiates the whole incident of the fight on the frozen lake, as having no connection with Hrolf Kraki whatever. Apart from that he condemns the motive of seeking reward for past services as utterly unworthy and ignoble. Olrik also refuses to accept Saxo's explanation, which he considers improbable, but he substitutes for it one at least equally improbable, viz., that Aðils probably invited his step-son to Upsala with the intention of treacherously killing him, "this being a frequent *motif* of hero-saga." He leaves quite out of consideration the fact that, in such cases, some reason— or at any rate pretext—usually existed for these murder-

ous designs on the part of the host, and that here there is
no such reason. Hrolf has done his step-father no injury,
nor is he the possessor of great treasure which could have
given rise to the jealousy of Aðils. Dr Olrik discards
further the part played by Yrsa as a modern addition to
the story, but it is difficult to see what grounds he has
for so doing in the face of authority as early as that of
Skáldskapermál.

On a close examination, it will be seen that the only
features of the episode of the Upsala visit which remain
unchanged in the various sources are the following:
(1) the *raison d'être* of Hrolf's visit to Upsala was to
obtain money from Aðils, (2) Hrolf's mother Yrsa was,
at the time of her son's visit, in Upsala as Aðils' wife.

The *Beowulf* contains no suggestion of Eadgils' (Aðils')
marriage with a Danish queen; according to it the only
relative of Hrothulf (Hrolf Kraki) in Sweden was his
aunt, the sister of Halga (Helgi) and Hrothgar (Hroar),
who married King Onela (cf. *Beo.* l, 62). There is however no reason to doubt the fact of Aðils' marriage
with Yrsa, which is well substantiated in Scandinavian
tradition.

If we look at the chronology of the *Beowulf* we shall
see that at the time of Beowulf's visit to King Hrothgar
(Hroar), Halga (Helgi) was in all probability already
dead. Hrothgar himself was already a very old man
(cf. *Beo.*, l. 357), and according to all Scandinavian traditions the life of Halga (Helgi) who was his elder brother
was cut short at a comparatively early point in his career.
By this time too, Hrothulf (Hrolf Kraki) was already
grown up, in fact in both *Beowulf* and *Widsith* he is
represented as ruling jointly with his uncle Hrothgar

(cf. *Wids.* ll. 45–49; *Beo.* ll. 1074 ff., 1163 f., 1181 ff.). It is a circumstance worthy of notice that only several years after Beowulf's exploit at the Danish court, does Eadgils (Aðils) appear for the first time in the *Beowulf* story. He and his brother Eanmund, while apparently still young men, fled into Gautland in order to escape the vengeance of their uncle Onela, and it was some years later that Eadgils (Aðils) overthrew Onela, and became king of Sweden in his stead (*Beo.* ll. 2379 ff., ll. 2391 ff.) (cf. also *supra*, p. 28).

This survey of the chronology of the Swedish and Danish royal families as contained in the oldest known records makes it impossible for us to accept the account of *Hrolfss.*, according to which Helgi was treacherously slain by Aðils while on a visit to Upsala. The evidence of the *Beowulf* shows that in all probability Helgi (Halga) and Aðils (Eadgils) were not even contemporaries, and the latter cannot, under any circumstances, have been more than an infant when Helgi's death took place. Hrolf (Hrothulf) himself must have been many years senior to Aðils (Eadgils), if, at the time of Beowulf's visit to the Danish court, he was already of an age to rule, and we may thus infer that his mother Yrsa was quite an old lady by the time that Aðils (Eadgils) was of a marriageable age. This being so, it seems more than probable that Aðils, in marrying a person so much his senior as we know Yrsa must have been, had some ulterior motive which has not been directly preserved in tradition.

Among the various reasons assigned for Hrolf's visit to Upsala, that of the *Skjǫldungasaga* (as contained in *Skáldsk.* cf. *supr.* p. 76), which should be the most reliable,

we are obliged to reject, as it is most unlikely that Hrolf
would have sent forces to take part in a campaign against
Áli (Onela) his uncle by marriage. But at all events
Áli was defeated and slain by Aðils (with the help of
Bǫðvar-Bjarki, cf. *Skáldsk.* Ch. 44) who then succeeded
him as king of Sweden. It was a common practice
amongst early Northern nations for a conqueror to marry
the widow of his predecessor in order to improve his
position amongst his new subjects (e.g. the marriage of
Cnut after his conquest of England in 1017 to the widow
of Athelred the Unready). Thus it would have been a
very natural thing for Aðils to take to wife the widow
of Áli—who, it must be remembered, was the sister of
Hrolf's father, and who belonged to an earlier generation
—notwithstanding the probable disparity of age between
them.

We find then on the one hand Aðils married to a
woman so much his senior that we cannot conceive his
motives in marrying her to have been other than political
ones: we have on the other hand discovered a motive
which might very well account for a marriage of this
nature: it remains for us to fit, if possible, marriage and
motive to one another.

The chief point to be noticed in this connection is the
relationship between Helgi and the wife of Aðils.

Yrsa*, Aðils' wife, was the daughter, and at some
time in her life, the wife of Helgi (Halga); the widow of

*

Beowulf		*O.N. Tradition*
Healfdene		Halfdan
Halga ——— ? = Onela		Yrsa = Helgi = Ólof
Hrothulf		Hrolf Yrsa = Aðils

King Áli (Onela) whom, as we have seen, it would have been quite natural for Aðils to have married on his accession to the Swedish throne, was the sister of Helgi (Halga). All versions of the story of Yrsa lay stress on her illegal marriage with Helgi, by which she became the mother of Hrolf Kraki, and it seems conceivable that Scandinavian tradition may have substituted a marriage between father and daughter for one which was originally between brother and sister, and for which parallel cases may be found in Northern tradition*.

Were this the case the name of Yrsa would supply the gap in *Beowulf*, l. 62, where a word beginning with a vowel is required for the alliteration: as the sister of Helgi (Halga) and the wife of Onela (Áli) her figure acquires new significance, and her marriage with Aðils is at once satisfactorily explained†.

If Yrsa were really the sister of Helgi and the missing name in *Beowulf*, l. 62, this would establish the truth of the origin attributed to Hrolf, and would bring him into line with the long roll of heroes of the migration period, so many of whom sprang from an illicit union of brother and sister (cf. p. 83). The attempt to show that the story

* I owe this suggestion to Mr H. M. Chadwick.

† This leads on to a further suggestion regarding the motive underlying Hrolf's visit to Upsala. All authorities agree that he went in order to obtain from Aðils a certain sum of money; we are led to infer that this money should have been paid before, but that it had been wrongly withheld by Aðils who was of a miserly disposition.

It is possible that what Hrolf went to fetch from Sweden was the "mundr" of his mother Yrsa, i.e. the bride-price, due to the relatives of the bride, without the payment of which no marriage was legal: thus the main object of his visit and of his action in extorting the "mundr" from Aðils would ultimately be to ensure the proper status and dignity of his mother as queen of Sweden (but *vide inf.* p. 141 f.)

of Hrolf's incestuous birth arose merely by the analogy of similar cases, would, if successful, seem to prove too much, as these cases themselves might be accounted for with as much likelihood in exactly the same way.

HEOROWEARD.

The Heoroweard of *Beowulf*, who was the son of Heorogar (*Beo.* ll. 2161–2), seems to correspond in name to the Hiǫrvarð of Scandinavian tradition (Saxo, Hiartuarius); but Scandinavian writers do not hint at any blood relationship between him and his brother-in-law Hrolf Kraki, while on the other hand, they do not seem to have any clear conception of the political situation which underlay Hiǫrvarð's attack and defeat of Hrolf Kraki at Leire.

Hrolf's fall at Leire is the chief theme of *Bjarkamál*, and here the only motive assigned for Hiartuarius' attack is the ambition of his wife Skuld: the soldiers of Hiartuarius are called in *Bjarkamál* Goths or Swedes (Saxo, pp. 65 f.). All later Scandinavian sagas in describing the incident lay stress on the treachery of Hiǫrvarð and Skuld as the sworn vassals of Hrolf Kraki, but none of them give any satisfactory explanation of the nationality of Hiǫrvarð's army, and no two accounts agree as to who and what Hiǫrvarð himself actually was.

The identification of Hiǫrvarð with the O.E. Heoroweard would supply the key to the situation. Heoroweard was the son of Heorogar, Hrothgar and Halga's elder brother, and thus had a claim to the Danish throne, prior to that of his cousin Hrothulf (Hrolf Kraki) but one which he—perhaps like Hrethric (*vide inf.* p. 100)—was unable to make good, on account of Hrothulf's superior power. In order to save his own life, he may, therefore, have sworn homage to Hrothulf, a pledge which, according to Scandinavian tradition, he afterwards broke. But none of the Northern sources, without exception, have any idea that Hiǫrvarð had an excuse for his treachery in the existence of a valid claim to the throne of Denmark, and as matters at present stand we have not enough evidence to prove conclusively his identity with the O.E. Heoroweard. It is, however, more probable than not that the two are the same, and that the events related in the Scandinavian sagas were in reality the outcome of the political situation, which is hinted at in the *Beowulf*, but which was subsequently—after the lapse of centuries—completely forgotten (cf. *D. H. D.* pp. 38–42).

Hrothgar and Hrothulf.

The most serious discrepancy between the account of the Danes in *Beowulf*, and that contained in Scandinavian tradition, concerns the person and character of Hrothgar (Scand. Ro, or Hroar).

We have seen that in no Scandinavian authority does Ro play an important part : his personality is, on the other hand, distinctly colourless. He died early and was succeeded by his brother Helgi, Helgi in his turn being followed by the great Hrolf Kraki. In *Hrolfss.* the insignificance of Hroar is emphasized yet more, for according to it, he did not reign at all in Denmark, but went to Northumberland where he married and settled, leaving his brother Helgi in undisputed possession of the Danish throne.

But the evidence of *Beowulf* regarding Hrothgar (Hroar) points all the other way. He is everywhere referred to in terms of the greatest admiration and esteem, and stress is laid, throughout the poem, on the length and glory of his reign (cf. *Beo.* ll. 1769 ff.).

At first sight it seems as if some confusion must have taken place between the two kings, as the part played by Hrothgar in O.E. tradition seems to correspond so exactly to that filled by Hrolf Kraki in Scandinavian records. In that case, though the bulk of evidence would favour the supposition that Hrolf Kraki was the more outstanding of their two men, it is all evidence of a late date—in no case earlier than the twelfth century—while on the other hand, the testimony of *Beowulf*, although standing alone, is several hundred years earlier than that of the Scandinavian records, and therefore cannot be lightly disregarded.

But there is another possible explanation of the difficulty. Both *Beowulf* and *Widsith* represent Hrothgar and Hrothulf (Hrolf) as reigning together in Denmark in accordance with a practice which we frequently find amongst early Teutonic peoples, viz. that in any case where there were two or more adult members of a royal family, they reigned as joint kings in the country. Both poems also lay stress on what seems to have been a remarkable fact and very contrary to custom, namely, the friendly relations which existed between these joint rulers Hrothgar and Hrothulf (cf. *Wids.* ll. 45–49, *Beo.* ll. 1074 ff., l. 1163 f., ll. 1181 ff., l. 1018 f.). As Hrothulf was the nephew of Hrothgar, and presumably a much younger man, it is very probable that he survived his uncle, and continued to reign alone after Hrothgar's death. If this was so, one can well see how his fame might in the course of centuries have come to entirely overshadow that of Hrothgar, and how, when written records came to be made, this glorious epoch of Danish history was associated primarily with the name of Hrolf Kraki.

On the other hand, the fame of Hrothgar may have reached England during that ruler's lifetime, and before it became eclipsed by that of his nephew. Indeed, it looks as if this must have been the case, as we have no evidence that England had any communication with the Baltic countries between Hrothgar's reign and the end of the eighth century, when the Danish invasion began. This explanation would also account for the very minor part played by Hrothulf in *Beowulf.*

THE HALL HEOROT.

The scene of Beowulf's exploit against Grendel is the great Heorot, which is said to have been built by Hrothgar, and is described with reverential admiration by the poet as the national hall and sanctuary of the Danes (*Beo*. ll. 67–85).

The seat of the Danish kings was, according to the unanimous testimony of Scandinavian literature, Hleiðrgarðr (Leire) on the island of Sjaelland (Zealand), the building of which is attributed in a good many authorities to Hrolf Kraki. In other references, however, we read of a castle of Hleiðrgarðr having existed in very much earlier times (cf. *Yngls*. Ch. 31, where it is represented as being from the beginning the ancestral home of the Skjǫldungar) and having been built by the founder of the dynasty.

The Leire of to-day is a tiny village whose present

insignificance contrasts so strongly with the accounts of
its former glory that some scholars have found it difficult
to believe that it could ever have been the site of a royal
residence. But not many miles from Leire stands Roeskilde, which is an important town: it was formerly capital
of Denmark and is the ancestral burial-place of the
Danish kings. Roeskilde means "the fountain of Ro,"
and tradition connects the name of Ro with the building
of the town. In view of these facts, it is somewhat difficult to say whether the Heorot of the *Beowulf* is to be
identified with Leire or with Roeskilde.

Some light is thrown on the question by Dr Olrik, who
has no doubt that the present Leire does represent the
old Hleiðrgarðr, and is sure moreover that its former
greatness is no fable, but has a solid foundation in fact.
For through all tradition, the one thing which stands
firmly established about Hleiðrgarðr is its connection
with Hroar and Hrolf: that remains though all else goes.
There is nothing, however, to show that it was a royal
residence after the sixth century, and it is very possible
that it was destroyed in the last great fight, when Hrolf
Kraki met his death at the hands of the treacherous
Hiǫrvarð (cf. *Bjarkam.*, Saxo, pp. 59–66). The fall of a
great king is always the starting-point for epic narrative,
and probably the position of Leire in song and story is an
attempt of the scalds to develop and enhance its former
glory, which had come to such an untimely end.

The view that Leire played a part in national poetry
long after it had ceased to exist, and that it lived, so to
speak, on its past reputation, would account satisfactorily
for its later insignificance compared with the neighbouring
Roeskilde. Another fact may have contributed to Leire's

loss of importance in mediaeval times: its great natural strength against any attack by sea was no longer a matter of such importance once the political status of the Danes was assured; the attention of the nation was then naturally turned rather to the increase of their commercial prosperity, than to the necessity of self-defence, and this led to the growth of Roeskilde (*D. H. D.* pp. 188–200).

As the difficulty of regarding the modern village of Leire as the site of the ancient Hleiðrgarðr has thus been cleared up, it seems more likely that Heorot is to be identified with it than with Roeskilde, and the fact that Hleiðrgarðr is represented throughout Scandinavian records as the national hall and sanctuary of the Danes would be in favour of this. The importance attaching to Roeskilde as the burial-place of the Danish kings probably dates only from Christian times. The tradition that a castle of Hleiðrgarðr existed in very early times is no argument against its identity with Heorot, for it is quite conceivable that, being built of wood, it might have been burned down (as we hear in *Beo.* ll. 82–3 that it was), and re-built by Hrolf Kraki.

HRETHRIC.

According to the *Beowulf* (l. 1189) Hrothgar had two sons, Hrethric and Hrothmund. Hrothmund is otherwise unknown, but Hrethric has been identified by Sarrazin, Olrik and others with the Roric (Hraerek, Roricus) who is a personage of considerable importance in Scandinavian tradition, although authorities are at variance with regard to the actual circumstances of his life. The following account of him is almost entirely

based on the evidence which has been collected by
Dr Olrik (cf. *D. H. D.* pp. 28–34, 167–175), and which
in some cases has led him to somewhat startling conclusions, especially in his interpretations of the *Beowulf*
and *Widsith.*

Starting now as always from *Bjarkamál,* we find that
Rolvo (Hrolf) slew Rǿricus the son of the covetous Bǫkus.
The words which describe the incident are put into the
mouth of Hjalto (Hjalti), and the passage is as follows*:
"But let us who honour our king...go forth in the way
the king taught us : our king who laid low Rorik the son
of Bok the covetous (*qui natum Bǿki Rǿricum stravit
avari*) and wrapped the coward in death. He was rich
in wealth, but in enjoyment poor, stronger in gain than
bravery : and thinking gold better than warfare, he set
lucre above all things, and ingloriously accumulated piles
of treasure, scorning the service of noble friends." Hjalti
goes on to tell how Rorik, when he was attacked by the
navy of Hrolf, spread out treasure before his city gates
in the hope of staying the fury of the enemy, and thus
saving his own life. But Rolf the righteous assailed him,
slew him, and captured his vast wealth, and shared among
worthy friends what the hand of avarice had piled up in
all those years.

But Saxo knows another Roricus surnamed Slyngebond, a brave and warlike ruler, and the son of Hotherus
who followed Hiartuarius on the Danish throne (cf. Saxo,
ed. Holder, pp. 82 ff.). This person appears as Rökil
Slaghenback in Sven Aagesen's chronicle, where he is
the direct successor of Hrolf Kraki. According also to
the genealogy of the Icelandic *Lgfǎg.,* Hrolf Kraki is

---

* Saxo Grammaticus, Books i—ix, translated by O. Elton, p. 75.

succeeded by a Hraerek, who however is here surnamed *Hnauggvanbaugi* (covetous of rings or treasure) and is described as *Ingiallz syn*, i.e. the son of Ingjald. Three generations further down in the genealogy of *Lgfdg.* comes *Hraerekr Slaungvanbaugi*, the son of Halfdan (cf. Genealogies, p. 273).

In the later version of the lost *Skjǫldungasaga*, represented by Arngrim Jonsson's fragmentary Latin transcript (*Aarb. f. nord. Oldkynd.* 1894, pp. 104 ff.) (= A) and the recently discovered *Bjarkarímur* (Finnur Jonsson, Copenhagen, 1904) (= B), Raerecus (Hraerekr Sløngvanbaugi) (B) is represented as the son of Ingjalldus (Ingjald). According to A, he and his brother Frodo (Froði) kill Roas (Hroar) in revenge for their father's death, and after Rolfo Krake's death Raerecus divides the kingdom with Rolfo's son Walldarus (Arngr., Ch. XII–XIII). According to B, the relationships are the same, and here also Ingjald has been murdered by Hroar and Helgi. Hraerek then comes on board Hroar's ship, throws the ring Sviagris into the sea, and is lamed by the two brothers in revenge. He goes home and dies soon afterwards (*Bjr.* VII). In the *Hrolfss.* a similar story is told of Hrók (Hrørek ?) who kills Hroar after throwing his ring into the sea; but Helgi avenges his brother's death by crippling Hrók (*Fas.* I, pp. 24 ff.). Thus Scandinavian sources all know a Roric (Hraerek Roricus) who is contemporary with Hrolf Kraki, and is surnamed *Slanganbogi* (*Slanggenbøghi*), while in the oldest Icelandic genealogies he has apparently become two personalities, for we find *Hraerekr hnøggvanbaugi* and his grandson *Hraerekr slǫngvanbaugi* (*Lfdg.*). The same confusion occurs in Saxo: for according to the *Bjarkamál* (Saxo's version) Røricus was the son of

c.   7 the covetous B*ø*kus. *B*øki avari* would be in Old Danish *hins nygga B*øks* (O.N. *hn*øggva Baugs*): this, as has been pointed out by Sarrazin (*Engl. St.* xxiv, 144 f.) and Olrik (*D. H. D.* p. 33), can scarcely be anything but a mistake for the epithet which we have already seen applied to Roric, viz. *hn*øggvanbaugi*, perhaps in the strong form *hn*øggvanbaugs*, in which the genitive of a noun *baugr* (= ring) has been taken as the genitive of a proper name. This emendation also fits the description of R*ø*ricus, which follows, so exactly that in consideration of the age of the *Bjarkamál* there can be little doubt that it was the term originally applied to him. It is easy to understand the scribal error which later on reproduced *hn*øggvanbaugi* as *sl*øngvanbaugi* (Saxo *Slyngebond*). The latter was, too, a more complimentary term and applied equally well to the R*ø*ricus of *Bjarkamál*, who threw down his treasure in order to appease the anger of his enemy. The mistake, as we have seen, led in some cases to an erroneous belief in the existence of the two Rorics (Saxo, *Lf*ær*g*.), to the further consequences of which we probably owe all the stories of later Scandinavian tradition (*Hrolfss.*, *Bjr.*, Saxo) which relate the throwing of the ring by Roric (Hraerek, Hrok, R*ø*ricus) into the sea: they are merely late inventions to account for the curious surname of "ringslinger," the origin of which was unknown.

Apart from the story of the ring, the later accounts of Roric in Scandinavian literature agree as to the main facts of Hroar's murder at his hands, and the subsequent vengeance taken for that murder (usually by Helgi), but vary in almost every other circumstance of the narrative.

The clue to this tangle of conflicting evidence, says Dr Olrik, is to be found in the oldest records, viz. the

Beowulf and *Widsith,* which, taken in conjunction with *Bjarkamál,* alone give the true explanation and the right sequence of events. Certain passages in the O.E. poems (*Beo.* ll. 1014–1019, 1163–1168, *Wids.* ll. 45–49*) contain for Dr Olrik a clear reference to an impending catastrophe in the Danish royal house. For the present, peace reigns in Denmark: Hrothgar and Hrothulf rule as joint sovereigns in love and goodwill. But evil days are in store: treachery will part those who were bound by oaths of friendship and ties of blood-fellowship.

For the key to all these dismal prognostications we are referred by Dr Olrik to the *Bjarkamál,* which relates how Hrolf Kraki overcame and killed Roric (Rǿricus). After Hrothgar's death dissension arises between the

---

* *Beowulf,* ll. 1014–1019.

> Faegere gethaegon
> medoful manig mâgas thara
> swîth-hicgende on sele tham heán
> Hrôthgar and Hrôthulf. Heorot innan waes
> freóndum âfylled ; nalles fâcen-stafas
> theod Scyldingas thenden fremedon.

[Hrothgar and Hrothulf the stout-hearted kinsmen took full meetly many a cup of mead in the high hall. Heorot was filled within with friends; by no means did the people of the Scyldings then use treachery.]

ll. 1163–1168.

> tha cwôm Wealhtheó forth
> gán under gyldnum beáge, thaer thâ gôdan twegen
> saeton suhter-gefaederan : tha gyt waes hiera sib aetgaedere,
> aeghwylc ôthrum trŷwe : swylce thaer Ûnferth thyle
> aet fôtum saet freán Scyldinga : gehwylc hiora his ferhthe treówde
> thaet he haefde môd micel theáh the he his mâgum naere
> ârfaest aet ecga gelâcum.

[Then came forth Wealhtheow to go under a golden circlet, where the two good men, uncle and nephew, sat: as yet there was peace between them, each to the other true. Unferth the "thyle" sat there likewise at the feet of the Lord of the Scyldings : each of them trusted to his heart that he (i.e. Unferth) had a mighty courage, though he might not have been true to his kinsman at the play of swords.]

cousins Hrethric and Hrothulf, and Hrethric is killed
by the powerful Hrothulf; for nothing would check more
fatally the growth of this young kingdom than internal
strife, and Hrothulf would have no alternative but to
suppress promptly the first indications of civil unrest
by the assertion of his superior power (*D. H. D.* pp. 14–18,
29–34). Such is Dr Olrik's reconstruction of this passage
of Danish history. The invention in late Scandinavian
tradition of the story attributing the murder of Hroar
to Roric (Hraerek, O.E. Hrethric), who as we see was
originally Hroar's (O.E. Hrothgar's) son, he ascribes to
a desire in the first instance to exculpate Hrolf (O.E.
Hrothulf) from blame, and to make his action in killing
Roric appear as a deed of righteous vengeance. The saga
then became independent of Hrolf, and the figure of Helgi
was added as the most suitable avenger of his brother
Hroar (*D. H. D.* pp. 167–175).

This explanation of the historical significance of the
Hrethric of the *Beowulf* is extremely ingenious, but it
rests solely on the evidence of *Bjarkamál*, which is made
to serve as the excuse for reading into the O.E. poems
much which is not really there. It is a manifest ab-
surdity to say with Dr Olrik (*D. H. D.* p. 330) that the
tragic climax of the *Beowulf* is the struggle for the Danish
throne between two rival branches of the great Skjǫldung
family. The most that the O.E. poems can be said actually to contain is a hint of surprise at the friendly
relations existing between Hrothgar and his nephew
Hrothulf; in the light of events incontrovertibly known
to have taken place later than the action of the *Beowulf*,
these references might perhaps be regarded as prophetic
utterances. But the difficulty lies in our complete

ignorance of later events; for the sole authority of the *Bjarkamál* with its one reference (*qui natum Bøki Røricum stravit avari*) admittedly corrupt, and conceivably pointing to some person other than the Hrethric of *Beowulf,* is not conclusive, and is certainly not a sufficient foundation for the airy erection of hypotheses which Dr Olrik has built upon it.

HROTHGAR'S WARRIORS.

In addition to the members of the Danish royal family, the *Beowulf* poet mentions by name four of the warriors in Hrothgar's service : Unferth, Wulfgar, Aeschere and Yrmenlaf; but, as it is only in the case of Unferth that the references consist of more than a passing allusion, and as, further, none of these characters are known in any other source, it is impossible to make even a conjecture as to their historical significance.

Aeschere and Yrmenlaf were brothers (l. 1324). The former was a doughty warrior and trusted thegn and counsellor of king Hrothgar (ll. 1323 ff.). He was snatched away by Grendel's mother on the night after Beowulf's first victory, when the monster, burning to avenge the death of her son, made a raid on Heorot (ll. 1281 ff.). The old king was overcome with grief at the loss of his knight and companion in arms (cf. Bugge, *P. B. B.* XII, 65 ff.).

Wulfgar was a prince of the Wendlas (ll. 348) and the herald of the Danish king ; Beowulf and his knights were received by him at the gate of Heorot on their arrival (ll. 325 ff.). The Wendlas were perhaps the people of Vendill, which is the most northerly point of Jutland (cf. *supr.* p. 70).

Unferth is described as the "orator" (*thyle*) of King Hrothgar (l. 1165): his place was at the foot of the throne, and both Hrothgar and Hrothulf relied on his fidelity, although he had apparently betrayed and murdered his own brothers (ll. 587, 1166 ff.). He was a man of a surly and jealous disposition, for on Beowulf's arrival at Heorot he sought to injure his reputation by taunts (ll. 499 ff.): later on, however, he forgot his malice in admiration, and even went the length of lending Beowulf his famous sword Hrunting, when he was arming for his descent into the mere in search of Grendel's mother.

Dr Olrik regards both the character of Unferth and his rôle in *Beowulf* as having a purely allegorical significance. The connection in which Unferth is mentioned in the poem (l. 1165; cf. *supra*, p. 99) is a sign (says Dr Olrik) that he was involved in the subsequent feud between the joint sovereigns of Denmark, which is the "tragic climax" of the poem. In fact Unferth may probably be looked upon as himself the promoter of this feud, and in this light his figure may be compared with that of the wicked counsellor Bikki in the Ermanric saga, and other similar characters. His very name is symbolic of the part which he plays in the story, according to Dr Olrik's interpretation—*Unferth* = *unfrith* = strife (cf. *D. H. D.* pp. 25–27).

There is no justification whatever for this fanciful explanation of Unferth's appearance in *Beowulf*, either in the poem or elsewhere, and it is impossible to attach value to it, the more so as the practice of giving names of abstract significance to real characters is one scarcely known in Scandinavian hero-legend.

THE HEATHOBEARDAN IN BEOWULF.

The tribe of the Heathobeardan mentioned in *Beowulf* cannot be identified with any certainty. Various attempts have been made to prove that they were the Langobards (Grein in Ebert's *Jahrbuch*, IV, pp. 260–285) or the Heruli (Müllenhoff), but without success.

The story of Frotha and Ingeld as told in *Beowulf* has already been given : a similar story is contained in the sixth book of Saxo's Danish history, but occurs in quite a different setting (Bk VI, pp. 200–215, ed. Holder), and the same set of events appears in a very much disguised form in Icelandic tradition.

Saxo's account is as follows :—

Frotho IV, King of the Danes, was treacherously slain by Swerting, King of the Saxons, a tributary sovereign who wished to regain his independence. At the same time, Frotho slew Swerting. Frotho was a wise, just and merciful ruler, and was beloved of all men : he was succeeded by Ingellus, who was as vicious as his father was virtuous. He was a glutton and debauchee, and was lost to all sense of honour. Ingellus made peace with the sons of Swerting, his father's murderer, heaped favours on them, and took their sister to wife.

News of Ingellus' shameful deeds reached Starcatherus, an old warrior who had formerly fought for Frotho, and who was at that time sojourning in Sweden. He was stung with anger and grief at the behaviour of the son of his old master, and straightway set off for Denmark in the hope of being able to rouse the sluggish spirit of Ingellus to action. On his arrival Ingellus was away hunting, and insults were heaped on Starcatherus by the queen, who did not know who he was: but when the king returned and recognised the rough-mannered stranger to be Starcatherus, "he rebuked his wife and charged her roundly to put away her haughty tempers, and to soothe and soften with kind words and gentle offices the man she had reviled." But Starcatherus would have none of her: instead of partaking of the sumptuous banquet which followed, he arose in wrath and denounced Ingellus for his gluttony, and for his unfilial spirit in forgetting to avenge his father, and in allowing Frotho's murderers to occupy the seats of honour at his table.

The severe rebuke of Starcatherus at last kindled a spark in the torpid soul of Ingellus: presently this spark blazed forth into flame, and Ingellus, mindful only of the shameful deed of the sons of Swerting, rushed on them with drawn sword, and with the help of Starcatherus slew them all, thus tardily avenging his father's death (Saxo, pp. 189–215).

It is clear that this story is essentially the same as that told of the Heathobeardan in *Beowulf* (ll. 2022–2069), but instead of representing Frotho and Ingellus as kings of the Heathobeardan and contemporary with Hrothgar of the Danes, Saxo has represented them as Danish kings thirteen generations later than Hrothgar.

In *Langfeðgatal*, Frode and Ingjald his son also appear as Danish kings, but here their names occur before those of Helgi and Hroar, Ingjald being only one generation earlier than these two.

But a reminiscence of the Heathobeardan, described in the *Beowulf* as Hrothgar's contemporaries, seems to be preserved in the Hothbroddus, king of Sweden, mentioned by Saxo (p. 51) as the father of Athislus and Hotherus, and the slayer of Ro. An account of the relations between Hothbroddus and the kings of Denmark has been given earlier in this chapter (p. 73), and the fact that Hothbroddus was defeated and killed, and his kingdom made subject by a Danish king, confirms the evidence as to the fate of the Heathobeardan, which we already possess.

In Hothbroddus, which is apparently the same word as Heathobeard, we have an instance of the personification of a tribe or people as one man. Instances of this process are frequent in ancient times; cf. Hunding(us) (Saxo, p. 51) and the Hundingas (*Wids.* L, 23), Hading(us) (Saxo, p. 19) and the Hjaðningar (*Skáldsk.* Ch. 50).

According to O.N. tradition (with the exception of *Yngls.*) Halfdan was killed by his brother—who appears variously as Froði or Ingjald—and avenged by his sons Hroar and Helgi, who themselves narrowly escaped death at the hands of their uncle* (cf. *supr.* pp. 63 f.). A narrative similar in detail to that of Hroar and Helgi's revenge as told in *Hrolfss.*, and probably derived from Norse tradition, occurs in the seventh book of Saxo; here it is related of the Danish king, Frotho V, who murdered his brother Harald(us) and was killed in revenge by Harald's sons, Halfdan (Haldanus) and Harald(us) (Saxo, pp. 217 f.).

With regard to the background or framework of the events forming our story, Old English, Icelandic and

---

* In *Skjǫlds.* (Arngr. Jonss. and *Bjr.*) Ingjald and Halfdan are brothers the sons of Froði. Halfdan is murdered by Ingjald and avenged by his own sons Hroar and Helgi. According to Arngrim's version however, Halfdan had previously taken vengeance for the murder of his father Froði by the Swedish earl Sverting, by killing Sverting's twelve sons as in Saxo: and Ingjald, at Starkað's instigation, had put away his wife, Sverting's daughter, for a similar reason.

Danish traditions are strikingly at variance with one another. In the O.E. poems, the Danish kings (Scyldings, O.N. Skjǫldungar) and the Heathobeardan are represented as two separate dynasties, and the struggle between them appears as a tussle for supremacy between petty kings, before the power of the Danish kingdom was firmly established. In Icelandic tradition, however, the struggle between Halfdan and his sons, on the one side, and Froði and Ingjald, on the other, has become a blood-feud between two competing branches of the Skjǫldung family : there is no longer any question of rival dynasties. Again Danish tradition (Saxo) represents both Frotho and Ingellus as kings of the Danes, and has transferred the whole story to a much later period : the murderer of Froði is here, as in Arngr. Jonsson's *Skjǫlds.*, Swerting, who is no longer a Swedish earl, but king of the Saxons, although in both cases a vassal of the Danish sovereign.

In the matter of detail, it is to be noted that different sources choose for elaboration different features of the story. For example, in the O.E. poems, Ingeld's revenge is described, while the occasion of that revenge, viz. the murder of his father Froði, is only mentioned in passing. But in Icelandic sources, it is Froði's murder on which emphasis is laid : it was itself a deed of vengeance and nothing is said of the revenge for that revenge except in Arngrim's version of the *Skjǫlds.*, according to which Hroar was killed by the sons of Iugjald ; while the revenge story proper is introduced in a different connection*. Saxo has preserved, as we have seen, accounts both of Frotho's crime and murder

* See note on p. 105.

(pp. 217 ff.), and of Ingellus' revenge* (pp. 199 ff.);
probably also that of the final defeat of the Heathobeardan by the Danes (p. 53). But that he had no
clear idea of the real significance and interdependence
of these incidents is shown by the way in which he
has treated them in his history: for they are introduced at altogether different periods, and are tacked on
to the persons of kings separated from one another by
generations.

Little doubt can be entertained that the strife of the
Danes and the Heathobeardan was in reality the outcome
of a situation such as is described in *Beowulf* and *Widsith*,
viz. a bloody struggle between two dynasties of petty
kings for political supremacy. The probability seems to
be that the Heathobeardan were originally one of the
several tribes who occupied lands on the western Baltic :
they were, perhaps, in common with the Danes, one of
the seven tribes mentioned by Tacitus (cf. *sup.* p. 62)
as united by the cult of the Goddess Nerthus. In the
constant struggles which mark the gradual consolidation
of every great state, the Danes appear to have gained
the upper hand, and to have gradually absorbed various
other originally independent peoples, of whom the Heathobeardan were one.

The distinctive name and character of these peoples
were in time consequently lost, while the names of some
of their former rulers survived; and these names have
apparently been incorporated with the genealogies of the

---

* Here we are told even the name of the *eald aescwiga*, viz.
Starcatherus, and a long description of him is given ; in fact Starcatherus
(O.N. Starkað) is one of the chief characters of Saxo's history, and of
Northern tradition in general.

Danish royal families by later historians, who knew nothing of them, further than that they were the names of kings who had once ruled in Denmark. These historians were thus—as perhaps also in the case of Hiǫrvarð—driven to invent a fresh explanation for facts, whose real underlying causes had been meanwhile completely forgotten *.

The account of the feud between the Danes (Scyldungas, O.N. Skjǫldungar) and the Heathobeardan resolves itself into a long story of revenge and counter-revenge. The first episode in this story of which we hear anything is the murder of Healfdene (Halfdan) by Froda (Froði) or Ingeld (Ingjald), which is recorded by O.N. authorities; this would be quite in harmony with the course of after events in the *Beowulf*, but in view of the evidence of *Yngls.*, viz. that Halfdan died and was buried at Upsala, it cannot be accepted without reservations† (cf. also pp. 130 ff., 69, 135). The Danes avenged themselves for Healfdene's death by killing Froda (*Beo.* ll. 2047 ff., Icel. Sagas, Saxo, Bks VI and VII). Apparently a battle took place (*Beo.* ll. 2047 ff.) in which Hrothgar (Hroar) and Halga (Helgi)—or possibly Hrothgar and Hrothulf

* What has happened in the case of Froda and Ingeld appears to have also taken place with regard to Waermund and Offa, who were in reality kings of Angel, but whose names have become incorporated with the genealogies of Danish kings (cf. Ch. IV, on Offa).

† Dr Olrik regards the O.N. evidence as worthless, and prefers to accept the statement of Saxo, Sv. Aag. and other mediaeval Danish chronicles that Halfdan killed his brother and took the kingdom (*D. H. D.* pp. 175 ff.). But this seems to have been in the first instance a corruption, which was then perpetuated by later writers, the more so as Halfdan, in spite of his crime, is reported to have died a peaceful death—a circumstance which causes the chroniclers great astonishment (but cf. *inf.* pp. 130 ff.).

(Hrolf)—defeated the Heathobeardan (*Beo*. l. 2051), and in which Froda (Froði) fell by the hand of Swerting (Saxo, Bk VI, p. 189; Arngr. Jonss., Ch. IX).

At a later date—probably after the lapse of several years (cf. *inf*. p. 111), and perhaps after another battle in which the Danes inflicted a signal defeat on Ingeld at Heorot (cf. *Wids*. ll. 45–49, *inf*. p. 110), Hrothgar (Hroar) gave his daughter Freawaru in marriage to Ingeld (Ingjald) in the hope of bringing the strife to an end. Freawaru took with her as page or aide-de-camp a young nobleman, the son of the warrior who had slain Froda (viz. Swerting)—an arrangement which, under the circumstances, can scarcely have been intended as an insult, and can, therefore, only be characterised as extremely tactless on the part of King Hrothgar. This young Dane actually wore the armour of the murdered Froda, and boasted openly of the Danish victory amongst the Heathobeardan, until at last Ingeld, roused by the exhortations of the old warrior (Starkað), murdered him one night, after which he apparently fled from the country (*Beo*. l. 2061 f.).

These events, viz. Ingeld's marriage and the murder of the *faemnan thegn*, seem to have taken place in Denmark, at or near Heorot, where we may suppose Ingeld to have settled with his bride. *Beo*. l. 2061 f.* can hardly refer to anyone but Ingeld, and they certainly imply that after killing the young Dane he effected his escape, owing to his knowledge of the country. It would

* *Beo*. l. 2061 f.

him se òther thonan
losath lifigende, con him land geare.

[The other got away thence with his life because he knew the country.]

be quite in accordance with the customs of these times
for a warrior to settle down amongst his wife's relations
rather than to take her back to his own country (cf. Hroar
in *Hrss.*, Sigurð in *Vǫlss.*, etc.): indeed the chief object
of such marriages was, in many cases, to cement and
strengthen the newly formed bond of friendship between
those who had previously been enemies.

The course of events after this point is obscure. There
is clear indication (*Beo.* ll. 82 ff.) that Ingeld returned
subsequently to Heorot with an army, and succeeded in
burning down the hall. This battle may have had fatal
consequences for the Danes, and it is quite possible that
Hrothgar himself was killed*. Many scholars believe,
however, that this engagement is identical with the one
mentioned in *Wids.* ll. 45–49, and that the passage does
not point to events which took place before Ingeld's
marriage. In that case the result would be just the
reverse—a Heathobeardan instead of a Danish defeat.

The chief difficulty of any attempt to reconstruct the
course of the Heathobeardan struggle is the question of
chronology, and especially the point in the story to which
the *Widsith* passage (ll. 45–49) should be assigned. With
regard to the actual date of any of the events mentioned,
we have extremely little to go upon. Beowulf's visit to
king Hrothgar probably took place about the year 500 A.D.,
or possibly a little earlier (cf. Ch. i). At that time
Hrothgar was an old man and had reigned for a long
time (cf. *Beo.* ll. 357, 608, 1769, &c.). The story of
Ingeld's marriage and revenge, which Beowulf tells

* Cf. Saxo, ii, p. 52, according to which Ro (Hrothgar) was slain by
Hothbroddus, cf. Arngr. Jonss.'s epitome of *Skjǫlds.* Ch. xii, according
to which Hroar was killed by the sons of Ingjald.

Hygelac on his return to Geatland, must be regarded as a prophecy of future events, for when Beowulf was in Denmark, Freawaru's presence still gladdened the guests in her father's hall (*Beo*. ll. 2022 ff.). There is a chronological objection to the most usual interpretation of the episode referred to in *Wids*. ll. 45–49, viz. that it took place after the murder of Freawaru's thegn, and is identical with the battle hinted at in *Beo*. ll. 82 ff., and, therefore, the last incident in the struggle of which the O.E. poems show any knowledge. For after this battle, Hrothgar and Hrothulf are said to have ruled together "for a very long time*," and we have seen that Hrothgar was already an old man before Freawaru's marriage. The assumption that the *Widsith* battle took place very shortly before Ingeld's marriage to Freawaru is, of course, open to the same objection though in a lesser degree. On the other hand, it is possible that the *lengest* of *Wids*. need not be interpreted as meaning more than a few years, and again, as the quarrel between Danes and Heathobeardan seems to have continued intermittently for more than a generation, this great Danish victory may have taken place on some occasion other than the two which we have mentioned as possible. In the present state of the evidence there is no means of coming to a satisfactory conclusion on this point.

If we assume, however, that the Heathobeardan defeat of *Wids*. ll. 45–49, Ingeld's marriage to Freawaru, and the events subsequent to it, took place after Beowulf's

---

* *Beo*. ll. 1163 ff.

              Thaer thâ gôdan twegen
saeton suhter-gefaederan : thâ gyt waes hiera sib aetgaedere
aeghwylc ôthrum trŷwe.

visit to Denmark, we may assign as their approximate
date the very beginning of the sixth century*: the next
question is the date of Froda's death and the interval
which elapsed between that and Ingeld's revenge.

Taking as a starting-point the marriage of Ingeld
and Freawaru, we see that Ingeld and Hrothulf were
of the same generation, and consequently also Froda
and Hrothgar. Thus Froda was a generation later, and
probably a much younger man than Healfdene. This
makes us inclined to doubt the Icelandic tradition, according to which Hroar (Hrothgar) and Helgi (Halga)
executed revenge on Froði (Froda) while they were still
boys. Probably this story was an invention made by
Icelandic "sagamen" to balance matters, at the same
time that Froði (Froda) was moved up a generation
and represented as the brother of Halfdan (Healfdene).
Again it is highly probable that a considerable period—
probably fifteen or twenty years—lay between Froda's
death and Ingeld's revenge; for the admonitions of the
eald aescwiga Starkað only have point if they can be
taken as referring to an event, the memory of which,
though still an open sore in the mind of the old man,
was scarcely even a scar in that of the young. If Hrothgar
and Halga executed vengeance on Froda (in a battle as
has been suggested, cf. p. 108), the death of the last mentioned probably took place when Hrothulf and Ingeld were
still children, and hostilities between the two tribes would
in that case be suspended for some years, until Ingeld

---

* The presence of Starkað in the story prevents us from putting it
at any later date, for, as we shall see (cf. *inf.* p. 117), Starkað who was an
old warrior at this time is represented as serving in his youth kings who
flourished during the first half of the fifth century.

was grown up. But according to the *Grottas*. (cf.
p. 75), Hrolf (Hrothulf) was the avenger of Healfdene.
If Hrothgar (Hroar) with Hrothulf (Hrolf) instead of
Halga (Helgi) killed Froði, then Ingeld (Ingjald) would
already be a grown man, and very little time would elapse
between his father's murder and his own marriage and
revenge. But this second possibility is, from every point
of view, less likely than the first*, and chiefly because it
is˙ only if we can suppose a considerable time to have
elapsed between Froda's murder and Ingeld's revenge that
the rôle of Starkað receives its full poetical significance.

NOTE.—At this point ends the evidence of the Old
English poems: indeed with Hroar's death we have
already gone beyond them. But to judge from the
Scandinavian evidence which we possess, the Heathobeardan struggle seems to have continued into the next
generation, for we hear that Agnar, Ingjald's (Ingeld's)
son, was slain by Bǫðvar-Bjarki, the warrior of Hrolf
Kraki (cf. *Bjarkamál* in Saxo, II, 64; Saxo, p. 66; *Hrolfss*.
p. 104˙; *Bjarkarímur*, VII). In some sources we find for
the ˙second time the story of a wedding with a Danish
princess, here told of Agnar: strife breaks out, this time
at the wedding ceremony, resulting in the death of the
bridegroom by the sword of Bǫðvar-Bjarki, who is rewarded for his prowess by receiving the hand of the lady.
This story of a wedding disturbed by strife is combined
by Scandinavian writers with another already existing
motif, viz. the custom of bone-throwing at feasts. The
explanation of this is probably that here, as in many other
instances, the true significance of the events, viz. the

* Especially as the reading of *Grottas*. is uncertain.

struggle between Danes and Heathobeardan, had been forgotten, and it was therefore necessary to invent a new motivation for the story. The whole introduction of the wedding in connection with Agnar is probably due to confusion with his father Ingeld, for after Ingeld's marriage and its results it was extremely unlikely that Agnar would be on such terms with Hrolf as to make a similar experiment.

The Identity of Froda the Heathobeard.

Northern tradition knows many Froðis (Froda), in fact there is no more common name in the genealogies of the Danish royal family. We saw (p. 75) that the *Grottas.* (which is the earliest Scandinavian work dealing with these characters) has confused the Froði (Froda) who is said to have killed Halfdan (Healfdene) with Frið-Froði the peace-king, who is represented as living at the beginning of the Christian era, and whose reign symbolised the Golden Age of Denmark. But the figure of this peace-king has undergone duplication in Scandinavian tradition; besides the Frið-Froði of the gold-mill (*Grottas.*), the genealogies have a much later Froði surnamed "the Peaceful" (*hin friðsami*). It is to this later Froði that Saxo attributes the peace (Frotho III of the great Frotho biography, pp. 121–171), while he represents the Froði of the gold-mill as a viking king (Frotho I; cf. Saxo, pp. 38–57). The story of Ingellus' (Ingeld's) revenge for his father is told by Saxo of neither of these, but of yet another Froði (Frotho IV*, pp. 182–189).

* Frotho IV is surnamed by Saxo *largus*; by Sven Aagesen the same man is called *frithgothae largus* and appears as the peace-king; so that here also there are reminiscences of the confusion between Frið-Froði and Froði (Froda) the murderer of Halfdan (Healfdene).

Now, everything that we hear of the Heathobeard Froda in the O.E. poems points to his having been a viking or sea-king, and in *Widsith* (l. 47) the Heathobeardan army is directly called *wicinga cyn*. Neckel (*Z. f. d. A.* Vol. XLVIII, p. 184) indeed points out that Froda (Froði) has become the centre of a group of viking sagas quite apart from his significance as the father of Ingeld. This viking king Froði, surnamed "the Bold" (*hin frøkni*) and corresponding in character to the Froda of the O.E. poems, has in Saxo replaced Frið-Froði of the gold-mill (cf. Saxo, Bk II) as the characteristic of Frið-Froði has in the meantime been transferred to a later king, Frotho III; thus we find in Scand. tradition only the most thorough-going confusion regarding the identity of Froda the Heathobeard. The one thing certain is that he can have had originally nothing to do with the peace-king, i.e. Frið-Froði. Neckel (*Z. f. d. A.* Vol. XLVIII, p. 185) believes that the confusion first arose from the surname *hin friðsami* having been added to Frið-Froði in order to distinguish this king from the viking Froði *hin frøkni*. The double epithet, viz. *Frið-Froði hin friðsami*, thus led to a duplication of the figure of the peace-king*, in addition to the already existing *Froði hin frøkni*! Then came the further confusion in character between the viking king and the peace-king, which is not so incomprehensible as it appears at first sight. For Saxo's conception of the peace-king is that of a great legislator:

---

* Dr Olrik shows not only that the character of the same peace-king occurs twice in the genealogies, but that out of the long Danish genealogies of later date can be separated two parallel and partly corresponding groups, typical of the Heroic and the Viking Age of Denmark respectively (cf. Olrik, *D. H. D.* pp. 316–320).

the viking Froði (Froda) also gave his warriors laws: and not only has the viking king taken the place of the early Frið-Froði in Saxo's history, but some of his laws have even been transferred to Saxo's Frotho III (cf. Neckel, *Z. f. d. A.* Vol. XLVIII, p. 185).

It has been suggested that the Heathobeard Froda may be identical with the Froði of *Yngls.* Ch. 27, who is described as a king of Denmark, and who fights against and kills King Óttar of Sweden. In support of this suggestion, it may be said that these two kings of the same name must have been more or less contemporaries, that they both seem to have been sea-kings, and that we do not know of any other Froði (Froda) living at this time. There is unfortunately, however, not sufficient evidence on which to base a theory of their identity.

SIGEHERE AND ALEVIH.

In addition to the passage dealing with Hrothgar and Hrothulf, the *Widsith* contains two scanty references to early Danish kings, viz. l. 28*: "Sigehere reigned for a very long time over the Sea-Danes," and ll. 35 ff.†: "Alevih ruled over the Danes: he was the bravest of all these men (i.e. of the kings named), but he did not exceed Offa in valour."

A recent attempt to supply an historical background for the figures of Sigehere and Alevih has been made by Mr H. M. Chadwick in his book, *The Origin of the English*

---

* l. 28, Sigehere lengest Sae-Denum weold.

† ll. 35 ff.

> Offa weold Ongle, Alevih Denum:
> se waes thara manna modgast ealra:
> no hwaethre he ofer Offan eorlscype fremede.

Nation (Cambridge Univ. Press, 1907), Ch. IV, p. 146, note on the Early Kings of the Danes. Sigehere is identified as usual with the Sigarus of Saxo, Bk VII: Mr Chadwick, however, by an interesting chain of evidence, shows that Sigehere in all probability ruled over the Danes previous to the middle of the fifth century, and consequently before Halfdan and his sons, whereas in Saxo he is introduced at a very much later period.

The following are the main lines of Mr Chadwick's proof :—

Sigarus' chief exploit was the slaying of Hagbarð, the lover of his daughter Signy (Saxo, O.N. poetry): this Hagbarð had a brother Háki, a sea-king who, according to *Yngls.* Ch. 23, fought against Jǫrund, king of Sweden. In the genealogy of *Yngls.*, Jǫrund occurs four generations earlier than Aðils, the contemporary of Hrolf Kraki, and although some of the intervening kings are certainly mythical, there can be at least little doubt that Jǫrund lived before and not after Aðils. The story of Starkað points towards a similar conclusion, for this warrior as quite an old man (*Beo.* ll. 2041 ff.) is associated with Ingeld, while he says that he served King Haki in his earliest youth (Saxo, p. 214); and it is evident from the *Beowulf* and *Widsith* that Ingeld was a contemporary of Hrothgar and Hrothulf.

A further clue to the probable date of Sigehere's reign is that Sigar (Sigehere), Haki, and Hagbarð are intimately connected with Sigmund the Vǫlsung and his family in Northern poems and sagas; the allusions which associate them with one another occur too often, and are too definite, to be considered the result of an accident. Sigmund and his family have usually been regarded as fictitious, but there is nothing to show that the character of Sigmund was not historical: he is certainly brought into close relations with the historical Gunnar (Gundicarius, O.E. Guthere, mhg. Gunthhere) king of the Burgundians, who reigned between 400 and 437 A.D., a date which would correspond almost exactly to that which we have obtained from Sigehere from quite independent evidence.

The conclusion that Mr Chadwick comes to about Sigehere is best given in his own words:—"Now if Sigarr occupied the same throne as Hrothgar and Hrodwulf, as Saxo's account clearly indicates, it is plain from all that has been said that he must have been a predecessor of these kings. Further, since we have no valid reason for doubting that Healfdene was immediately succeeded by his sons, we may infer with the greatest probability that Sigarr preceded him also. On the other hand, if we are to believe Saxo's statement (p. 237) that Starkathr had come into contact with Sigarr, we shall have to suppose that this king lived until about the middle of the sixth century."

Mr Chadwick makes a further attempt to identify Alevih—whose name is associated with that of Offa in *Widsith* (ll. 35 ff.)—with Dan, who follows Offa in almost all Scandinavian genealogies * (cf. Sv. Aag., Saxo, *Langfðg., Flateyj.†*). This identification turns largely, however, on the exact translation of the lines in *Widsith* (ll. 35 ff.), where the names of Alevih and Offa occur side by side, and it is very doubtful whether there is enough evidence

---

* A knowledge of the contents of Ch. IV on Offa will help to make clear the line of argument in this section.

† Ed. C. R. Unger, Christiania, 1868, vol. I, p. 27.

to justify its acceptance, as the passage in question is
exceedingly obscure.

Mr Chadwick cites the genealogies mentioned above,
in all of which Dan follows the king called variously Olaf
or Uffo (= O.E. Offa) but is not said to have been his
son. In a second genealogy from *Flateyjarbók* (*Flat. B.*)
Dan's name is omitted, and instead of Olaf the son of
Vermund we find Olof the daughter of Vermund, and
the mother of Froði the Peaceful. Some explanation of
this entry is afforded by Arngrim Jonsson's epitome of the
lost *Skjǫldunga saga*, Chs. 4–7, where it is said that Danus
married Olufa, the daughter of Vermundus: the original
tradition may have been that Dan was the brother-in-law
and successor of Olaf (Uffo, Offa). Arngrim relates further
that Dan at the beginning of his reign ruled only over
Jutland, but that he later conquered Åleifus, king of
Selandia, and ruled over the whole of Denmark, to which
he gave its present name. Arngrim does not say who
this Åleifus was, but the name is obviously identical with
Olaf. This being so there may be some ground for the
identification of Alevih with Dan, and the very obscure
passage in *Widsith* may contain a reference to the same
event as that recorded in *Skjǫlds.* Ch. 4, viz. the conquest
of Offa by Alevih. A fact which suggests the connection
of Alevih with the royal family of Angel, quite independently of the above considerations, is that the name occurs
at a much later date in the Mercian royal family which
claimed descent from the Kings of Angel: the nephew of
Penda is called Alwih (Alewih): this would be explained
by the supposition of Alewih's marriage with the sister
of Olaf.

A difficulty in accepting Dan as an historical character

is his position as eponymous and hence mythical ancestor of the Danish people in *Skjǫlds.* and elsewhere. But it is quite possible that the name Dane may only have come into use about this time, as there is no early evidence for its existence (cf. p. 62), and it is perhaps possible "that it was originally a local name, perhaps that of the place from which Alevih's family were sprung."

If, however, we accept Mr Chadwick's suggestions as to the reigns of Sigehere and Alevih, we undoubtedly obtain results which add substantially to our knowledge of early Danish history. If Alevih be a contemporary of Offa, whose reign we are in a position to ascribe to the latter part of the fourth century (cf. *inf.* Ch. IV, on Offa), he may have lived well into the fifth century, for according to *Yngls.* Ch. 25, Dan lived to be an old man, although perhaps we cannot lay too much stress on this statement*. There can be but a short interval between him and Sigehere, who is said (*Wids.* l. 28) to have reigned for a long time. Again the death of Sigehere must bring us nearly up to the reigns of Healfdene and his sons Halga and Hrothgar. We know from the *Beowulf* that Hrothgar was contemporary with Hygelac, king of the Götar, who was killed between 512 and 520 on a marauding expedition against the Franks, and previous to this expedition Hrothgar is spoken of as having reigned for a long time *hund missera* (cf. *Beo.* l. 1769). Hrothgar was apparently succeeded on the Danish throne by his nephew Hrothulf (Hrolf Kraki), who reigned for some time. Hence if it is found possible to accept this reconstruction of early Danish history, we shall have succeeded in bridging over a period of about a hundred and fifty years, from the end of the fourth to

* Cf. Olrik, *Aarb. f. nord. Oldkynd.* 1894, p. 144 f.

the middle of the sixth century, the point at which all relations between England and the Scandinavian countries seem to have ceased, and for two hundred years after which Danish history is a blank.

HEREMOD.

Although Heremod cannot be identified with any known Danish king, there are no adequate grounds for denying his existence as an historical character. Heremod is alluded to in *Beowulf* on two separate occasions (ll. 901–915, 1709–1722), and the facts which emerge concerning him are shortly the following:—Heremod was king of the Scyldings—i.e. presumably the Danes; he had been at one time a great man, but subsequently there was a falling off in his strength and courage (ll. 901 f.), and his pride and cruelty were notorious. He killed even his own warriors, and became a source of great wretchedness to his people. He was betrayed into the hands of his enemies and expelled from his kingdom, to the sorrow of many who had hoped to see in him a deliverer, but had been disappointed. Subsequently his existence was a joyless and solitary one.

In the first of the two *Beowulf* passages (ll. 901–915), the fact that Heremod is brought into direct connection with Sigmund (ll. 875–900 describe Sigmund's fight with the dragon) is significant as suggesting that Heremod is the person mentioned in *Hyndluljóð**, v, 2. There it is said that Odin gave Heremod a helm and coat of mail, and Sigmund a sword.

* Cf. *supr.* p. 16.

In *Eíríksmál* * (ll. 15, 28), Sigmund and Sinfjǫtli are represented as welcoming Eírík at the gates of Valhall: in *Hákonarmál* (l. 38), which is more or less a copy of *Eíríksmál*, the place of Sigmund and Sinfjǫtli is taken by Hermod and Bragi.

SCYLD SCEFING.

NOTE.—This section on Scyld Scefing is entirely based on, and scarcely professes to be more than an abstract of, Mr Chadwick's most interesting chapter on "King Aethelwulf's Mythical Ancestors" in his recent book, *The Origin of the English Nation*. As the present work professes to deal only with the historical aspect of the traditions underlying the O.E. poems, the subject of Scyld lies, strictly speaking, outside its scope. It is to be hoped that all who are interested in the customs and rites, and in the wonderfully realistic mythology, of our primitive ancestors, will read Mr Chadwick's book for themselves. Of great interest is also Dr Olrik's chapter on Skjǫld., which presents an altogether new view of the story (*D. H. D.* pp. 223–277).

In *Beowulf*, the genealogy of the Danish royal family is traced back to the eponymous ancestor of the Scyldungas, Scyld Scefing. The first fytte of the poem contains a panegyric on the reign of Scyld, and an account of the strange manner of his burial. "Lo! we have heard of the glory of the Spear Danes' warrior kings in days of yore—how the princes did valorous deeds! Often Scyld Scêfing took mead-benches away from troops of foes, from many tribes. The noble in-

* Cf. *supr*. p. 17.

spired awe from the time that he was first found helpless* :
for that he met with consolation, increased under the
heavens and throve in honours, until each one of those
who sojourned near, across the whale's road, had to serve
him and pay him tribute. A noble king was he!"

(The next fourteen lines describe the reign of Scyld's
son, Beowulf.)

"Then, at the fated hour, Scyld, full of exploits, departed to go into the keeping of the Lord : and they, his
fast friends, carried him to the water's edge, as he himself
had asked when he, protector of the Scyldings, governed
by his behests ;—when, dear ruler of his country, he had
long held sway. There, at the landing-place, the ring-
prowed vessel stood : the prince's ship, sheeny and eager
to start. They laid then the beloved chieftain, giver-out
of rings, on the ship's bosom—the glorious hero by the
mast. There were brought many treasures, ornaments
from far-off lands. Never have I known a keel more
fairly fitted out with war-weapons and battle-trappings,
swords and coats of mail. Upon his breast lay many
treasures which were to travel far with him, into the
power of the flood. Certainly they furnished him with
no less of gifts, of tribal-treasures, than those did who,
in his early days, started him over the sea alone, child
as he was. Moreover, they set besides a golden banner
high above his head, and let the flood bear him—gave
him to the sea. Their soul was sad, their spirit sorrowful.
Who received that load, men, chiefs of councils, heroes

* A better reading is with Sievers, *egsode eorlas*, with comma after
ofteah. Translation then runs, "Often Scyld Scêfing took mead-benches
away from troops of foes, from many tribes; he spread terror among the
warriors from the time that he was first found helpless."

under heaven, cannot for certain tell* " (ll. 1–11, 26–52).

The first part of the story—concerning the mysterious coming of Scyld—is only hinted at in *Beowulf*, viz. ll. 43–45, which have just been quoted. It is more fully preserved in the chronicles of Aethelweard and William of Malmesbury, in both of which, however, the story is told not of Scyld, but of Sceaf.

Aethelweard's account is as follows :—

" This Scef came to land in a cutter on an island in the Ocean which is called Scani : he was surrounded by weapons, and was a very young child and was unknown to the inhabitants of that land : nevertheless he was taken up by them, and they watched over him with great care as over one of their own kin, and later on they chose him as their king†."

According to Malmesbury the story runs thus :—

" He (i.e. Sceaf), as they say, was brought as a young child in a boat without oars to Scandza, a certain island of Germania, which is spoken of by Jordanes the historian of the Goths. He was asleep, and a sheaf of corn was placed at his head : because of this he was given the name of Sceaf (O.E. *sceaf* = sheaf), and he was received as a marvel by the dwellers in that region and carefully nurtured ; when he reached man's estate, he reigned in the town which was then called Slaswic, but now

---

* *Beowulf and the Fight at Finnsburg*, transl. into modern English prose by R. J. Clark Hall, M.A., Ph.D., London, 1901.

† Aethelweard's Chronicle, Bk III, Ch. 3 : Ipse Scef cum uno dromone advectus est in insula Oceani quae dicitur Scani armis circumdatus, eratque ualde recens puer et ab incolis illius terrae ignotus ; attamen ab eis suscipitur, et ut familiarem diligenti animo eum custodierunt et post n regem eligunt.

Haithebi. Now that district is called Old Anglia, and is situated between the Saxons and the Goths; the Angli came thence to Britain*."

Neither of these accounts makes any reference to the latter half of the story which is given in the *Beowulf* passage (ll. 28–52).

The story of Sceaf occurs only in the two chronicles just quoted, but the genealogy is given also in the A.S. Chronicle, although owing to a scribal error the name of Sceaf has dropped out of the Parker MS. (Ⱥ.)†. In the A.S. Chronicle Sceaf is represented as the son of Noah, and his is the first of the non-Biblical names. In William of Malmesbury and Aethelweard his name occurs nine generations above Wodan, and ends Aethelweard's genealogy ‡.

---

* Malmesbury, *Gesta Reg. Angl.* Bk II, Ch. II: Iste (Sceaf) ut quidam ferunt in quandam insulam Germaniae Scandzam de qua Jordanes historiographus Gothorum loquitur, appulsus naui sine remige puerulus, posito ad caput frumenti manipulo, dormiens, ideoque Sceaf nuncupatus, ab hominibus regionis illius pro miraculo exceptus et sedulo nutritus ; adulta aetate regnauit in oppido quod tunc Slaswic nunc uero Haithebi appellatur, est autem regio illa Anglia Vetus dicta, unde Angli uenerunt in Britanniam, inter Saxones et Gothos constituta.

† Another possible explanation of this circumstance is suggested by Prof. A. S. Napier, viz. that when the Parker MS. was written, *Sceaf* had very possibly not yet been invented.

‡ Subjoined are the portions in question of these genealogies :—

A. S. Chronicle.	*Malmesbury.*	*Aethelweard.*
Taetwa Beawing	Tetius	Beo.
Beaw Sceldwaing	Beowius	Scyld.
Sceldwa Heremoding	Sceldius	Scef.
Heremod Itermoning	Sceaf	
Itermon H(r)athraing	Heremodius	
Hathra Hwalaing	Stermonius	
Hwala Bedwiging	Hadra	
Bedwig Sceafing id ed filius Noe	Gwala	
	Bedwegius	
	Strephius.	

According to *Beowulf*, the first kings of Denmark were Scyld Scefing and his son Beowulf; the appearance of the forms *Beo* and *Beowius* in Aethelweard and Malmesbury respectively suggest that *Beaw* may be not a true West Saxon form, but due to dialectic peculiarity or scribal error, in which case it may correspond to the Danish king Beowulf of the poem. In the *Beowulf* the Danish king Beowulf is described as a popular and open-handed monarch : the only information which we possess about the Beo or Beaw of the O.E. genealogies is supplied by the Plantagenet Roll in the Library of Trinity College, Cambridge, in which the descent of Henry VI is traced back to Adam. This genealogy shows several affinities with the forms used by Malmesbury, and in it the son of Sceldius appears as Boerinus which is apparently a corruption of Malmesbury's Beowius. To this Boerinus are ascribed nine sons, from whom according to a note " are descended nine nations which inhabited the North, and which once upon a time invaded and acquired the kingdom of Britain*." It is probable that the introduction of these nine sons is due to the influence of Scandinavian tradition, for in *Flateyj.* I, 25, and *Skáldsk.* Ch. 64, we find a parallel instance in the nine sons attributed to Halfdan the Old†. It is to be noted further that the Plantagenet Roll contains the only information given by any of the genealogies about Sceldwea or Scyld in a note which says: " This Sceldius was the first inhabitant of

---

* Ab istis novem filiis Boerini descenderunt novem gentes septentrionalem inhabitantes qui quondam regnum Britanniae invaserunt et optinuerunt, viz. Saxones, Angli, Iuttii, Daci, Norwagenses, Gothi, Wandali, Geati et Frisi.

† Cf. also *Hyndl.* v, 14–16.

Germany*." The names of Sceaf and Beowulf do not occur in any Scandinavian genealogy. In most cases Skjǫld is represented as the son of Odin, but according to Saxo he is the son of Lotherus†.

We have already seen that the story which is told of Sceaf in the chronicles of Aethelweard and William of Malmesbury is undoubtedly part of the same tradition as the account given in *Beowulf* (ll. 26–52) of Scyld Scefing. We have, therefore, to seek an explanation of why the story should be told in the one case of Scyld and in the other of Sceaf.

It is impossible to suppose that the incident was originally told of Sceaf, and afterwards transferred to his son Scyld. For over and above the non-appearance of Sceaf in Scandinavian genealogies, and the note in the Plantagenet Roll in which it is said that Sceldius was the first inhabitant of Germany, we have the authority of the *Beowulf* which dates from several centuries earlier than Aethelweard and Malmesbury, and the terms in which the child Scyld is there described imply that his parentage was quite unknown. It is, therefore, impossible to regard the epithet *Scéfing* as a patronymic, it must rather be taken to mean "child of the sheaf," and the expression is satisfactorily explained by William of Malmesbury's version of the story, according to which the child Sceaf came to the island of Scandza in a boat with a sheaf of corn lying at his head. It is easy to understand how, later on,

* Iste Sceldius primus inhabitator Germaniae. The same note occurs in a Paris MS. and is quoted by Kemble in the Preface to the Introduction to his translation of the *Beowulf*.

† Cf. List of Genealogies in App. II. Other important Scand. genealogies to which reference should be made are those of Sv. Aag. *Skáldsk.* and *Lfdg.*

Scéfing was mistaken for a patronymic in consequence of which the whole story was transferred to Sceaf the supposed father of Scyld, as it was manifestly absurd that the mysterious coming and departure of the unknown ruler should be ascribed to any but the founder of a race or dynasty.

Dr Olrik opposes this explanation of *Scéfing* on the ground that the sheaf only appears in a very late version of the story (Wm of Malmesbury) at an age when heroic traditions were dying out in England. Malmesbury's *frumenti manipulus* is, according to him, merely a foundling *motif* introduced to account for the name of the hero, and the *Scéfing* of the Beowulf is a patronymic derived from Sceafa, king of the Langobards (cf. *Wids.* 32), whose presence in connection with Scyld is due to the English love of framing long genealogies!

But the introduction of the Langobard king into the story of Scyld is purely fanciful, and it is further most unlikely that the names Sceafa and Sceaf are the same*. Mr Chadwick has showed by a most interesting chain of evidence that the sheaf was not only an original element in the story of Scyld, but also that it was apparently a religious symbol among the heathen English by whom it was probably regarded as the manifestation of the corn deity (cf. Chadwick, *op. cit.* pp. 277–281).

There is no doubt that the O.E. Scyld, father and eponymous ancestor of the Scyldungas, corresponds to the Scandinavian Skjǫld, father and eponymous ancestor of the Skjǫldungar, although the characteristic facts related of Scyld in the O.E. poem are not recorded in Northern tradition. Skjǫld is said in *Yngls.* to have been the

---

* Cf. Chadwick, *op. cit.* p. 282, note.

husband of Gefion the plough goddess, and this would explain his association with the sheaf which was the symbol of agriculture.

The origin of the Scyld legend is very obscure, but all the available evidence goes to show that Scyld-Skjǫld was not an historical but a mythical character, probably first invented to account for the existence of his descendants the Scyldungas-Skjǫldungar. The word Skjǫldungar (Scyldungas) may be taken to mean "people of the Shield." Dr Olrik regards the Skjǫldungar as specifically the warrior class of the Danish nation, and Skjǫld as the personification of the warlike qualities of that class (*D. H. D.* pp. 271 ff.). Mr Chadwick tends to believe, on the other hand, that the name Scyldungas-Skjǫldungar implies the particular use of a shield by the people in question, perhaps in connection with a religious rite. He thinks that a sheaf and a shield together may have possibly been in the first instance the symbol of some deity, from which developed later the idea of the personification of Skjǫld.

The presence of the sea in the Scyld story is difficult to account for: it is possible that it is due to the influence of a similar story told in the A.S. Runic poem about Ing, who is the mythical ancestor of the Ingvaeones, one of the groups of tribes into which Tacitus classifies the Germani (Tac. *Germ.* Ch. 2). The name *Ingwine* occurs frequently in *Beowulf* in such expressions as *eodor Ingwina* (l. 1044), *frean Ingwina* (l. 1319), &c., and is apparently always synonymous with Scyldungas. It seems on the whole probable that Scyld (Skjǫld) was the successor of Ing as the putative ancestor and eponym of the Danish kings, and that he has taken over some characteristics which originally belonged to his predecessor.

There still remain for discussion Healfdene and Beowulf, who were, according to the *Beowulf*, the father and grandfather of Hrothgar respectively.

HEALFDENE.

Although little is said of Healfdene in the *Beowulf* there can be no doubt that he was an historical character, as the fact of his existence receives abundant testimony from Northern tradition. According to O.N. saga literature Halfdan (Healfdene) is commonly supposed to have fallen a prey to the jealousy of his brother Froði. But in *Yngls.* Ch. 25 we find the statements that Halfdan deposed the Swedish king Aun, reigned in Upsala in his stead, and died and was buried there. As these two accounts are clearly incompatible with each other the only alternative to rejecting one of them is the existence of two Halfdans, both kings of Denmark and both more or less contemporary with each other. In Arngrim Jonsson's extract from *Skjǫldungasaga* we do find two Halfdans (Halfdanus), but the first is merely a name, and it is clear from a comparison with other sources that this part of the genealogy has been duplicated (either by Arngrim or) by the author of the *Skjǫldungasaga*. The second Halfdan (Halfdanus, of *Skjǫldungasaga* corresponds in position to the Healfdene of the O.E. poems: his father is Froði (Frodo) who conquers the Swedish king Jǫrund (Jorundus) and exacts tribute from the country (*vid. sup.* p. 77): Froði also takes as a prisoner of war Jǫrund's daughter, who becomes the mother of Halfdan (Arngr. Jonss. *Skjǫlds.*

Ch. 9). These circumstances of his father's conquest and his own birth might well be thought by Halfdan, when he was grown up, *to constitute a claim to the Swedish throne.*

Saxo offers us in his Danish history a choice of four Halfdans: of these, the first, who is the father of Roe (Hrothgar) and Helgo (Halga), is only a lay figure and need not be further considered, as his personality is probably to be looked for in one of the late kings of the same name. Now of these three Halfdans, two are obviously the same (cf. Saxo, Bk VII, pp. 216–224, 241–247): they are brought into contact with the same characters, perform the same exploits (for which one gains the name of "Biargramm"), *both are said to have been victorious over the Swedes, while the first actually became king of Sweden.* It is said of the first that he died childless, while the second fell in battle.

The remaining Halfdan of Saxo is represented as the son of Eric Málspaki, the brother-in-law of Frotho III, the peace-king, and *as a king of Sweden* (cf. Saxo, Bk VI, pp. 173, 189), but in this capacity no further information is given about him.

The double figure of Halfdan Biargramm occurs in Saxo very much later than do Ro and Hrolf Kráki, but Saxo's chronology is thoroughly untrustworthy, as we have already seen more than once. According to Arngr. Jonsson's *Skjǫlds.* Ch. 10, Halfdan's wife and the mother of Hroar and Helgi (Hrothgar and Halga) was Sigrid (Sigrida) (cf. p. 78). In Saxo, Bk VII, just as there are two Halfdans so are there two Sigrids (Syritha), also apparently the duplication of one character. Both are near relations of king Sigar (Sigehere) and Halfdan is brought

9—2

into intimate connection with the first, for although he is not said to have married her himself, he interposed to prevent her marriage with a low-born suitor during the actual course of the wedding ceremony*. This association in Saxo of Halfdan Biargram (Haldanus Biargrammus) and Sigrid (Syritha) taken with the statement of *Skjǫlds.* Ch. 10, that Halfdan married Sigrid, and the date which we have already found for Sigar (Sigehere) and his family (cf. p. 118), suggests that the whole incident has been transferred by Saxo to a date much later than that at which it really took place. In that case Halfdan (Halfdanus) of *Skjǫlds.* Ch. 10, the father of Ro (Roas) and Helgi (Helgo), is identical with Halfdan Biargramm (Haldanus Biargrammus) of Saxo, Bk VII, and in the latter we find the real personality of the Halfdan of Bk II (Haldanus, father of Roe and Helgo), who, as we have seen, is little more than a name. Halfdan Biargramm's (Haldanus Biargrammus') relations with Sweden are further just what we should expect from the account of Halfdan's origin contained in *Skjǫlds.* (Ch. 9); and both authorities agree so well with the narrative of *Yngls.* Ch. 25† that it can scarcely be doubted that the Halfdan there referred to is the same person, viz. the father of Ro and Helgi‡. Thus the conclusion which we have reached is that at the time with which we are

---

* It is worth noting that Halfdan Biargramm II who married Guritha (this form may well be a corruption of Syritha), the grand-daughter of Sigar(us) (Saxo, pp. 245 ff.), only gained his bride by entering and killing a rival suitor during the marriage feast.

† See p. 69.

‡ Although it is not actually stated, this is the natural inference from *Yngls.* 29, where Helgi is said to be the son of Halfdan, as the Halfdan of *ib.* 25 is the only king of that name previously mentioned.

dealing there was only one king Halfdan reigning in Denmark, who was the father of Hroar (Ro) and Helgi, and who, therefore, corresponds to the Healfdene of *Beowulf*, the father of Hrothgar and Halga ; it is very possible that the Halfdan (Haldanus) represented by Saxo as king of Sweden may be merely another aspect of the same character. We are, therefore, confronted by the obscure if not insoluble question of the conflicting evidence regarding this king, especially the manner of his death ; to this we shall have to return later.

If the claim of a Danish king to the throne of Sweden, and the temporary realisation of this claim during Halfdan's reign, can be accepted as facts, we at once obtain results of historical value, for an explanation is offered of the mysterious relations of the Danish kings with Upsala during the period which we are considering (cf. *sup.* p. 89). If Helgi and Hrolf Kraki claimed the throne or, as is perhaps more likely—the over-lordship of Sweden, by right of descent from a king who had conquered the Swedes, viz. Froði (*Skjǫlds.* Ch. 9), or Halfdan (*Yngls.* Ch. 25), we need seek no further for the motive of the various expeditions of these Danish kings to Upsala and the covertly hostile attitude of Aðils towards them : their incentive would be all the stronger if Halfdan's body lay buried at Upsala, which was a possibility (*Yngls.* Ch. 25). From this point of view the marriage of Halfdan's (Healfdene's) daughter to Áli (Onela), a king of the conquered country, acquires political significance ; such marriages of a conquered king with the daughter of the conqueror were common (cf. Ingeld and Freawaru), and in this way Halfdan (Healfdene) would hope both to bring hostilities to an end and to confirm his suzerainty over the vanquished nation.

BEOWULF.

According to the *Beowulf*, the father of Healfdene was named Beowulf. This person as we saw (p. 126) is perhaps identical with the Beowius of Malmesbury and the Boerinus of the Plantagenet Roll. According to the practically unanimous testimony of Scandinavian tradition the father of Halfdan was Froði*, and where obvious repetition or confusion with Froði the father of Ingiald (Ingeld) has not taken place, this Froði usually represents the second of the peace-kings, *hin friðsami*. As the two peace-kings were originally without doubt one and the same person† it is possible that Halfdan's father was in reality the king known in Northern tradition as Frið-Froði, who owed his name to the peace and prosperity which marked his reign. In any case the father of Halfdan certainly must have been an entirely different personality from Froði (O.E. Froda) the Heathobeard, the father of Ingjald (O.E. Ingeld) and a viking king (*hin frøkni*).

Common to all Old Icelandic literature is a tradition that a certain King Froði was guilty of an exceptionally dastardly crime—probably fratricide—and it is difficult to believe that a belief so widespread had not any foundation in fact. In *Grottas.* this crime is attributed to Frið-Froði, which is usually considered to be due to

---

* It is, however, to be observed that the nine sons attributed to Halfdan the Old in *Skáldsk*. Ch. 64, and *Flateyj*. i, 25, all of whom were founders of famous dynasties, form a curious parallel to the nine sons attributed to Boerinus in the Trinity College Library Roll (cf. *sup.* p. 126) and suggest that there is some ground for connecting Boerinus with Halfdan.

† Olrik, *D. H. D.* pp. 316–320; *Z. f. d. A.* xLVIII, p. 185; cf. also *supr.* p. 114.

confusion. But it is not inconceivable that *Grottas.* may be correct, and that Frid-Frodi's reign was marred by the murder of his brother (Áli as in Arngrim's *Skjǫlds.* ?). For the confusion between Frid-Frodi and Frodi (O.E. Froda) the viking king (*hin frøkni*) and the father of Ingjald (Ingeld) has been already discussed, and as the latter was known to have been at war with Halfdan's (Healfdene's) family, it is easy to see how his influence might lead to the substitution of Halfdan's name for that of Áli as the murdered brother of Frid-Frodi. If these suggestions, which are, it must be admitted, of a somewhat hypothetical nature, could be substantiated, there would be no longer any difficulty in accepting the statement of *Yngls.* Ch. 25, that Halfdan (Healfdene) died and was buried at Upsala.

The main difficulty in regarding Frid-Frodi as the father of the Healfdene (Halfdan) of the O.E. poems is that his reign will then come into conflict with the dates which we have found for Sigar (Sigehere). As we saw (p. 118) Sigar must have been alive about the middle of the fifth century, and at the beginning of the sixth century Hrothgar had been reigning for a long time (*Beo.* l. 1769). Thus the intervening space is barely enough to cover the reigns of the two kings Frid-Frodi (?) and Halfdan, the first of which must by implication have been of considerable length, even although we accept the statement of *Yngls.* Ch. 25 that Halfdan reigned for several years not in Denmark but in Upsala.

On the other hand, Halfdan's father, whoever he was, was certainly not Sigar, and it is quite possible that he may have been a king contemporary with Sigar, but reigning in a different part of the country. Tradition connects Frið-Froði with Jutland*, while Sigar is associated with Sjaelland†.

This seems the most satisfactory solution of the difficulty and removes the only serious obstacle towards identifying the Danish king Beowulf of the O.E. poem with the peace-king Froði of Northern tradition. This identification in the nature of things can be at present only hypothetical, but it is to be hoped that before long some fresh evidence may come to light which will convert the hypothesis into a certainty.

THE RING SVIAGRIS.

The ring Sviagris is very often mentioned in the accounts of the dealings between Halfdan's (Healfdene's) family and the Swedish kings. It is described as a gold "ring‡" (*Skáldsk.* Ch. 44) (the heavy necklace referred to by Saxo, p. 55, is doubtless the same jewel), and all sources lay stress on its great value.

According to *Skáldsk.* Ch. 44, Sviagris was one of the treasures for which Hrolf stipulated as the acknowledgment of his assistance rendered to Aðils against Áli, "King of Uppland" (Onela), and to obtain which, owing to Aðils' subsequent refusal to give them up, Hrolf undertook his expedition to Upsala. There is no need to repeat the part played by Sviagris in the Danes' flight to Fyrisvellir except to emphasize the fact that it alone availed to check Aðils' pursuit, as his desire to regain it was even keener than his hatred of his enemy Hrolf. It

---

* *Skáldsk.* Ch. 43, Saxo, p. 169, *Skjǫlds.* Ch. 3.

† Saxo, p. 228.

‡ In Old Icelandic *hringr* was a generic term for any gem which was circular in form, viz. ring, bracelet or necklace.

is to be observed, however, that while *Skáldsk.* affirms Sviagris to have been an heirloom in Aðils' family[*] Arngrim's *Skjǫlds.*[†] says quite distinctly that it belonged to Hrolf, and that his forefathers had won it in battle[‡].

In *Hrolfss.* Chs. 7, 8, we find an account of a very precious ring which was the property of King Helgi, but which is not specified by name. It passed from him into the hands of his brother Hroar who coveted its possession, but from whom it was stolen at the instigation of his sister Signy. *Bjarkarímur* contains the same story of the theft of a ring from Hroar, and here we are told that the ring was no other than the famous Sviagris. Hrolf Kraki afterwards obtained possession of it, and "sent it to his mother." If any value is to be attached to the suggestion that Hrolf's mother was Helgi's sister and the wife of Onela (cf. *Beo.* l. 62 and *sup.* p. 89), it seems possible that Sviagris may have been in the hands of Onela at some time—perhaps up to his defeat by Aðils on Lake Wener.

The fact that Sviagris was such a coveted possession suggests that there was attached to it some very special significance, quite apart from its intrinsic value. The word means "sucking pig of the Swedes." Now the pig appears to have been an animal sacred to the Swedish kings[§],

---

[*] *Skáldsk.* Ch. 44 : " Svíagris, er átt hǫfðu langfeðgar Aðils."

[†] Arngr. Jonss. *Skjǫlds.* Ch. 12 (repr. *Aarb. f. n. Oldk.* 1894) : "Quod cernens Danus, Adilsum nummulis aureis non inescari, promit annulum ingentis pretii, quem majores ipsius praedae loco a devictis olim Sveciae regibus reportarant, eumque Adilso obviam projecit."

[‡] In the *Skjǫlds.* the motivation of the whole incident is somewhat different. Hrolf has the ring with him when he goes to Upsala.

[§] Chadwick, *op. cit.* p. 248 f.

probably from its association with Frey (or Freyja) the deity from whom they traced their descent. It is tempting to believe that this "ring" Sviagris was some religious symbol—perhaps even the emblem of royalty of the Swedish kings. If this were so it would be easy to understand both Hrolf's claim to it, on account of the conquests of his grandfather Halfdan, and the eagerness of the Swedish tributary kings first to regain it, then to keep it from each other, and from their common enemy the king of Denmark.

IV.   SUMMARY OF EVIDENCE ON DANISH TRADITION IN THE LIGHT OF ITS HISTORICAL VALUE.

It will now be well to summarize briefly the results which we have obtained from the foregoing investigation of Danish tradition regarding the persons and events mentioned in the O.E. poems.

As has been already noticed the Danes are not found mentioned by name before the sixth century, although there can be no reasonable doubt that they existed as a nation from very much earlier times. The Danish kingdom appears to have been originally insular, and to have thence spread to the mainland of Jutland, although it is difficult to say when this movement of national expansion first began. If we can accept the very probable conjecture of Mr Chadwick, that the Dan of *Skjǫlds.* who conquered Åleifus (= Olaf = Uffo or Offa, king of Angel, cf. Ch. IV), is identical with the doubtless historical Alevih, who is associated with Offa in *Widsith,* we shall have some evidence for the presence of Danes on the mainland in the end of the fourth or beginning of the fifth century*.

The appearance of Alevih in the guise of Dan the eponymous ancestor of the Danish people, might be accounted for by the possibility that the name Dane itself only came into use about this time: and against the common acceptation of all eponymous ancestors as necessarily mythical, speaks in this case the circumstance that no attempt is made to represent Dan as the head of the dynasty from which the Danish kings trace their descent: he appears in most genealogies six or seven generations below Odin and Skjǫld†.

We take then as a starting point the reign of Alevih-Dan which is probably to be dated in the first quarter of the fifth century: thus the period of Danish history which falls under our consideration consists approximately of the fifth and the first half of the sixth century, after which all evidence of communication between England and the Baltic countries ceases for about two hundred years.

To the first half of the fifth century must belong, as we saw, the reign of Sigar (Sigehere) which apparently lasted till c. 450 (cf. p. 118). There is also some ground

* Hnaef, of the Finn episode in *Beowulf*, who appears to have been a Jute, is described as the officer of Healfdene (*Beo.* 1. 1069), and his men are called Danes (1. 1090). This would be indirect evidence of the presence of Danes on the mainland in the middle of the fifth century. This point will be made clearer when we come to discuss the chronology of the Finn episode (cf. Ch. v).

† Although the second name in Saxo's genealogy is that of Dan, who is apparently regarded as the eponymous ancestor of the Danes, it is to be noted that the Dan who succeeds Uffo, and who, therefore, corresponds to the Dan of the *Skjǫldungasaga*, at present under discussion, occurs seventeen generations from the head of the genealogy.

for believing that the reign of the Froði, known in Danish tradition as the great peace-king, covered the middle years of the fifth century, perhaps partly overlapping with that of Sigar. This last assumption presents no serious difficulties, for not only are the names of these two kings associated with entirely different localities (cf. p. 136), but there is every evidence that Denmark was at this time not yet a united kingdom under one monarch. We can discern throughout this period a constant fierce struggle for supremacy between king and king, and tribe and tribe, in which the Danes finally gained the upper hand (absorbing some of their enemies and reducing others to the position of tributary states), but which lasted at any rate until the days of Hrolf Kraki.

There seems no reason to doubt that Healfdene, Hrothgar, Halga, Hrothulf are all historical, and that they all ruled as kings of the Danes. Healfdene (Halfdan) was, according to the *Beowulf*, the son of Beowulf, king of the Danes. This person is altogether unknown in Scandinavian tradition, but it is not impossible that he may be identical with the peace-king Froði (cf. p. 135 f.). Hrothgar (Ro, Hroar) and Halga (Helgi) were brothers, the sons of Healfdene (Halfdan), and Hrothulf (Hrolf) was almost certainly the son of Halga (Helgi). The presence of, and the part played by Hiǫrvarð (Heoroweard) in Northern tradition, seems to lend colour to the belief that he and his father Heorogar (who was according to the *Beowulf* the elder brother of Hrothgar and Halga) are also historical characters. Ro and Hrolf Kraki (= Hrothgar and Hrothulf) were apparently for a time joint kings of Denmark in Leire, and Helgi

(Halga) while he lived seems to have been a sea-king*. After Ro's death, Hrolf Kraki continued to reign, as sole king of the Danes. All authorities lay stress on the unusually amicable dispositions of Ro and Hrolf, and the friendly relations which existed between them. Whereas most countries which had more than one king were in a state of constant war, owing to the rival claims and jealousies of their different rulers, Ro and Hrolf occupied the same throne for many years, at peace with one another, so that their reign was a time of unprecedented prosperity for Denmark. According to Scandinavian tradition Hrolf Kraki was indeed the King Arthur of the North, whose court was the meeting-place for all the greatest warriors then living. His castle of Leire (Hleiðrgarðr), which is probably represented by the Heorot of the *Beowulf*, was the traditional seat of the Danish kings from the earliest times.

Close relations, although superficially of a mysterious nature, seem to have existed between Denmark and Sweden during this period, but there are indications of a satisfactory explanation in the view commonly expressed by Northern authorities, that Denmark held suzerainty over Sweden from the time of Halfdan (or perhaps from that of his father Froði) onwards. Such a state of affairs would account for the constant visits—either of a covertly or of a directly hostile nature—made by Danish kings to

* Although all Northern kings of this early age were in a sense sea-kings it is necessary to distinguish between those—if for the sake of clearness we may call them so—" land-kings " like Ro and Hrolf Kraki, who only used the sea as their highway, and the sea-kings proper, who had no landed possessions but who, like Helgi, regarded the sea as their only realm, and spent their whole lives in viking cruises. Cf. also Snorri in *Yngls.* Ch. 29, *supr.* p. 72.

Upsala during this time, and in particular would seem to offer the best solution of the mystery surrounding Hrolf Kraki's famous expedition to the Swedish court. In this connection, it may further be said that there does not seem any reason to discredit the part played by Yrsa in Northern tradition as mother of Hrolf Kraki and afterwards wife of Aðils. I am inclined to believe further that Yrsa is identical with the person whose name is omitted in *Beo.* l. 62, that she was the sister rather than the daughter of Helgi, and was the wife of Áli (Onela) previous to her marriage with Aðils.

The fact that Bǫðvar of Gautland (Götland) was in the service of Hrolf Kraki, taken with the evidence of the *Beowulf* that Beowulf reigned over the Geatas, is perhaps an additional proof of the over-lordship of Hrolf Kraki in the southern part of Scandinavia.

We may accept as historical the chief events of the Heathobeard struggle, which apparently flickered on fitfully for two or three generations, ending in the incorporation of the Heathobeards with the Danish nation. In the present conflicting state of evidence there can be no certainty as to the circumstances attending the death of King Halfdan, but the crushing defeat inflicted by the Danes on the Heathobeards, involving the death of their king Froda (Froði), the marriage of Ingeld (Ingjald) to Hrothgar's (Hroar's) daughter Freawaru, Ingeld's subsequent revenge for his father's death at the instigation of the old warrior, and the burning down of Heorot at his hands, have all a strong claim to be regarded as historical. Appearances seem to point further to the fall of Hrothgar (Hroar) in battle against the Heathobeards, possibly on the same occasion as that on which Heorot was burnt down, although there is no direct evidence in confirmation of this. Forming a link between the age of Hroar (Hrothgar) and Hrolf (Hrothulf) and the earlier times of Sigar and his contemporaries, stands the figure of Starkað —the *eald aescwiga* of *Beo.* l. 2042—who grew old in his armour, and served under many kings of different nationalities, notably (for us) under the Heathobeard Froda (Froði) and his son Ingeld (Ingjald)*.

It is possible that Hroar (Hrothgar) left a son Roric (Hrethric) who attempted to set up a claim to the throne against Hrolf Kraki (Hrothulf), but who was speedily crushed by his powerful cousin; but this view is to be accepted with reservations, as it is not supported by any substantial evidence. Very probably Hrolf Kraki (Hrothulf) fell at the hands of Hiǫrvarð (Heoroweard) in an attempt made by the latter to assert his prior claim to the Danish throne; whether that event is accurately represented by the accounts of Saxo and others and of the *Hrolfss.* there is, however, considerable reason to doubt (cf. *inf.* Ch. III, p. 154).

It is now possible—and will be, for the sake of clearness, convenient—to collect in tabular form the chief results which we have obtained. We have found cause to believe that the O.E. heroic poems, and, to a certain extent, Scandinavian poems, sagas and chronicles of a later time, preserve much genuine historical information about the leading persons and events of Danish history in early times, and particularly in the fifth and first half of the sixth century. The kings who appear to have flourished during this period—and whose actual existence a nearer study of the sources makes more and more

* For further information about this character cf. Chadwick, *op. cit.* p. 149 and note.

probable—taken as far as possible in chronological order, with hypothetical dates, are the following:

Alevih (Dan). End of fourth and beginning of fifth century.

Sigar (Sigehere). First half of fifth century till c. 450 (perhaps reigning only in Sjaelland).

Froði—The peace-king—middle years of the fifth century (perhaps reigning only in Jutland) = Beowulf, Danish king mentioned in *Beo.* ll. 53 ff.?

Halfdan (Healfdene). Before c. 475.

[Helgi (Halga), sea-king in latter half of fifth century.]

Hroar (Hrothgar), c. 475—c. 570.

[Rorik (Hrethric)?]

Hrolf Kraki (Hrothulf), joint king with Hroar and succeeding him—c. 550.

Hiǫrvarð (Heoroweard)? reigned for a short time.

Thus all the Danish kings mentioned in the *Beowulf* and *Widsith* are accounted for with the exception of Scyld Scefing and Heremod. The former cannot be considered as other than mythical, and therefore does not concern us further. There has also been a common tendency to regard Heremod as mythical, owing to the absence of any known historical background for his figure. But this decision is a somewhat arbitrary one. It is true that Heremod's identity is wrapped in obscurity, but the circumstantial detail with which he is described in the *Beowulf* implies that he had at one time been a well-known personality, and is certainly in favour of his existence as an historical character, probably as a king in Danish lands. The way in which he is associated with Sigmund suggests that Heremod is perhaps to be assigned to the first half of the fifth century (cf. p. 122).

CHAPTER III

THE SWEDES.

THE Swedes (Svear) are also called in A.S. Scylfingas (*Beo.* l. 2381), in Scand. (O.N. saga lit.) Ynglingar.

The relationships of the Swedish royal family in *Beowulf* are as follows:

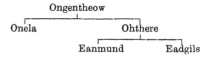

In l. 2603 Wiglaf is spoken of as *leod Scylfinga*; again in l. 2813, Beowulf, addressing Wiglaf, speaks of *ússes cynnes Waegmundinga*, where he clearly classes himself along with his hearer: this would seem to show that both Beowulf and Wiglaf claimed descent from a man named Waegmund, and the epithet *leod Scylfinga* as applied to Wiglaf has been supposed to signify some relationship between the Swedish royal family and the house of the Waegmundings (cf. Müllenhoff, *Anz. f. d. A.* III, pp. 176–178).

On these lines the following hypothetical genealogy has been constructed:

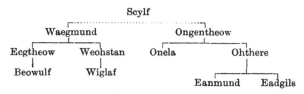

Nor must it be forgotten, as bearing upon the hypothetical character of the above table, that there is considerable uncertainty as to the exact meaning of *leod Scylfinga*, for which there are other possible interpretations besides "prince of the Scylfings."

I. THE SWEDES IN BEOWULF.

In the scattered references to the Swedes which are made in the *Beowulf*, the fortunes of this people are closely bound up with those of their neighbours the Götar, and for an account of the campaign between Ongentheow, king of Sweden, and Haethcyn and Hygelac, the princes of the Götar, the reader is referred to Chap. I, p. 26 f.

Ongentheow was apparently succeeded on the Swedish throne by his son Onela, who seems to have married the only daughter of King Healfdene of the Danes (*Beo.* l. 62).

Onela's nephews, Eanmund and Eadgils, the sons of his brother Ohthere, rebelled and were banished from the kingdom; they fled to the court of Heardred, the young king of the Geatas (Hygelac, his father, having meanwhile perished in the hapless expedition against the Franks), where they found protection and kindness (ll. 2379 ff.). They were, however, followed by Onela, who attacked and killed Heardred (l. 2388); probably in the course of the same campaign Eanmund was slain by Weohstan, who seems to have been in Onela's service.

Weohstan deprived the dead warrior of his helm, sword and coat of mail, and laid them at the feet of Onela, who returned them to him as a gift. After many years Weohstan bequeathed these trophies to his son Wiglaf, Beowulf's faithful follower (ll. 2609-2625).

Onela returned to Sweden victorious (l. 2389 f.) : after a time Eadgils, supported by Beowulf, now king of the Geatas, made an expedition to Sweden against his uncle (*he gewraec syththan cealdum cear-síthum*). The enterprise was successful : Eadgils defeated and killed Onela, and reigned as king of Sweden in his stead (ll. 2391-2396).

II.   (1) References to the Swedes in Latin Historians.

Tacitus.

Jordanes (Migne, *Patrologia*, I, 69).

Saxo Grammaticus (ed. Holder ; Bks I–IX, English transl. by O. Elton, London, 1894).

(2) References to the Swedes in Scandinavian Authorities.

Hrolfssagakraka, Fas. I, pp. 1 ff.

Skáldskapermál (Sn. Edd. ed. Wilken, Paderborn, 1877, pp. 101 ff.)

Bjarkarímur.

St Ólafssaga, Ynglingasaga (Heimskr.).

Skjǫlds. (Arngr. Jonss., *Aarb. f. nord. Oldkynd.* 1894, pp. 83 ff.).

Tacitus, *Germ.* Ch. XLIV *. The earliest reference to the Swedes is by Tacitus (*Germ.* Ch. XLIV) who wrote at the end of the first century; he mentions the Suiones as having a curious, despotic form of government, and says further that they had fleets and lived in the ocean, i.e. in islands.

Jordanes† says that the Suethans like the Thuringians used the best horses.

It is impossible, in dealing with Scandinavian authorities, to separate from one another the extracts dealing with the Swedes and the Danes, and an account of the relations between these two nations during the period under our consideration has already been given in Chap. II, to which the reader is referred. Two extracts from the *Ynglingasaga*, which are of exclusively Swedish interest, are here given:

Ch. XXVIII. *The Marriage of King Adils.* "Adils was the name of Óttar's son, who took the kingdom after him: he was king for a long time, and was very wealthy, and some summers he went on viking expeditions (*i viking*). King Adils came with his army to Saxland, over which ruled a king named Geirdjóf, while his wife was called Álof the mighty: there is no mention of their having had children. The king was not in the

* Tacitus, *Germania*, Ch. XLIII: "Trans Lugios Gotones regnantur, paulo iam adductius quam ceterae Germanorum gentes, nondum tamen supra libertatem, protinus deinde ab Oceano Rugii et Lemovii: omniumque harum gentium insigne rotunda scuta, breves gladii et erga reges obsequium."

Ch. XLIV. "Suionum hinc civitates ipso in Oceano, praeter viros armaque classibus valent, forma navium eo differt quod utrimque prora paratam semper adpulsui frontem agit."

† Jordanes, *Get.* III: "¡Alia vero gens ibi moratur Suethans, quae velut Thuringi equis utuntur eximiis."

country. King Aðils and his men plundered there: some drove down herds to slaughter on the strand. Slaves, both men and women, had tended the flocks, and all of these they took with them. Amongst the company was a maiden, wondrously beautiful: her name was Yrsa. King Aðils took her home with the rest of his booty. Yrsa was not put with the other bondwomen. It was soon clear that she was wise and learned, and shrewd in all respects. She was much admired and chiefly by the king; thus it came about that Aðils made her his wife. Then Yrsa was queen of Sweden and was eminent among women."

Ch. XXIX (last part of chapter). "King Aðils was very fond of good horses: he had the best horses of that time. One horse of his was called Slǫngvir, and another Hrafn, which he took from the dead King Áli. And of it was born another horse called Hrafn which he sent to Heligoland to King Goðgest. King Goðgest rode it and could not pull it up, until he fell off its back and was killed: that was at Ömd in Heligoland. King Aðils was at the sacrifice to the *disir* and was riding his horse round the temple of the *disir*: the horse stumbled and fell, and the king was thrown, and his head came against a stone, so that the skull was broken and his brains lay on the stones. That was his death. Aðils died at Upsala and is buried there. The Svíar called him the powerful king."

III. COMPARISON OF EVIDENCE WITH REGARD TO THE SWEDES.

Several points relating to Swedish tradition have already been discussed in connection with the subject of the preceding chapter, particularly the story of Yrsa.

Generally speaking, the accounts of *Skáldsk.*, *Hrolfss.* and Saxo vary only in points of detail with regard to the period of Swedish history with which we are dealing (i.e the period corresponding to the events described in *Beowulf*), the general outline of the story being the same in all three cases as far as Aðils is concerned. In the *Yngls.* a somewhat different aspect is imparted to the story. Some points which are of minor importance in the other are omitted altogether. The campaigns of Óttar and Froði for example, which are described in *Yngls.* at comparative length, are not mentioned in any of the other authorities with which we have been dealing; whereas Hrolf Kraki's visit to Sweden, on which so much stress is usually laid, is here passed over with the barest mention.

A point on which different authorities are considerably at variance is that of the genealogy of the Swedish kings. No genealogy of Swedish kings is given in *Hrolfss.* and *Skáldsk.*, but according to Saxo, Aðils (Athislus) and Óttar (Hotherus) were brothers, the sons of Hothbroddus, king of Sweden, and Hothbroddus was the son of Regnerus. According to *Yngls.* on the other hand, Aðils was the son of Óttar, who was the son of Egil.

We come now to compare the sum total of Scandinavian evidence with that of *Beowulf.* First, as regards the genealogies: according to *Beowulf*, Ongenthe w, king of Sweden, had two sons, Onela and Ohthere : Ohthere had, in his turn, two sons, Eanmund and Eadgils, of whom the younger succeeded to the throne after having defeated and killed his uncle Onela.

Ongentheow has entirely dropped out of Swedish tradition, where he has been replaced by Egil, a totally different personality; but the great age of the *Beowulf* justifies us in accepting Ongentheow rather than Egil as the historical father of Óttar (Ohthere)*.

Further, there is no mention in any Scandinavian authority of a king of Sweden whose figure corresponds to that of Onela, Eadgils' uncle and predecessor in *Beowulf*, but *Yngls.* and *Skáldsk.* both relate that Aðils was at war with a certain King Áli of Uppland, who belonged to Norway; in this campaign, Aðils—according to *Skáldsk.* —obtained help from Hrolf Kraki, who sent his twelve berserks (amongst them Bǫðvar-Bjarki) to his assistance. A decisive battle was fought on the frozen Lake Wener (Vaenir), in which Áli was killed.

All the evidence we possess tends to show that King Áli of Uppland in *Skáldsk.* and *Yngls.* must be identical with King Onela of Sweden in *Beowulf*. In support of this, we have firstly the identity of the two names Onela and Áli, and secondly the similar circumstances which are reported concerning both.

Both Onela and Áli were at war with Eadgils-Aðils; in both cases Aðils called in foreign assistance against his foe. It is true that in one case the help came from the Danes, and in the other from the Geatas, but the link between the two lies in the person of Beowulf-Bǫðvar. According to *Beowulf*, it was Beowulf who helped Eadgils to wrest Sweden from his uncle Onela; in *Skáldsk.* Bǫðvar's name is the first among those of twelve berserks sent by Hrolf Kraki to Aðils' assistance.

As has been elsewhere shown, there is a good deal of evidence in support of the view that Bǫðvar-Bjarki

* From an examination of the sources, it seems indeed possible that both the Egil of *Yngls.* and his father Aun are mythical characters.

and Beowulf are identical.   Without further ado this
would solve the difficulty that it was in one case the
Geatas, in the other the Danes, who rendered assistance
to Aðils.

The fact that Áli (Onela) appears in Scandinavian
tradition as a Norwegian king is probably due to confusion
arising out of the word Uppland.   There was both a
Swedish and a Norwegian Uppland : the former was in
the heart of the Swedish kingdom, and consisted of the
country lying immediately round Upsala, whereas the
latter was a general name for the Norwegian highlands.
As the Swedish king had his capital in Upsala, it was
natural that he should be called king of Uppland, and
thence it is easy to see how a confusion might arise in
later times between the two Upplands, and how the
names of one or more Swedish kings might, in consequence,
drop out of the genealogies.

In the case of Onela and Áli, it is probable that this
is what took place, and that Áli was really a king of
Sweden, as *Beowulf* reports him to have been.   In this
case again, the evidence of *Beowulf* is more trustworthy
than that of the sagas on account of its greater age, and
also because, in marked contrast to the Scandinavian
authorities, it contains a circumstantial account of the
events which led up to the campaign between Eadgils
and Onela.

This view receives confirmation from the site of the
battle between Aðils and Áli, which, according to Scandinavian authorities, took place on the ice of Lake Wener
(Vaenir).   The lake separating Götland from Sweden (i.e.
Svealand) would be the most natural place for a Swedish
army to meet a force coming from Götland, as the *Beowulf*

reports Eadgils to have done. In the poem itself the battle between Eadgils and Onela is described thus:

Lines 2393 ff.

" Folce gestepte
ofer sae sîde sunu Ôhtheres
wigum and waepnum : he gewraec syththan
cealdum cear-sîthum cyning ealdre bineât *.".

Is it too far-fetched to suppose that this "cold sorrow-bringing journey" is more than merely an alliterative expression, and is really a reference to the battle on the frozen lake ?

There still remains for discussion Wiglaf, who comes into prominence in the last section of the *Beowulf*, viz. in the course of Beowulf's struggle with the fire-spitting dragon. Wiglaf is the more interesting, inasmuch as, with the exception of Beowulf himself, he is the only figure which stands out from the dimness of that last shadowy contest, with a tangible presence, and some semblance of claim to an actual flesh and blood existence. Wiglaf was apparently a Swedish warrior in the service of Beowulf, and was the only thane who did not desert his master at the hour of need, but stood by him to the end. The poem also gives some information about Wiglaf's father, Weohstan. Weohstan was, we are told, in the service of Onela, king of Sweden ; he is probably identical with the Swedish Vesteinn mentioned in *Kálfsvisa*, *Skáldsk*. Ch. 48. The hortatory speeches of Wiglaf are reminiscent of those made by Hjalti in *Bjarkamál*, but the only character in northern tradition whose name presents any likeness to that of Wiglaf is Vǫgg, the

* "Beowulf supported Ohthere's son with a host over the wide waters, with warriors and weapons : the latter subsequently executed vengeance by a cold hostile journey : he deprived the king of life."

faithful servant and avenger of Hrolf Kraki. The form
of the name which occurs in Saxo, viz. Wiggo, looks like
a hypocoristic, and it is tempting to connect it with
Wiglaf, although the double consonant and short vowel
present considerable difficulties in the way of identifying
the two names. But in addition to this similarity of name
the figures of Wiglaf and Vǫgg have certain features in
common. Both were Swedes; both left their first master
for a new one, in one case Beowulf, and in the other Hrolf
Kraki; both play a similar part in relation to their new
master; and both receive from him rich gifts. It is not
necessary to emphasize anew the intimate association of
Hrolf Kraki with Bǫðvar-Bjarki, and, further, the extreme
likelihood that the latter is identical with Beowulf.

Thus, in view of the foregoing suggestions, it is far
from clear whether Vǫgg, Wiggo (Wiglaf?) was originally
connected with Hrolf Kraki or with Beowulf-Bjarki.
This again raises the whole question of Hrolf Kraki's fall
at Leire, and makes it not altogether inconceivable that
the narrative as it stands may have been substituted for
one which, in the first instance, had Bǫðvar-Bjarki
(Beowulf) as its hero, and that the *Bjarkamál* may be
a reproduction, however corrupt and mutilated, of the
speeches of Wiglaf and Beowulf in the last fyttes of the
O.E. poem.

IV. HISTORICAL FACTS UNDERLYING THE SWEDISH
TRADITIONS IN BEOWULF.

It must be remembered that Sweden, at the time
with which the *Beowulf* deals, by no means corresponds
to the kingdom of Sweden at the present day, which

comprises Sweden (i.e. Svealand), Götland and Skaane. Sweden and Götland were originally politically separate countries, while Skaane, until comparatively recently, belonged to Denmark. The Sweden of the sixth century (Swiðjoð) consisted of what on modern maps appears as the province Svealand.

In *Heimskr. St Ólafss.* Ch. 76, which dates from the early thirteenth century, there is a geographical description of Sweden (Swiðjoð). It is said to consist of:

- *a.* Suthrmannaland.
- *b.* Vestrmannaland or Fiathrundaland.
- *c.* Tíundaland.
- *d.* Áttandaland.
- *e.* Siáland.

Most of these divisions can still be traced on modern maps.

Although there is no adequate reason to doubt the historical value of Ongentheow, Onela and Ohthere as kings of Sweden, the only king for whose life there is really satisfactory evidence is Aðils (Eadgils of *Beowulf*). Again, taking as a starting-point the date of Hygelac's expedition to the Rhine, we must place the reign of Aðils some time before the middle of the sixth century.

Nowhere does the character of Aðils appear in a very favourable light, in fact it is noteworthy that all authorities represent him as being of an avaricious and mean disposition. The remarkable unanimity displayed with regard to this point would seem to indicate that it was no mere myth, but had solid foundation in historical fact. Yet in *Yngls.* it is stated that Aðils was remembered among the Swedes as " the powerful king " (Ch. 23).

The evidence of Jordanes (*Get.* Ch. 3), who says that the Suethans, like the Thuringians, used the best horses, is valuable confirmation of the evidence of *Yngls.* Ch. 23, regarding the attention which Aðils paid to horse-breeding.

It seems almost certain that at the time with which we are dealing, Sweden (as probably also Götland) was a tributary kingdom to Denmark, and that Aðils was a vassal of Hrolf Kraki. It is impossible to affirm this with certainty, as our evidence is not thoroughly trustworthy, but every allusion points in the same direction, and we know in addition that Hrolf Kraki was famous throughout many lands on account of his conquests.

The account of Aðils' campaign against Onela, the reigning king of Sweden, who was probably his uncle, the assistance given to Aðils by his allies the Gautar under Beowulf-Bǫðvar, and his subsequent success in obtaining the Swedish crown, may be accepted as historical. The story of Yrsa is in all probability also founded on fact*.

* Cf. Ch. II, pp. 82 ff.

CHAPTER IV

I. OFFA.

OFFA is mentioned both in *Beowulf* and in *Widsith*. The following is a rough translation of the passages in the two poems, which contain allusions to him:

Widsith, ll. 35–44. "Offa ruled over Angel, Alevih over the Danes. He was the bravest of all these men, yet he did not surpass Offa in deeds of valour. But Offa, while yet a boy—at an earlier age than any other man—won the greatest of kingdoms. No one at the same age has performed a greater deed of valour. Single-handed he fixed his frontier with the Myrgingas at Fifeldor. The Engle and the Swaefe have ever since kept to the line won by Offa*."

Beowulf, ll. 1931–1962. (The poet has been dwelling on the virtues of Hygd, the wife of Hygelac: suddenly, without any explanation, he breaks off in quite a different direction.)

"A certain queen, Thrytho, was a woman of proud and fierce spirit. No man dare gaze on her face save her husband, without paying the penalty of imprisonment and death. This is not a queenly custom, but the 'ale-drinkers'

* Translation by Mr H. M. Chadwick.

report that Thrytho performed fewer wicked deeds since the time when she first came over the sea at her father's behest, to become the wife of Offa.

" She observed her pledge towards the prince, and was renowned for her goodness at his court. Offa was a warrior, keen in battle and held in wide esteem. He was the kinsman of Heming and the descendant of Garmund. His son was Eomaer*."

II. OTHER AUTHORITIES FOR OFFA.

Mercian Genealogy in A. S. Chron. under year 755 and other Chronicles.

Vitae duorum Offarum, or *Legend of St Albans*, ascribed to Matthew Paris.

Saxo Grammaticus.

Sven Aagesen (Langeb. *S. R. D.* I, pp. 42–64).

In the genealogy of the Mercian kings the name of Offa occurs twice. Offa II we know to have been king of Mercia from 757–796, and an account of his reign is given in the A. S. Chron., but there are no references in history to his ancestor Offa I, whose name occurs twelve generations earlier in the genealogy†.

We may at once dismiss the idea that the above-quoted passages contain any allusion to Offa II, since apart from any other consideration the *Beowulf* had probably reached its present form considerably before the middle of the eighth century, when Offa II's reign commenced.

The *Legend of St Albans*, or *Vitae Offarum*, has been ascribed to Matthew Paris, a monk of St Albans who died

---

* Translation by Mr H. M. Chadwick.

† Cf. Appendix II, with list of genealogies.

about 1259, although it is now generally supposed to have
been the work of an earlier writer, which was used by him;
the ostensible object of the work was to account for the
founding of the monastery of St Albans. The legend is
shortly as follows :—

VITA OFFAE I.

A certain king of the West Angles named Warmundus
(probably here West Angles = Mercians), famous for having
founded the city of Warwick, had one son Offa. Offa was
a man of great stature and tremendous strength, but he
was blind until his seventh year, and dumb until his
thirtieth. Some of the Mercian nobles, led by Riganus,
conspired against Offa, and on the ground that he was
physically unfit to reign, demanded the kingdom. Riganus
himself hoped to be chosen as successor to the throne.
The old king Warmundus, in great perplexity, called a
council to consider what should be done, as he himself
was too old to lead an army to battle. But in this crisis,
Offa prayed that he might receive the gift of speech, and
his request was granted ; the difficulty was then solved,
for Offa forthwith volunteered to lead the king's army
against the rebels.

The two armies met on the opposing banks of a deep
river. Offa dashed across the river, and engaged the two
sons of the rebel leader, Hildebrandus and Sueno, both of
whom he killed. The rebel army was completely routed
and Offa returned home victorious. His father Warmundus
resigned the throne in his favour, and died soon afterwards. He was buried at Gloucester.

One day, Offa, while out hunting, heard the voice of
someone in distress. He found it to proceed from a

maiden, who told him that she was the daughter of the king of York. Her father had wished to seduce her, and she had fled away into the woods. Offa took the maiden home with him, and she became his wife. Subsequently he had by her twin children.

Some years after this incident, the king of Northumbria appealed to Offa for help in war against the Scots. Offa went to his assistance and was victorious.

He then wrote to his nobles giving an account of his successes, and despatched his letter by a messenger. But on the way south it was intercepted by the king of York, who at last saw an opportunity for achieving revenge for the flight of his daughter. For the original letter he substituted a forged one, which announced a great disaster to Offa's army. According to the letter, this misfortune was directly due to divine wrath against Offa for having married his wife, and directions were given that she and her children should be exposed in the woods, and maimed or killed. These orders were followed. Mother and children were turned out into the forest and the children were killed. They were, however, restored to life by the prayers of an anchorite, who then took them, along with their mother, home to his cell and hid them there.

When Offa returned, the treachery of the king of York was discovered, but it was only after a long and painful search that he came upon the anchorite, who restored to him his wife and children. At the suggestion of the anchorite, Offa vowed to build a monastery as a thank-offering, but he forgot all about his promise until the time of his death, when he exhorted his son to fulfil the neglected vow. The fulfilment of the promise was postponed from generation to generation until the days of Offa II.

Vita Offae II.

(What follows is only a partial account of the *Vita Offae II*, which is very long and contains much that has no bearing on the present subject.)

Thingferth, a Mercian prince, had a son Winifrith, who was lame, and could neither see nor hear. Thingferth and his wife, remembering the story of Offa, prayed that Winifrith might become sound, and took a fresh vow to build a monastery. Their prayer was answered, and their son healed. After he was cured, Winifrith received the name of Offa.

In the meantime, a certain noble, Beornred, revolted, and killed many of the leading men in the kingdom. Thingferth and his wife fled before him, but Offa remained behind and defeated Beornred, and was then elected king.

One day there drifted to the shore a small rudderless boat, bearing a girl who was almost dead from starvation and exposure. She gave her name as Drida and said that she was a relative of Carolus, king of the Franks. The reason that she had been cast adrift she gave as her refusal to accept offers of marriage from certain persons of ignoble blood. The truth was, however, that Drida had been condemned to death for some crime, the nature of which is not stated; but on account of her royal blood, the punishment was commuted to exposure in a rudderless boat. Offa received Drida well, and she was fed and carefully tended until health and beauty were restored. Then Offa married her, although much against the will of his parents, who from the first had not believed her story. After her marriage Drida was called Quendrida. Offa

and Quendrida had three daughters.   The eldest married
Brithricus (Berhtric) king of Wessex, the second Aethel-
redus (Aethelred) king of Northumbria, and the third
was promised to Albertus (Aethelbert) king of East
Anglia.

By this time Quendrida had come out in her true
colours. She was a cruel, scheming woman who hated
her husband, and desired above all things to get rid of
him. She was angry that her daughters should all marry
Englishmen, and would have liked to marry them to
foreign princes, who would then have helped her to
destroy Offa. She therefore conspired against the life of
Albertus, and caused him to be secretly murdered, one
day while he was on his way to visit his bride. Shortly
afterwards, Quendrida was herself murdered by robbers at
the very spot on which Albertus had fallen, and Offa, full
of gratitude at being delivered from the plots of his wife,
fulfilled the vow made long before by his ancestor, Offa I,
and founded the monastery of St Albans.

The historical evidence regarding Offa II which is
contained in the A. S. Chron. confirms the account of the
Vita Offae II, according to which Offa obtained his
kingdom by defeating the rebel Beornred. There is,
however, no reason to suppose that the very peculiar
circumstances under which Offa I fought were repeated
in the case of Offa II as Matthew Paris reports them to
have been.

A story which strikingly resembles that told of Offa I
in the *Legend of St Albans* is related by the Danish
historians Saxo (pp. 106–117) and Sven Aagesen. Sven
Aagesen wrote in the year 1185, and Saxo was engaged on
his work at the same time, but it was not completed

until the beginning of the twelfth century. The accounts of the story given by these two writers are so much alike as to be almost identical.

Wermundus, the son of Vigletus, was king of Denmark: during his reign the province of Sleswic, which formed part of the kingdom, was governed by a man named Frowinus.

Athislus, king of Sweden, invaded Denmark in the neighbourhood of Sleswic : Frowinus, who led the defending army, met Athislus in single combat and was killed. Wermundus then gave the government into the hands of Keto and Wigo*, his sons.

Keto and Wigo determined to avenge their father's death, and went to Sweden, where they lay in wait for Athislus. Seizing their opportunity, they fell on him together and killed him, but their action was generally considered most discreditable to their honour, although Wermundus was satisfied to have got rid of his enemy by any means, fair or foul.

Wermundus had one son, Uffo, the child of his old age, who was a man of enormous size and strength, but who for many years was afflicted with dumbness. According to Sven Aag. Uffo did not speak from his seventh to his thirtieth year, and his silence was due to shame on account of the disgraceful action of Keto and Wigo in killing Athislus. Uffa was in a position to feel this disgrace very keenly, as he was married to the daughter of Frowinus.

---

* In the genealogy of Wessex we find the descendants of Wodan given as follows :

Wodan—Beldaeg—Brand—Frithungar—*Freawine*—*Wig*, &c.
In Saxo : *Frowinus*—*Wigo*.

In his old age Wermundus became blind; an embassy came to him from the king of Saxony*, proposing that, as Wermundus was blind, decrepit, and unfit to rule, Denmark should be handed over to him. If Wermundus would not agree to this proposal, let his son come out and fight against the son of the sender of the challenge. Wermundus was deeply stung by these taunts, but he answered that although old and blind, he would himself accept the challenge and go out to fight. Just at that moment, however, Uffo stepped forward and spoke for the first time. He offered to fight single-handed against the son of the king of Saxony and any other warrior whom he might choose to support him. The reason he gave for wishing to fight against two men instead of one was that by so doing he hoped to wipe out the disgrace which lay upon the Danes on account of the death of Athislus through Keto and Wigo.

An island on the river Eider was chosen as the scene of the duel, and great crowds of onlookers flocked thither to witness the combat. Uffo went down alone to meet his opponents. The old Wermundus was also guided down to the river and he stood on the bridge, ready to throw himself down, should his son suffer defeat. But Uffo cut to pieces, first the Prince of Saxony and then the other Saxon champion, and thus retrieved the glory of the Danish nation, which had been lost through the murder of Athislus. The kingdom of Saxony was then handed over to the Danes, and was governed by Uffo after his father's death.

* This is Saxo's version: according to Sven Aag. the embassy was sent by the Emperor.

III. COMPARISON OF EVIDENCE WITH REGARD TO OFFA.

The story of Uffo as told by Saxo and Sven Aagesen obviously refers to the same events as that of the *Vita Offae I*, and Uffo the son of Wermund is clearly the same person as Offa the son of Warmundus. In both cases the king's son, who has been dumb until his thirtieth year, recovers his speech under similar circumstances, and overcomes singlehanded, by a river, two champions of an opposing army. Further, the genealogy of Uffo's ancestors given by Saxo corresponds to that of Offa's ancestors in the Mercian genealogy:

	Saxo.		Mercian Gen.	
	Vigletus.			Wihtlaeg.
	Wermundus.			Wermund.
	Uffo.			Offa.

There are, however, certain discrepancies between the accounts of Saxo and Sv. Aag. on the one hand and the *Vita Offae* on the other, the chief of which are the following :

1. According to Saxo and Sv. Aag. Wermundus and Uffo were kings of the Danes, and Uffo's combat took place on the frontiers of Schleswig and Holstein. According to Matthew Paris, Warmundus and Offa were kings of the Mercians, and all the events connected with them took place in England.

2. According to Saxo and Sv. Aag. the attack on Wermundus was the act of aggression of a foreign king, whereas in the *Vita Offae* the enemies of King Warmundus were rebel nobles.

3. In Saxo and Sv. Aag. the whole quarrel between Wermundus and the king of Saxony (or the Emperor) was settled by the result of Uffo's duel, while in the *Vita*

Offae a pitched battle took place of which the duel was but one episode.

It is evident that these three accounts—viz. those of Saxo, Sv. Aag., and the *Vita Offae I*—tell the same story as that related by *Widsith*, ll. 35–44, of Offa, king of Angel, where we find again the description of Offa's great prowess, and of his momentous single-handed combat with the invaders (see p. 157). *Widsith* is, however, in disagreement with the other authorities in regard to Offa's age at the time of the incident described. Whereas the *Vita Offae I*, Saxo, and Sv. Aag. all represent him as a man of about thirty years of age, he is described in *Widsith* as *cniht-wesende*, "while yet a boy," and this epithet is emphasized by the words which follow—viz. "at an earlier age than any other man." To explain this, it has been suggested that in the original account of the story the expression used with regard to Offa's age at the time of the duel may possibly have been *thritig missera* (thirty half-years, i.e. fifteen years), which later writers may have misinterpreted as thirty years.

If we now turn back to the *Vita Offae I* we see that Offa I is there represented as a king of Mercia, and that the whole scene of the story is laid in England.

According to the genealogies, Offa I was the ancestor of Penda, king of Mercia*.

In the A. S. Chron. (MS. Ӕ) under the year 626, there stands an entry in which it is said that Penda, who began to reign in that year, was fifty years of age, and that he reigned for thirty years. According to this reckoning, Penda was born in the year 576, and was eighty years of age when he died in the year 656. But there are good

* Cf. list of genealogies in Appendix ii.

reasons for regarding it as improbable that this chronology is correct, or that Penda was born as early as the year 576. For example :

1. On his death in 656, Penda left quite a young family, as his youngest son resigned the throne as late as the year 704.

2. Penda's sister, who was married to Coenwalh, king of Essex, was divorced by her husband between the years 640 and 650, and it is extremely unlikely that she should have been the sister of a man who was at that time between seventy and eighty years of age, the more so as Coenwalh, who died in 673, is said by Bede* to have been cut off by a premature death.

3. Penda was engaged in wars up to the time of his death, an activity which would have been, to say the least, surprising in a man of eighty years old.

Although the combined weight of these considerations makes it barely possible that Penda can have been born as early as 576, we may assume that he was at any rate well on in years at the time of his death in 656, and for purposes of calculation, the year 600 may be taken as the approximate date of his birth. If we reckon back, allowing thirty years for each generation, we get the year 360 A.D. as the approximate date of the birth of Offa I. But this is the pre-British and pre-Christian period of the English nation, and if there was a King Offa I, he must have ruled over the Angles on the Continent, and not in England. Thus the authority of Matthew Paris, in so far as he represents Offa I as king of Mercia and a Christian, cannot be accepted.

Wermund and Uffo are represented in Saxo as kings

* *Hist. Eccl.* iii, 7.

of the Danes, but they are never mentioned in connection with the islands, which were the stronghold and seat of government of the Danish kingdom. On the contrary, all the places mentioned in the story of Uffo, e.g. Sleswic, Eider, &c. are situated in the southern part of the Jutish peninsula, i.e. in, or near, the district which was the former home of the English and which ancient writers called Angel* (Ongel, Oghgul). In *Widsith*, l. 35, Offa is definitely said to have reigned over Angel. A possible explanation of this anomaly is that Wermund and Uffo came to be regarded as Danes, because they were known to have ruled over a country which later belonged to Denmark. When the Danes acquired possession of S. Jutland they became heirs, so to speak, of existing local traditions of which the story of Uffo would naturally be one, and Wermundus, which is the usual form in Saxo and Sven Aag., and which is English or Frisian and not Danish, would lend colour to this supposition†.

The hypothesis which has been put forward to account for the presence of an English form Wermundus in Danish tradition—viz. that the Danes first acquired the story of Offa during the period of their invasions of Britain— would fail to account for the continental forms such as Frowinus and Uffo which occur in the Scandinavian authorities, and also for the localisation of events in their version of the story.

Saxo, Sv. Aag., and other writers were apparently quite familiar with the spot on which Uffo's duel took

---

* Cf. H. M. Chadwick, *op. cit.* pp. 103 ff.

† Mr Chadwick believes that the Danes, when they settled in the basin of Eider, probably in the fifth century, "adopted the language of the natives, though at the same time without losing consciousness of their own nationality" (*op. cit.* p. 140).

place—viz. on an island in the river Eider (Saxo, pp. 115, 402). This island is said to be the one on which part of the town of Rendsburg stands: the spot is called by Peter Olavus, Kunungskamp (*S. R. D.* i, p. 84), which name is perhaps preserved in Kampen, formerly one of the parishes of the same town (*S. R. D.* i, p. 152, note). According to *Wids.* l. 43, Offa fought his single combat at Fifeldor (*bi Fifeldore*): no place of that name is known: but it is not altogether inconceivable that the name should be connected in some way with *Egidora*, which is the older form of Eider. The last part of the word is the same in both cases, and *fifel*, which in O.E. = monster, might possibly represent *egi*, if the latter is connected with O.E. *ege* = terror.

Nor was the story of Offa first brought to England by the Danes. For the names of Offa and Wermund occur in genealogies previous to the Danish invasions, and the authority of *Beowulf* and *Widsith* is also of an earlier date *. There does not appear to have been any communication between England and the Baltic countries from the middle of the sixth century up to the time of the Danish invasions (*vid. sup.* p. 53), so that with regard to the story of Offa (Uffo) we are driven back upon the only possible conclusion—viz. that English and Scandinavian tradition has developed independently at any rate since the sixth century. The English invaders carried with them to their new home the remembrance of the exploits of their national hero, while the story lived on on

* It is impossible to say with any certainty when these poems were composed, but according to the best authority they seem to date in the first instance from not later than the very beginning of the seventh century.

its native soil, and became incorporated in the annals of the Danish nation of which Angel afterwards became part.

Saxo relates that in the reign of Wermundus, Denmark was constantly harried by the incursions of Athislus, king of Sweden. There are two curious facts to be noted about this Athislus. In the first place, he always attacked the Danes in the neighbourhood of Sleswic, whereas the obvious point for a Swedish attack on Denmark would have been either Skaane in the south of Sweden, or the island of Zealand. In the second place, the fact that Uffo, king of Denmark, killed single-handed two warriors who were Saxons, hardly seems a sufficient equivalent for the murder of Athislus, king of Sweden, by two Danish champions who attacked him simultaneously.

According to *Widsith*, l. 42, it was against the Myrgingas that Offa fought in single combat. This people probably occupied territory between the Elbe and the Vistula and in the neighbourhood of the Angli, but the name Myrgingas appears to have been rather a dynastic than a tribal one, else it is difficult to account for the omission by other authorities of all mention of the tribe, which appears to have been one of considerable importance. We learn, further, from *Widsith* that the leader of the Myrgingas was a prince named Eadgils.

Now Swedish tradition preserves the name of only one King Adils, who reigned in the middle of the sixth century and with whose figure we are already familiar. As the events of the story of Offa must have taken place before the sixth century, it is obvious that this King Adils is not the same person as the Athislus referred to by Saxo in connection with the story. It has, however, been suggested that Eadgils mentioned by Widsith as the leader of the Myrgingas is identical with Athislus who, according to Saxo, harried Denmark in the reign of Wermund.

The figure and deeds of Athislus would acquire far more significance if it could be proved that he belonged to the country south of the Eider instead of being, as Saxo reports, king of Sweden.

The explanation given above is rendered more probable by further considerations :

If Athislus came from the south, his most natural point of attack on the Angles would be Sleswic. The action of Uffo in killing two Saxon warriors, in order to atone for the disgrace which had rested on the Danish nation since the death of Athislus, would also be more easily explained, and would further link the story of Saxo to that of Widsith, in which Offa fights against the Myrgingas, whose leader is said in the same poem to be Eadgils (Athislus).

Again, Widsith represents Eadgils of the Myrgingas as contemporary with Ermanric, king of the Goths (cf. *Widsith*, ll. 88–98), whose death we know to have taken place shortly before the year 375 A.D. (Ammian. XXXI, 3, 1). Eadgils must, therefore, have lived in the middle and latter half of the fourth century. But 360 was the year which we have seen cause to regard as the approximate date of the birth of Offa I, so that he must have been a considerably younger man than Eadgils. Uffo's duel did not, however, according to Saxo, take place until some time after the death of Athislus, and this chronology would therefore be quite in agreement with the theory that the latter is identical with Eadgils, prince of the Myrgingas, the patron of Widsith.

It is, however, difficult to come to any definite conclusion regarding the nationality of Offa's opponents, for
Myrgingas, as we have seen, is possibly a family or
dynastic rather than a national name. Saxo calls them
Saxones (p. 116), while in Sven Aagesen's chronicle they
appear as Alamanni (*S. R. D.* i, pp. 45–47).

At the end of the passage in *Widsith*, containing an
allusion to Offa (ll. 43 f.), it is said that "the *Engle* and
Swaefe have ever since kept to the line won by Offa." It
is not clear from this whether the *Engle* and *Swaefe* were
allies or enemies, though the natural interpretation would
certainly be that they were the two compounding parties
to a bargain which was the means of bringing some
previous disagreement to an end. The most that can be
definitely inferred from the passage is that the *Engle* and
Swaefe must have been neighbouring tribes.

Now from the evidence of classical historians (most
important in this respect are Strabo and Tacitus) the
term Suebi (Suabi) appears to have been a group-name
covering a number of tribes, all of which lay in or round
the basin of the Elbe. Hence in all probability the Suabi
(*Swaefe*) mentioned in *Widsith* were the North Suabi,
occupying the western part of Holstein and thus bordering
on the Angli (*Engle*) on the south and south-west.

On behalf of the supposition that the *Widsith* poet, in
mentioning this people of the North Suabi, is referring to
Offa's enemies, there are one or two circumstances which
must be taken into account. We have seen that, in
Sv. Aagesen's narrative, Offa's opponents are called
Alamanni: now the Alamanni are sometimes called Suabi*.

---

* Cf. Paulus Diaconus, *Historia Langobardorum*, iii, 18; ii, 15; Greg.
Tur. *Hist. Franc.* ii, 2.

Again, if the Athislus of Saxo was, as has been suggested, identical with the Eadgils described in *Widsith* as Prince of the Myrgingas, Offa's opponents, it is quite possible that this king was originally designated *Swebe kyning*, and that for the subsequently forgotten term *Sweba* was substituted the more familiar *Svea* by later Danish writers.

On the whole there seems good reason to believe that the people against whom Offa fought his single combat, who appear variously as Myrgingas, Saxones, Alamanni, are also referred to in *Widsith*, l. 44, as the *Swaefe*, and that they belonged to the northern branch of the great congeries of tribes situated round the basin of the river Elbe, described collectively by classical historians as the *Suebi** (Suabi).

We have still to consider the allusion contained in the passage from *Beowulf* (ll. 1931–1962), usually known as the Offa Episode, which was cited at the beginning of the chapter. The Offa referred to, as has been seen, cannot be Offa II, the historical king of Mercia, but any doubt which may still exist on this point is dispelled by the reference in *Beo.* ll. 1960–1962, where he is spoken of as the descendant of Garmund and the ancestor of Eomaer, thus occupying a position analogous to that of Offa I in the Mercian genealogy.

The bulk of the *Beowulf* passage deals with Thrytho, Offa's wife, whose character is represented in a most unfavourable light, though to her credit it is said that her morals and manners underwent a considerable improvement after her marriage. This Thrytho, strangely enough,

* The information here given with regard to Offa's enemies is borrowed entirely from Mr Chadwick, cf. *op. cit.* pp. 124 ff.

corresponds in name and character to the Quendrida of the *Legend of St Albans*, who was the wife not of Offa I, but of Offa II. The historical wife of Offa II was Cynethryth (not Cwenthryth, which would correspond to Quendrida), and the only historical evidence regarding her character is contained in a letter from Alcuin to Egfrith, Offa's son, in which the words occur "Disce a patre auctoritatem a matre pietatem*." This allusion does not justify us in believing Cynethryth the monster she is represented to be in the *Vita Offae II*. According to the A. S. Chron., Aethelberht (Albertus in *Legend of St Albans*) was put to death by Offa. There is no authority earlier than that of the twelfth century† for implicating Cynethryth in the murder.

Nothing is known historically of the wife of Offa I. The story of the *Vita Offae I* does not bear the impress of a genuine narrative, and may very probably have been invented merely to suit the purposes of the legend (i.e. to account for Offa's vow to build the monastery of St Albans); it thus appears that great confusion arose in later English tradition both between the two Offas and between their wives, and that in particular the attributes of the wife of Offa I were, quite unjustifiably, transferred to the wife of Offa II.

IV. Historical Facts underlying References to Offa in Beowulf and Widsith.

In the case of Offa, the historical background for the events recorded in *Beowulf* and *Widsith* seems less hazy than usual, owing to the unanimity which exists between

---

* Jaffé, *Bibl. Rer. Germ.* vi, p. 267.
† Cf. Florence of Worcester, i, 62, 63.

the accounts given in the poems and those contained in other records.

The combined evidence of all authorities gives us the following well-substantiated facts, which there is little difficulty in accepting as historical.

In the second half of the fourth century there reigned over the country of Angel (the district between the Slee and Rendsburg) a king named Waermund. Waermund was an old man and had one son, Offa, who was apparently as a boy awkward, uncouth and generally unpromising, but who, as he advanced in life, won an unrivalled reputation for strength and courage.

On one occasion preparations were made for attacking Angel by a hostile power, whose territory presumably lay to the south or south-west of the river Eider; there is some ground for identifying the invaders with the people known to classical historians as the North Suabi. Their object appears to have been to reduce Angel to the condition of a tributary state, but no battle took place: for according to agreement, the dispute was settled by a single combat on an island in the river Eider, in which Offa killed two picked champions of the opposing army, thereby fixing once and for all the frontier of his father's kingdom. After this signal victory, Offa became king of Angel, and his fame went abroad as that of the most valiant of kings*.

There is good ground for accepting as historical the fact that Offa I had a wife as notorious for her vicious habits as her husband was famous for his bravery. It is

* Some reference to the subsequent history of Offa and his possible relations with the Alevih of *Wids.* l. 35 has already been made in the preceding chapter, cf. p. 119.

not necessary to repeat the story of the strange arrival of this woman in Offa's country, of her marriage with Offa, and his subsequent discovery of her true character. It may seem rash to accept this story on the sole evidence of *Beowulf*, but weight is added to this evidence by the narrative of the author of the *Vitae Offarum*, who knew and told the same story, although, owing to some confusion, he believed it to refer to the wife not of Offa I but of Offa II.

CHAPTER V

FINN.

I & III*. The epic fragment *Finn* and the Finn episode in *Beowulf* are all that have come down to us of a lost Finn saga: the Fragment probably formed part of a whole epic on the subject of the Finn saga, the rest of which has disappeared.

Both the Finn episode and the Fragment are extremely obscure, and have hitherto baffled the efforts which have been made to reconstruct the saga with even approximate certainty. The Finn episode, in about one hundred lines, sketches in outline the course of events in a quarrel between Finn the king of the Frisians, and Hnaef and Hengest, whom it calls Danes. The Fragment seems to consist of a more detailed account of one of the episodes of that quarrel. The general course of events in the Finn saga as contained in the *Beowulf* passage (ll. 1068–1159) may, with the help of the references in *Widsith* †, be provisionally reconstructed as follows:

Finn, the son of Folcwalda, ruled over the Frisians. His wife was probably Hildeburh, the daughter of Hoc.

---

* No Scand. or other authorities contain evidence with regard to this saga.

† *Wids.* l. 27: "Fin Folcwalding (weold) Fresnacynne."

       l. 29: "Hnaef (weold) Hòcingum."

We learn from *Widsith* that Hnaef ruled over the Hocings,
and from *Beowulf* that he was the vassal of Healfdene.   It
is probable, too, judging from *Beo.* l. 1074, that he was
a near relative, perhaps a brother, of Hildeburh.   This
Hnaef visited the court of Finn, along with a retinue of
warriors, the chief of whom was called Hengest.   Strife
broke out between Finn and his guests, and there is
certainly the suggestion of foul play on one side or the
other, though it is not clear on which (*Beo.* ll. 1068 ff.).
In the fight Hnaef was killed, and also apparently one
or more of Hildburh's sons (cf. l. 1074).   Finn's fighting
force was so much impaired by the damage inflicted on it
by Hnaef's men that Finn was obliged to come to terms
with Hengest, who had taken command after Hnaef's
death.   Hnaef's men received treasure in compensation
for their losses, and solemn oaths of peace were exchanged
(ll. 1085 ff.).   The bodies of the slaughtered warriors, i.e.
of Hnaef and the son or sons of Hildeburh, were solemnly
burned on one pyre, in the presence of the sorrowing
queen (ll. 1108–1124).

Through the winter and on into the next spring, peace
was preserved between Finn and Hengest; perhaps Hengest became Finn's sworn vassal through the acceptance
of a sword, Hunlafing (cf. ll. 1143 ff.).   But when icy
winter had relaxed its hold on sea and land, and spring
was fully come, thoughts of vengeance began to stir in
Hengest's mind, and he thought more, as we are told,
of the possibility of accomplishing his revenge than of
setting out on a sea-voyage (i.e. of escaping from Finn's
land) (ll. 1127–1141).   From this point onwards the course
of events is not quite clear, but it would appear that
Guthlaf and Oslaf, two warriors also mentioned in the

Fragment (Guthlaf and Ordlaf) as accompanying Hengest, were the instigators of an attack upon Finn, the result of which was that the Frisians were completely defeated, while Finn himself was killed and his queen taken prisoner along with much treasure, and carried home by the Danes (ll. 1146–1159).

Such being the outline of the course of events, the difficult question arises of assigning to the more detailed events described in the *Finn* Fragment their proper place in the story. The Fragment is evidently part of the description of a treacherous attack made by Finn on the hall where the Danes were passing the night. Hengest exhorted his men to fight bravely (ll. 11–13) and posted some of his best warriors to hold the doors. At one door were stationed Guthlaf and Ordlaf, at the other Sigeferth and Eaha (ll. 16–18). The only two warriors mentioned as apparently belonging to Finn's band are Garulf and Guthere (l. 20). Of these we hear that Garulf was slain, presumably in a fight with Sigeferth (l. 33). The defenders of the hall, i.e. Hnaef's men, numbered sixty. For five days they held the doors without losing a single man (ll. 39–44).

It is difficult to see in this story either of the two fights alluded to in the Finn episode in *Beowulf*, as the circumstances under which it took place do not seem to apply exactly to either.

In the second battle of the Finn episode, in which Finn was defeated and slain, it is explicitly stated that Guthlaf and Oslaf were the attackers, which scarcely seems to tally with the account of a surprise night attack by Finn, for there can be no doubt that in the Fragment the Frisians were the attacking party. It is

also difficult to identify the first fight of the Finn
episode, *Beo.* ll. 1068–1085, with the battle described
in the Fragment. *Beo.* l. 1068, *thâ hie se faer begeat*,
does not seem to indicate that the first attack was
made by the Frisians: nor does it appear from ll. 1071–2
that any treachery practised was on the part of Finn
(i.e. if we take *Eotena* as referring to Hnaef and his
followers, a point to the discussion of which we shall
return later on).

The alternatives which remain to us with regard to
the fight described in the Fragment are to suppose either
that it formed the latter stage of one or other of the
struggles referred to in the Finn episode, or that it
described some fight which the Finn episode entirely
passes over, though this latter supposition is unlikely.
It might very well be a description of part of the first
struggle, and refer to the events immediately following on
Hnaef's death, when we might suppose that the strangers
took up as strong a position as possible in anticipation of
a counter-attack. The *heatho-geong cyning, Finn,* l. 2,
would then aptly enough denote Hengest, on whom the
command had just devolved (in fact *Finn,* l. 17, *and
Hengest sylf,* seems to imply that he *was* meant by
heatho-geong-cyning), and the losses which the defenders
evidently inflicted on the Frisians would tally well with
Beo. ll. 1080 ff., *Wîg alle fornam Finnes thegnas,* &c.
Finn, ll. 41–42, also give a good meaning if they can be
taken to refer to the speedy vengeance which Hnaef's
followers meted out to the Frisians for the death of their
master*.

* " I never heard of better recompense given for sweet mead than
that with which Hnaef was requited by his followers."

This hypothesis* seems to fit the facts related in the two poems better than the other theory which has been propounded respecting *Finn* by Möller and others. These scholars hold that the *Finn* Fragment refers to part of the last struggle between Hengest and Finn, that it is the *grimne gripe* after which Guthlaf and Oslaf made their last attack on Finn. But the Finn episode in *Beowulf* certainly implies that the second struggle between Hnaef's followers and the Frisians took place altogether on the initiative of the former, and that Guthlaf and Oslaf came across the sea in order to accomplish their purpose. There is nothing either in the *Beowulf* or in the Fragment to imply that Hengest was killed, and that Guthlaf and Oslaf then assumed command and defeated Finn. Indeed such an idea is far-fetched and very improbable†.

A somewhat difficult point in the Finn episode is the use of the word *Eoten-*, which occurs four times—three times as a genitive, *Eotena*, and once as a dative, *Eotenum*. It has been taken both as referring to the Frisians and to Hnaef's men.

In the first case, l. 1072, the use of the word is ambiguous; there is nothing to show to which party it refers. In the second case, viz. l. 1088, *Eotena* seems clearly to refer to Hnaef's men: *hie*, which is the subject of the clause, must denote the same persons as the *hig* in l. 1085, which is the subject of the principal clause, and which evidently refers to the Frisians.

---

* Cf. also Kögel, *Gesch. d. deutsch. Litt.*, Vol. I, p. 166.

† It should be noted that nowhere in the Finn episode is Hildeburh explicitly stated to have been the wife of Finn, but from the context we are justified in assuming this to have been the case. She is not mentioned at all in the Fragment.

We find the word a third time in l. 1141, *he Eotena bearn inne gemunde*. *He* = Hengest about whom the previous lines have spoken; whether *Eotena* refers to his own people or to the opposing party, i.e. the Frisians, depends on the sense in which *gemunde* is taken. Commentators who wish to make *Eotena* correspond to *Fresna* translate *gemunde* as "remember," i.e. take vengeance on : but it is much more natural to suppose that the feeling described by *gemunde* was one of sorrow for lost friends, in which case *Eotena bearn* refers of course to Hengest's own men.

l. 1145.—*mid Eotenum*.

The allusion contained in *mid Eotenum* is difficult, as the passage is obscure, but the key to the explanation is perhaps contained in *Hunláfing*, cf. l. 1143 : this Hunlafing was apparently a sword, which became the property of Hengest.

In Arngrim Jonsson's extracts from the lost *Skjǫld-ungasaga** there is an account of a Danish king Leivus, the father of seven sons, three of whom were named Hunnleivus, Oddleifus, Gunnleifus. Two of these names, viz. Oddleifus and Gunnleifus, are clearly identical with Ordlaf and Guthlaf who are mentioned in the *Finn* Fragment, l. 16, as fighting on the side of Hengest, and who appear in *Beo.* l. 1148 as avenging the death of Hnaef on Finn. (In this case, we may assume Oslaf to be a scribal error for Ordlaf.) A further confirmation of this is supplied by *Beo.* l. 1090, where Hengest's men are called Danes. The coincidence between the third name Hunnleivus and the Hunlafing of *Beo.* l. 1143 is too striking to be accidental, and at once places the

* *Aarb. f. n. Oldkynd.* 1894, pp. 104 ff.

whole passage in close relation to Ordlaf and Guthlaf, whom we know to have been warriors fighting on the side of Hengest.

The form of Hunlafing (cf. Hrunting, Miming) would suggest that it was the name of a sword, originally the property of a warrior named Hunlaf (Hunnleivus ?), which (cf. ll. 1143, 1144) apparently passed at this time into the possession of Hengest: the words of l. 1145, *þaes waeron mid Eotenum ecge cûthe*, are in that case spoken of Hunlafing, and their most natural significance would be that the sword was famous amongst the nation or tribe to which its owner belonged, i.e. *mid Eotenum*. But we have already seen good reason to associate Hunlafing with Ordlaf and Guthlaf, Hengest's men ; this being so, we are justified in inferring that the allusion contained in *mid Eotenum* is to the followers of Hengest—the " Dene " —rather than to the followers of Finn.

The form *Eotena* may be identical with the Scandinavian name for the inhabitants of Jutland, the O.E. forms of which would be O.E. *Eotan**, Anglian *Eote*, earliest Anglian **Juti* (= Bede's *Juti, Jutae*); E.W.S. *Jete*, L.W.S. *Yte*†. The gen. form *Eotena* shows, like *Seaxna* and *Miercna*, the genitive plural termination of nouns of the weak declension (cf. Sievers, *op. cit.* § 264, note), and the dative *Eotenum* for *Eotum* has taken the *n* from the genitive (cf. Sievers, *op. cit.* § 277, note 1, dat. pl., *nefenum* for *nefum* from nom. sing. *nefa*).

Bede calls the invaders of Kent and of the Isle of Wight *Jutae* and *Juti*, and in the A.S. Bede *Terra Jutarum* is rendered by *Ytenaland* and *Eotaland*. A.S. *eo* and O.N. *io* represent a Teutonic *eu*. The primary

† An -*i* stem, like *Engle*, cf. Sievers, *A. S. Grammar*, § 264.

form of the word must have been *Eutan-* and Bede's *Juti* would point to a stem *Eutia-*, which is probably the same as that underlying the form *Ytum* in *Widsith.*

From *Eutan* would regularly develop O.N. *Jótar* and original O.E. *Eotan.* *Juti* and *Eotan* are analogous forms to *Frisii* and *Fresones* which exist alongside of one another.

Möller has brought an objection against this explanation on the ground that the Danish word *Jydir*, which is the modern name for the inhabitants of Jutland, points to a form with original initial *j.* But it is difficult to understand how this can be, for initial *j* is always lost in Scandinavian languages. It seems more probable that the Danish form *Jydir* is due to a compromise between two forms *Jótar* and *Ytir*, the latter of which would correspond to the A.S. *Yte.*

In the *Finn* episode, Hnaef's men are spoken of indiscriminately as *Eotena* and as Danes ("Dene," *Beo.* l. 1090) and vassals of King Healfdene, a Danish king. This is somewhat curious, but it should be noted that the singer was telling his story at the court of a Danish king, which might well account for his desire to ascribe the prowess of Hnaef and Hengest to vassals of Healfdene.

In the Fragment the nationality of Hnaef and Hengest and of their followers is not designated in any way.

IV. HISTORICAL BACKGROUND OF THE FINN SAGA.

The sole link, by which we can in any way connect the Finn saga with history, lies in *Beo.* l. 1069, where Hnaef is described as a warrior of the Danish king Healfdene. Healfdene was the father of Hrothgar, in

whose reign the events described in the first part of
Beowulf took place, and from Gregory of Tours' Chronicle
we are enabled to assign these events to some date early
in the sixth century. Hygelac's expedition against the
Franks and Frisians took place probably about the year
520*.

Hrothgar the Dane was reigning then in the early
years of the sixth century. He was an old man, and had
been king for many years (ll. 1769–70). From this we
conclude that Healfdene, who was the father of Hrothgar,
and under whom Hnaef and Hengest flourished, must
have been reigning about the middle of the fifth century.

As we cast about for something whereby we may
further link this curious story of the Finn saga to known
historical events, the question naturally arises whether
Hengest of the Finn saga can possibly be identical with
the familiar Hengest who, along with his brother Horsa,
was one of the first Teutonic invaders of Britain. According to Bede† and the A. S. Chronicle, in the year
449 A.D. Hengest and Horsa, who are called Juti or Jutae,
came to Britain with a band of warriors at the invitation
of the British king Wyrtgeorn or Vurtigernus (Vortigern).
Nennius, in the *Historia Britonum*, § 3, dates the coming
of the Saxons in the year 428–9, and differs from Bede
and from the A. S. Chronicle in the reason which he
assigns for their coming. Three ships, he says, were

* According to this Chronicle, the expedition of Chochilaicus took
place between the years 512 and 520. The invaders were defeated by
Theodoric of the Franks and his son Theodobert. Now Chlodovech
(Clovis), the father of Theodoric, was born in 466; it is therefore
scarcely possible that he should have had a grandson of age to fight
much earlier than 520.

† *Hist. Eccles.* i, 14 f., ii, 5.

driven into exile from Germany, and came to Britain under Hengest and Horsa.

In support of the theory of the identity of the two, the following considerations might be urged :—

1. The two Hengests were more or less contemporary with one another. According to Bede's chronology, the Jutae came to Britain under Hengest and Horsa in 449 A.D.; from the evidence of *Beowulf* we learn that the Hengest of the Finn saga must have been alive about the middle of the fifth century.

2. Both warriors seem to have belonged to a tribe of the same name, i.e. if we take the *Eotena* of the Finn episode to refer to the men of Hnaef and Hengest, which is on the whole the more probable interpretation. Bede* calls the invaders of Kent under Hengest and Horsa *Juti*; and it has been shown that these two forms are derived from the same stem, and are probably the same word.

3. Nennius speaks of Hengest and Horsa as exiles from their own country. If, as is hinted in *Beowulf*, Hengest made terms with Finn after the death of Hnaef, and indeed became his vassal (cf. ll. 1085–1091, 1143–1144), such a discreditable action might well make it impossible for him ever to show his face again in his own country†.

4. The story of Finn and Hengest must have been very familiar to the mind of the person from whom Nennius derived his genealogy of Hengest and Horsa: for in this genealogy we find that the name of Folcwald has slipped in, as father of Finn the mythical ancestor

* *Hist. Eccles.* i, 15.

† Cf. account of Cynewulf's murder in A. S. Chron. under the year 755.

of Wodan, replacing that of Godwulf which is found in
all other genealogies *.

5. The name Hengest is an uncommon one. It is
not found except in these two cases, and its occurrence
side by side with that of Horsa looks very much as if it
were some kind of nickname.

All this evidence certainly tends in the same direction,
but against it we must put the fact that the year 520,
which is our only approximate date for the life of Beowulf,
and after which he is reported to have reigned fifty years,
is a very long way removed from 449, when, according to
our hypothesis, the father of the man to whom Beowulf
rendered a great service must have flourished. On the
other hand, at the time when Beowulf killed Grendel,
Hrothgar is spoken of as a very old man ; this must have
been several years before Hygelac's fatal expedition to the
Rhine, as is evident from the fact that after Hygelac's
death his son Heardred was old enough to reign, whereas,
on the occasion of Beowulf's victorious home-coming after
slaying Grendel, Queen Hygd is described in terms which
indicate that her marriage was still of very recent date.

Taking, however, everything into account, the balance
of probability seems on the whole in favour of accepting
the Hengest of the Finn saga as the same Hengest who
later on sought a new home across the seas in Britain.

The identity is far from complete, but the alternative
of such a curious and extensive coincidence of names
and events in wholly different versions is one not easily
accepted.

* Compare list of genealogies in Appendix II.

CHAPTER VI

DEOR*.

THE first two strophes of *Deor* (ll. 1–13) give in very compressed form the story of the Wêland saga. The reference contained in the third strophe is unknown. There is not sufficient ground for associating it with certain events of the Ermanric saga as Grein has proposed doing†. The most probable translation of the lines (14–16) is: "Many of us have heard that Geat's affection for Maeth-hilde was boundless, so that his anxious love robbed him entirely of sleep‡." We may compare this with what is said of the God Frey in *Skirnismál*. Frey had for long nourished a hopeless passion for a maiden named Gerda (Gerðr). After much persuasion, the maiden gave her consent to his suit, on the condition that he should wait for a certain length of time before gaining her. During this time of waiting, Frey's impatience and longing were so great that he could not rest for a moment, and at night all sleep went from him.

---

* For a description of the poem cf. Introductory Chapter.

† Cf. Grein, *Sprachschatz z. d. Bibl. der ags. Poesie*, under *Maeth*.

‡   "We thaet maeth hilde mongo gefrugnon:
       Wurdon grundlease Geates frige,
       Thaet him seo sorglufu slaep alle binom."

The name Maeth-hilde is quite unknown : that of Geat is found at the head of the older English genealogies. It is possible that the Geat of *Deor* may be identical with the Geat who is represented as the divine ancestor of the O.E. kings, and there may be also some significance in the fact that a similar story to that told of him in *Deor*, is in *Skirnismál* told of Frey, the divine ancestor of the Danish kings*.

The fourth strophe appears to contain an obscure allusion to the Ostrogothic saga-cycle of Ermanric and Dietrich. It may be translated thus : " Dietrich held the castle of the Maerings for thirty years : that was known to many†."

According to German hero saga‡, Dietrich of Bern was exiled from Italy by his uncle Ermanric, and was driven to take refuge at the court of the Hunnish king Attila. He remained with the Huns for thirty years, before he succeeded in regaining his inheritance. Maeringaburg as a place name is unknown, but the natural inference from these lines is that it was the name of some castle where Dietrich lived during the years of his exile, and that it was therefore probably situated in Hunnish territory. In a fragmentary *Lay of Theodoric the Goth*§ which is inscribed on an ancient runic stone in East Götland, Sweden, Theodoric (Dietrich) is called "Prince of the

---

* Some scholars think that the name *Gapt*, which heads the Gothic genealogies in Jordanes, is a corruption of *Gaut*, and is identical with the *Geat* of the English genealogies. It seems very doubtful whether this emendation is correct, for in Jordanes' orthography the name corresponding to *Geat* would be *Got*.

†   " Theodric âhte thritig wintra
           Maeringa burg : thaet waes monegumcûth."

‡ *Dietrich's Flucht, Rabenschlacht, Nibelungenlied*, &c.

§ *Corpus Poeticum Boreale*, I, 59.

Maerings " (*skati Maringa*) : this is the only other known occurrence of the name.

Strophe V is a clear reference to Ermanric, its discussion will therefore be reserved for the chapter on the Ostrogothic cycle.

Strophe VI, in which the poet relates some details of his own career, bears upon the Heodeninga, or Hildesaga, to a discussion of which, with that of the Wêland saga, it is proposed to devote this chapter.

(a) HILDE SAGA.

I. HILDE SAGA IN OLD ENGLISH.

I.   *Deor*, ll. 35 ff.

> " Thaet ic bi me sylfum secgan wille,
>   thaet ic hwîle waes Heodeninga scôp,
>   dryhtne dyre : me waes Deor nama.
>   âhte ic fela wintra folgath tilne,
>   holdne hlaford, ôth thaet Heorrenda nu,
>   leothcraeftig monn, londryht gethah,
>   thaet me eorla hleo aer gesealde.
>   Thaes ofereode, thisses swâ maeg * ! "

Waldere, B, ll. 8, 9.

> " Thaes the hine of nearwum Nithhades maeg,
>   *Wêlandes bearn, Widia* ût forlêt†."

Widsith, l. 21.

> ‡ " Hagena weold Holmrygum and Heoden Glommum."

---

* " This I myself will say, that I was for a time court poet of the Heodeningas, dear to my lord, Deor was my name. I had a good office and a gracious lord for many years, until now Heorrenda, a man skilled in poetry, has received the domain with which the king formerly presented me."

† " Because that from danger Nithhad's kinsman, Wêland's son Widia did rescue him."

‡ " Hagena ruled over the Holmrygas and Heoden over the Glommas."

II. Other Authorities for Hilde Saga.

Skáldskapermál, Ch. L.

Fornaldar Sǫgur I, *Sǫrlaþáttr.* (pp. 391 ff.).

Saxo Grammaticus.

Gudrun.

Vǫlsungasaga.

Skáldsk.

(Ch. L.) "There was a battle called the storm or shower of the Hjaðningar, and the weapons of the Hjaðningar were firebrands or staves. And thus runs this story : A king who was called Hǫgni had a daughter named Hild ; a king named Heðin, the son of Hjarranda, carried her off as spoil after a battle : at that time Hǫgni had gone to the assembly of kings. But when he heard that his kingdom was harried and his daughter taken away, he set out with his army after Heðin, and learned that he had sailed northwards along the coast. When king Hǫgni came to Norway he learned that Heðin had sailed across the sea to the west ; then Hǫgni sailed after him, right to the Orkney islands, and when he came to the one which is called Haey there were Heðin and his men. Then Hild went to meet her father and offered him peace on behalf of Heðin ; on the other hand she said that Heðin was ready to fight, and Hǫgni need expect no quarter from him. Hǫgni answered his daughter curtly, so when she met Heðin, she told him that Hǫgni did not wish for peace, and bade him prepare for the combat: and so both of them prepared to go up to the island and to lead on their men. Then Heðin called to Hǫgni his kinsman and offered him peace and much gold as expiation of his crime. Then Hǫgni

answered: 'You offer me this too late, if you are anxious
to make peace, because now I have drawn from the sheath
Dainsleif, the sword which the dwarfs made, which shall
be death to a man each time it is bared, and it never fails
at a blow, and the wound which it inflicts never heals.'
Then Heðin answered: 'You boast there of your sword,
but not of the victory: I call that a good (sword) which
never fails its master.' Then they began the combat
which is called the battle of the Hjaðningar; and they
fought that whole day, and in the evening the kings
went to their ships. But in the night, Hild went to the
battle-field, and by her magic arts restored to life all
those that were dead : and the next day the kings went
to the field and fought, and likewise all those that fell on
the first day. Thus the battle continued one day after
another, so that all the men who fell and all the weapons
which lay on the field were turned to dust. But when it
dawned, all the dead men stood up and fought, and all
the weapons were renewed. Thus it is said in poems
that it will be with the Hjaðningar until the end of the
world."

SAXO GRAMMATICUS.

(v, 158-160.) Heðin (Hithinus) was a prince of an
important Norwegian tribe, who fell in love by hearsay with
Hild (Hilda) the daughter of Hǫgni (Höginus) a Jutish
chieftain. Heðin's love was returned by the maiden, who
had heard of his prowess, and when the two met their
passion for one another knew no bounds.

Soon after this, Heðin and Hǫgni resolved to make
a raid together. Now Hǫgni was a big man of a fierce
disposition, while Heðin was short of stature and very
comely in looks. Before starting on their expedition,

Hǫgni betrothed his daughter to Heðin, and the two
chieftains swore an oath that if either of them should
be killed, his death should be avenged by the sword
of the other. The raid proved, however, successful,
and Heðin and Hǫgni returned home, having won
a great battle off the Orkneys, and captured a number
of ships.

But certain slanderous tongues accused Heðin to
Hǫgni of having seduced his daughter before they were
betrothed, which was at that time counted a great crime.
Hǫgni believed the report and collected a fleet in order to
attack Heðin who was busy collecting tribute on behalf
of King Froði (Frotho) from the Slavs. As the result of
the battle which took place between them, Hǫgni was
defeated and retired to Jutland.

By this action, Heðin and Hǫgni broke the peace
which had been instituted by Froði. The king enquired
into the cause of the quarrel between the two princes, and
as no satisfactory settlement could be arrived at, he
decreed that the question should be decided by single
combat. In the duel which ensued, Hǫgni, by reason of
his superior size and strength, had the advantage; but he
spared Heðin out of kindness, for in these times it was
counted a shameful action to deprive a weaker adversary
of his life.

Seven years afterwards, Heðin and Hǫgni met again
in battle and wounded each other so that they both died.
It is said that Hilda longed so ardently for her husband
that she each night restored to life by her spells those
who had fallen in the battle, in order that they might
renew their struggle the next day.

Sǫrlaþáttr.

The Introduction to the *Sǫrlaþáttr* is a page out of Norse mythology : the argument is briefly as follows :—

Loki robbed Freyja of a necklace which the dwarfs had made for her, and gave it to Odin. When Freyja demanded her necklace from Odin, he refused to give it up except on condition that Freyja should bring about a strife between two kings, each of whom had twenty kings under him. The fight between these two kings was to be ordered in such a way that those who fell should rise up at once and fight again, until some Christian man should be brave enough to enter into the battle and bring it to an end.

The *Sǫrlaþáttr* relates how these conditions were fulfilled, and how the Goddess Freyja thus regained her necklace.

The narrative of the *Sǫrlaþáttr*, in so far as it affects Heðin and Hǫgni, is the following :

Hǫgni was son of Halfdan, king of Denmark, and his friend and brother-in-arms was Sǫrli, son of Erling, king of Uppland in Norway. Sǫrli was killed by certain vikings of the Baltic. On hearing of this, Hǫgni sailed to the Baltic in order to avenge the death of his friend. He there conducted a most successful campaign, and returned home having conquered and brought into subjection, it was said, no less than twenty kings.

There reigned at that time in Africa (Serkland) a king named Hjarandi ; he had a son Heðin who was of great size and strength, and who had acquired great fame by his brave deeds. He had gone on campaigns against Spain and Greece and twenty kings paid him tribute.

Heðin was once going through a forest, when passing he saw, seated in a clearing, a large, comely woman, who told him, in answer to his enquiry, that her name was Gǫndul*. They fell into conversation together, in the course of which Gǫndul told Heðin that the only king in the world who could compare with him in prowess was Hǫgni of Denmark.

Heðin determined, therefore, to seek out Hǫgni; accordingly, when spring came, he set sail in a vessel with three hundred men, and after sailing for a whole year reached Denmark in the following spring.

When Hǫgni heard of the arrival of this great monarch he made a feast in Heðin's honour. Afterwards the two kings rode out, and vied with one another in various feats of strength and skill, but they were in everything so equally matched that none could say which was the greater, notwithstanding that Heðin was considerably the younger of the two. Then they swore oaths of eternal brotherhood, and Hǫgni set out on an expedition, leaving Heðin at home to guard his kingdom, and his wife Hervǫr, and his fair daughter Hild. One day while Heðin was walking in the woods, he saw, as before in Africa, the woman Gǫndul seated in a clearing. She gave him a potion to drink which made him forget all that had happened in the past. She then told him that it was a blot on his honour to have no wife, while Hǫgni had already a wife of noble birth, and that the only way in which he could retrieve this disgrace was by carrying off Hild by force in her father's absence, and by killing her mother by crushing her on the rollers when he launched his ship.

* Gǫndul was in reality a Valkyrie, and was thus possessed of supernatural power.

13—2

Heðin went home, still under the influence of the drug, and followed the advice which Gǫndul had given him. He prepared to set sail with Hild, and caused his boat to be launched over the body of Hervǫr, her mother, in spite of Hild's entreaties that he should wait until her father's return, when he would receive freely that which he insisted on taking by force, namely, her hand in marriage.

When everything was ready for their departure, Heðin went back to the wood, where he again found Gǫndul. She gave him another potion, and he lay down and slept by her side. When he awoke he remembered as in a flash all that had happened, and realised the mischief he had done. Then he got up quickly and sailed away, taking Hild with him.

When Hǫgni came home he was told that Heðin had carried off his daughter and his ship Halfdanamant, and had killed his wife by rolling the ship over her. Hǫgni was very angry, and immediately pursued Heðin with a fleet, but it always happened that Hǫgni reached in the evening the port from which Heðin had sailed the previous morning. He at last, however, succeeded in overtaking him at Haey in the Orkneys.

When Hǫgni came near, Heðin spoke to him and told him that he had killed his wife and carried away his daughter while under the spell of evil witchcraft. In token of penitence, he therefore offered to restore to Hǫgni his daughter and the ship, with men and money in compensation, and promised to turn his back on northern lands for ever. Hǫgni replied that he had intended from the beginning to bestow Hild on Heðin in marriage, and that as far as that question was concerned there was peace between them : but what he would not forgive was the murder of his wife, and he therefore bade Heđin prepare for battle.

Then Heđin and Hǫgni and all their men fought and killed one another : but no sooner were they killed than they rose up and fought again. In this way the battle continued until Olaf Tryggvason* became king of Norway, when it was brought to an end by the intervention of one of his warriors, according to that which Odin had fore-ordained.

M.H.G. Epic Gudrun.

The saga underlying the M.H.G. epic *Gudrun* is undoubtedly the same as that which we find in *Sǫrlaþáttr*, and in the accounts of the story of Heđin and Hǫgni given by Saxo and Snorri. It is not proposed to enter upon a discussion of the relation to one another of the two parts of the *Gudrun*. The question whether the Gudrun saga grew out of the Hilde saga or whether it was of independent growth lies outside the limits of this essay, but a brief survey of the story of Hilde as contained in the *Gudrun* is sufficient to show that, taken by itself, it is merely a German version of the Scandinavian story of Heđin and Hǫgni.

Hagen, king of Ireland, and his wife Hilde had a fair daughter Hilde. The report of Hilde's beauty reached King Hetel of the Hegelingen, who was therefore fired with a desire to win her as his wife. He knew, however, that Hagen was a cruel and fierce king, who would kill

* Olaf Tryggvason reigned 995–1000 : by this time the Norwegians had become Christians.

any man whom he suspected of having designs on his daughter, and that there was therefore no hope of winning Hilde except by strategy. Hetel, therefore, gathered together from neighbouring countries a little band of chosen warriors willing to undertake the adventure, the chief of whom were Wate of Sturmland, Frute of Denmark, and Horand the singer. Hetel equipped a ship for them, and provided them with soldiers for their expedition.

The envoys, on their arrival in Ireland, were received as guests, and courteously treated by wild Hagen and Hilde his queen. They purported to be traders carrying rich merchandise, who had been exiled by King Hetel from their home in the land of the Hegelingen. The strangers gained great favour at Hagen's court, and Horand, by his sweet singing, succeeded not only in gaining secretly the love of Hilde for his master, but also in winning her consent to a plan for escape.

The supposed traders then announced to Hagen the date of their departure, and the day before that which was fixed for setting sail they asked as a great mark of favour that Queen Hilde and her daughter might come and view the rich merchandise which they had in the ship. This request was granted, and when the two ladies came on board the ship with their following, the stratagem which had been planned was swiftly carried out. Hilde was separated from her mother, and with the utmost despatch anchor was weighed, and all sails were set for the land of the Hegelingen. Hagen gave chase, but overtook the fugitives only after they had arrived in Hetel's country. A great battle took place in which Hagen was in danger of his life. But Hilde interposed, and brought about a reconciliation between her father and Hetel.

Hagen then gave his consent to the marriage of Hilde and Hetel, after which he left the land of the Hegelingen, and sailed back to Ireland.

III. COMPARISON OF EVIDENCE WITH REGARD TO THE HILDE SAGA.

The story of Heðin and Hǫgni, as derived from Scandinavian sources and re-echoed in the mhg. *Gudrun*, forms a link between *Deor* ll. 35–41 and *Wids*. l. 21, where the names Hagena and Heoden are found side by side. These two names are plainly identical with Hǫgni and Heðin, and their juxtaposition in *Widsith* may be taken as signifying that the poet knew of the story which connected them. The occurrence in *Deor* of the names Heodeningas and Heorrenda at once suggests a connection with the same story.

In the *Skáldsk.* the battle between Heðin and Hǫgni is called *Hjaðinga víg*, i.e. the fight of the Hjathnings, and in the German version of the saga (i.e. in *Gudrun*) Hetel (Heðin) is represented as ruling the Hegelingas, which seems to be merely a corruption of Hetelingas*.

The cognate forms Heodeningas and Heoden (Hjaðningar and Heðin), and the fact that in *Widsith* Heoden is said to have ruled a tribe called the Glommas†, would seem to indicate that Heodeningas (Hjaðningar) was a dynastic rather than a tribal name. According to Saxo, Heðin (Hithinus) was prince of a Norwegian

---

* It has been suggested by Jiriczek (*Northern Hero Legends*, p. 135) that the form Hegelingas arose through confusion with the Bavarian place-name Hegelingas, as the *Gudrun* epic in its present form is almost certainly of Austro-Bavarian origin.

† Nothing is otherwise known of the existence of such a tribe.

tribe, while Hǫgni (Höginus) was a chieftain of the Jutes. According to *Widsith*, Hǫgni (Hagena) ruled the Holm-rygas, who are usually identified with the Ulmerugi, a tribe mentioned by Jordanes as living at the mouth of the Vistula. The account of *Sǫrlaþáttr*, which represents Hǫgni as king of Denmark and overlord of all Danish lands, and Heðin as king of Africa, is so obviously invented to suit the purpose of the legend that it need not be considered.

The accounts of Saxo, *Skáldsk.* and *Sǫrlaþáttr* display remarkable unanimity in their outline of the story of Heðin and Hǫgni. They vary only in unimportant details, and in that *Sǫrlaþattr*, in addition to the rest of the story, gives an account of the treatment which Hild's mother underwent at the hands of Heðin.

The German version of the story varies considerably, but the main facts, viz. the kidnapping of the princess and the pursuit of her father, are the same. The proof that we have here the same and not a similar story, is that the names of the characters correspond to those of the Scandinavian and O.E. versions*, while the respective characteristics of Hagen and Hetel correspond almost exactly to those of their Scandinavian prototypes. It should, however, be noted that while Horand, like the Heorrenda of *Deor*, is a court singer or *scóp*, Hjarandi is represented in *Skáldsk.* and in *Sǫrlaþáttr* as the father of Heðin.

---

* Hilde is identical with Hild, while Hagen, Hetel and Horand clearly correspond to O.N. Hǫgni, Heðin, Hjarandi, and O.E. Hagena, Heoden, Heorrenda, although the last-mentioned occurs in a corrupted form in O.E.

IV. HISTORICAL VALUE OF THE HILDE SAGA.

It is impossible to assign to the story of Heðin and Hǫgni its definite historical value. Though the facts on which it is based were of common enough occurrence in ancient times, yet the accumulation of circumstantial evidence with regard to this particular episode, and especially the correspondence of authorities, would seem to indicate that the story represented an actual historical incident. It may be said further that the extremely matter-of-fact nature of the reference to Heorrenda contained in *Deor*, ll. 35 ff., tells strongly against a mythical interpretation of the story.

The never-ending struggle between the two kings is peculiar to the Scandinavian version of the story, and is undoubtedly a later poetic addition. (For another interpretation cf. however Müllenhoff, *Z. f. d. A.* Vol. XXX, pp. 217 ff., "Frija und der Halsbandmythus.")

(*b*) WÊLAND SAGA.

I. WÊLAND SAGA IN O.E.

Deor ll. 1–12. Lines 1–5, which form the first strophe of the poem, relate in language so obscure as to be at times almost unintelligible the hardships which Wêland underwent at the hands of the King Nidhad, and especially how he was hamstringed by the king's orders.

Strophe 2, i.e. ll. 8–12, picture the plight of Beadohild after she had been seduced by Wêland : her fear because of the knowledge of her own pregnancy was aggravated by sorrow on account of the death of her brothers.

II. OTHER AUTHORITIES FOR WÊLAND SAGA.

Vǫlundarqviđa.
Thiđrekssaga.

VǪLUNDARQVIĐA.

The three young fairy maidens, Ǫlrun, Hlađguđ Svanhvit and Hervǫralvit, flew to the North, and alighted on the shores of a lake. They were taken to wife by the three heroes Egil, Slagfiđ and Vǫlund (Wêland) respectively. After seven years the maidens one day flew away during their husbands' absence from home. Egil and Slagfiđ skated southwards in order to try to find their wives, but Vǫlund remained at home hammering and forging golden rings in his smithy.

On one occasion while Vǫlund was out hunting, King Niđuđ of the Njars, to whom he was well known, marched with a large following to Vǫlund's home in the Wolf dales. In the hall Niđuđ's men found seven hundred rings threaded on bast. These they unstrung and strung again with the exception of one which they took away with them.

When Vǫlund returned he sat down to count his rings, and discovered at once that one of them was missing. He believed that his wife had returned during his absence and had taken the ring, and while sitting thinking over this strange occurrence he fell asleep. He awoke to find himself heavily fettered. This had been done by Niđuđ's soldiers. They dragged Vǫlund with them to the king's palace, where by Niđuđ's orders he was hamstringed in order to prevent his escape.

Then Vǫlund was taken to the king's smithy at Seastead, and compelled to work for him there. The ring which had been previously stolen from him was given to Bǫđvild (Beadohild), the king's daughter.

While Vǫlund worked in King Niðuð's smithy his one thought was how to revenge himself for the wrongs which he had suffered. He succeeded in enticing to his smithy Niðuð's two sons, whom he murdered. Out of their eyes, teeth and skulls he made jewels and goblets for the king and queen, and for Bǫðvild.

After this, Bǫðvild, having broken her ring, brought it to Vǫlund to be repaired. Vǫlund took advantage of Bǫðvild's visit to the smithy to seduce her, and to regain her ring, with which he was enabled to escape.

He flew away, and left Bǫðvild weeping for grief at her lover's departure, and from fear at the thought of her father's anger.

Alighting on the castle wall, Vǫlund then mocked Niðuð openly, and proclaimed aloud how he had murdered his sons and dishonoured his daughter. He then soared away, and Niðuð in sorrow sent for Bǫðvild, who confirmed the truth of all that Vǫlund had said.

THIÐREKSSAGA *.

(Chaps. 57–79.) †Velent was the son of the giant Vathe, who was born of King Wilkinus and a mermaid. He was apprenticed at first to a smith named Mimi, and afterwards to two dwarfs, through whose instruction he became the greatest of all living smiths.

Velent escaped from the dwarfs, and after tossing on the sea for eighteen days in a hollow tree-trunk which served him as a ship, he arrived in Jutland, which was ruled by a king named Nithung. He was well received

---

* *Saga Thithriks Konungs af Bern*, ed. C. R. Unger, Christiania, 1853. German transl. by F. H. v. d. Hagen : *Altdeutsche u. Altnordische Heldensagen. Wilkina- u. Niflunga Saga*. Breslau, 1872.

† Proper names are here given as in the German translation.

by Nithung, who gave him an office about his table (to
wit, the charge of three knives); he hid, for the time
being, his tree-trunk with all that it contained.

After a time Velent lost one of the king's knives ; in
the absence of Amilias, the royal smith, Velent went to
his forge, and forged a new knife exactly like the old one.
But this knife was sharper and better than any which
Amilias had ever made, as Nithung discovered as soon as
he used it. Amilias was angry that the work of another
should be preferred to his. He boasted that he was as
good a smith as Velent, and demanded that an opportunity
should be given for them both to make public trial of
their skill. To this King Nithung agreed. Amilias then
offered to produce in twelve months' time a suit of armour,
the strength of which should be tested by the blows of a
sword to be forged by Velent in the same length of time.

For the whole of the twelve months Amilias was busy
forging his armour, while Velent took less than half the
time to make his sword, Mimung, although he forged and
re-forged it three times before the temper of the blade
satisfied him. When the day of the test at last arrived,
Amilias put on the armour which he had made and strode
proudly through the market place : but Velent took
Mimung, and standing behind Amilias, he placed the
sword on the crest of the helmet, and pressed downwards.
He then asked Amilias what his sensations were. Amilias
answered that he felt as if cold water were trickling down
his back. Velent told him to shake himself, and when
Amilias did so, he fell apart into two bits, and so died.

After this, Velent's fame as a smith spread throughout
all Northern lands : he was known amongst the Vaeringiar
(says the saga) as Volond.

On one occasion King Nithung went out to attack another king. On the eve of the battle he remembered that he had left at home his stone of victory, without which it was vain to hope for success, and in despair, for he was very far from home, he promised to give the half of his kingdom and the hand of his daughter to anyone who would fetch him the stone by the next morning. This feat was accomplished by the smith Velent, but when he had obtained the stone and was on his way back to the king, he was stopped by Nithung's chamberlain, who attempted to make him give it up, at first by the offer of bribes, but finally by violence. Velent, however, slew the chamberlain and most of his men, reached the king with his prize before the battle had begun, and recounted to him all that had happened. Nithung, glad of any excuse whereby he might avoid fulfilling his promise, rebuked Velent severely for having killed his chamberlain, and drove him away without any reward. But owing to the stone of victory he won the battle and returned home after bringing his campaign to a successful close.

After a time Velent appeared at King Nithung's court in the disguise of a cook, and attempted to murder the king and his daughter by putting poison in their food. This was discovered, and as a punishment for his evil designs, Nithung ordered Velent to be lamed; but out of admiration for his skill, he gave the cunning smith silver and gold and a smithy in which to work.

Velent was, however, still intent on his revenge, and one day he enticed the king's daughter to his smithy, and seduced her. Shortly afterwards he succeeded in persuading the king's two young sons to pay him a visit, and them he murdered. Of their skulls he made a drinking-cup for the king, and out of their bones he fashioned all sorts of table utensils for the king's use. No suspicion fell on the smith with regard to the murder, on account of his clever ruse of making the boys walk backwards into his smithy after a fresh fall of snow, so that their footprints appeared to lead in the opposite direction.

After thus accomplishing his revenge, Velent made for himself a skin of feathers in order to escape from Nithung. Before he flew away, he lit on the highest tower of the king's castle, and proclaimed aloud the crimes which he had committed, namely the seduction of the princess, and the murder of her two brothers. He told the princess that he had left behind in his smithy armour and weapons which he had forged for the son whom she should bear him. This son was afterwards the famous Vithga (Ger. Witig, *Wids.* Wudga).

III & IV. DISCUSSION OF EVIDENCE REGARDING THE WÊLAND SAGA, AND OF THE HISTORICAL VALUE OF THE SAGA.

The Wêland saga is of Saxon origin, as has been shown by Jiriczek (*D. H. S.* I, pp. 11–54), but it quickly spread through all Teutonic countries, and even filtered through into Romance literature, for we find an old French version of the saga in addition to the many others which exist; in fact, no saga has been more popular or more widely cultivated than the Wêland saga from early times up till almost the present day. In the literatures of all early Teutonic peoples, the description of any weapon or armour as the work of Wêland was the highest praise which could be bestowed on it, and a sure criterion of its worth. As late as the eighteenth century there was an English tradition concerning the famous Wayland-Smith which was localised in Berkshire, where a certain prehistoric grave still goes by the name of Wayland-Smith's cave.

The three authorities which are of the greatest importance in a consideration of the Wêland saga are the three which have just been quoted, viz. O.E. *Deor*, O.N. *Vǫlundarqviđa*, and L.G. *Thiđrekssaga*; the first two because their evidence is of great antiquity, and because they are evidently closely connected with the original Saxon version of the saga; the third because, although late in date, it grew up on Low German soil in the very home of the Wêland saga, where the traditions concerning the cunning smith lived on through the centuries and are still alive at the present day.

From a consideration of these three authorities we seem forced to the conclusion that there is, in the case of the Wêland saga, less probability of the existence of an historical background for the events described than in the case of almost any other saga. Of course, the possible existence of an historical character, the prototype of the famous smith Wêland, cannot be denied, and in favour of his historicity it may be noted that in the *Thđs.* he is represented as the father of Witig (O.E. Wudga, Widia), a warrior of Ermanric, whose actual existence we have no reason to doubt. But the fact that the story of Wêland has been known and localised in so many different countries, and the existence from the most ancient times of similar stories in connection with legendary smiths of other lands, are both circumstances which speak strongly against the probability of the saga having had an historical basis.

Jiriczek explains the saga as the mythical expression of the wonders of the metal age superseding the former age of stone. This explanation seems quite an adequate one, as it can easily be imagined that there should at first appear to be something diabolical in the new inventions which the discovery of the action of fire on metal made possible, and that this strange power and its effects should be personified in the figure of the cunning smith and malignant spirit Wêland. Such a myth would from its nature be common to all peoples. According to Grimm * and Kögel † the name Wêland is altogether symbolical, and is either a participial formation connected with O.N. *vél* = "skill," "cunning," or a compound *wélwand* (*wand* = G. *gewandt*) = "versed in cunning works." It is, however, equally possible that the word Wêland is connected with Vulcanus, the corresponding figure of Roman mythology. The story of Gyges in classical mythology or folklore also offers many parallelisms.

* *Gram.* i, 462.   † *Ltg.* i, 1. 100 f.

CHAPTER VII

THE BURGUNDIANS AND WALDERE.

THE important position occupied in ancient Teutonic literature—especially in Scand. and mhg. records—by the tribe of the Burgundians, justifies a somewhat fuller treatment of the references made to them in the O.E. poems than might be otherwise deemed necessary. It has been found convenient to group the discussion of the Burgundians with that of the Waldere saga, as the two stand in partial relation to one another.

(a) THE BURGUNDIANS.

I. REFERENCES TO THE BURGUNDIANS IN O.E. POEMS.

(a) *Waldere,* Frag. A, ll. 25 ff., in which Hildeguth encourages her lover Waldere to do battle with Guthhere, who without due cause has come out to attack him.

(b) Frag. B, a dialogue between Waldere and Guthhere which takes place just before the combat, and in which the latter is addressed as *Wine Burgenda,* i.e. "Friend of the Burgundians."

(c) *Wids.* l. 19. *Burgendum (weold) Gifica.*

l. 65 :

> "And mid Burgendum, thaer ic beág getháh :
> me thaer Gûthhere forgeaf glaedliçne mâththum
> songes to laene : naes thaet saene cyning*."

II. FOREIGN AUTHORITIES CONTAINING EVIDENCE WITH REGARD TO THE BURGUNDIANS.

Historical.
Pliny (the elder).
Ptolemy.
Ammianus Marcellinus.
Prosper of Aquitaine (Migne, *Patrologia*, Vol. I, 51).
Prosper Tiro (*Recueil des Historiens des Gaules.* Bouquet. Paris, 1739).
Idatius. (Migne, *Patrol.* l. 51.)

Olympiodorus ⎱ (C. Müller. *Fragmenta*
Priscus ⎰ *Historicorum Grae-corum.* Vol. IV.)

Socrates.
Lex Burgundionum (Pertz. *Mon. Germ. Leg.* Vol. III, 533.)
Cassiodorus.

Legendary.
Edda Poems.
Prose *Edda.*
Vǫlsungasaga.
Nibelungenlied, and others.

---

* "I have been among the Burgundians, where I received a ring (bracelet). There Guthhere gave me the bright treasure in reward for my poem. He was not a slothful king."

III & IV. THE BURGUNDIANS IN HISTORY.

The earliest known reference to the Burgundians is made by the elder Pliny (*Nat. Hist.* IV, 99) who wrote about the year 79 A.D. He classes the Burgundians with the Goths as part of the Vandili, and therefore an eastern tribe*.

Ptolemy, writing in the second century, places the Burgundians between the Vistula and the Suebos (Warnow ?)†.

Ammianus (XXVIII, 5), writing about 380 A.D., speaks of the Burgundians as occupying the upper half of the Main basin during the second half of the fourth century. During the reign of Valentinian I (364–375), the Burgundians were allied with the Romans against the Alemanni.

The Burgundian language had affinities with Bavarian, Alemannic, and Gothic.

The Burgundians crossed the Rhine, and settled in and around Worms, probably after the year 406, which was the date of the great southerly migration of Vandals and Suebi.

According to Prosper of Aquitaine ‡ (c. 450) and Cassiodorus § the Burgundians gained a part of Gaul beside the Rhine in the year 413, at which time they

---

* "Germanorum genera quinque: Vandili, quorum pars Burgodiones, Varinnae, Charini, Gutones."

† ...μέχρι τοῦ Συήβου ποταμοῦ, καὶ τὸ τῶν Βουργουνιῶν τὰ ἐφεξῆς καὶ μέχρι τοῦ Οὐιστούλα κατεχόντων.

‡ Prosper of Aquitaine, under year 413: "Burgundiones partem Galliae propinquantem Rheno obtinuerunt."

§ Cassiodorus, under year 413: "Burgundiones partem Galliae Rheno tenuere conjunctam."

were already Catholic Christians, whereas all the other Christian tribes amongst the Teutons were Aryans.

Olympiodorus* relates that in 412 Gyntiarios, a prince of Burgundy, and Goar, an Alan, set up Jovinus as Emperor.

The Burgundian kingdom on the Rhine lasted until 436 or 437, when the Burgundians were almost annihilated by the Huns under Attila. Previous to this, however, in 435, the Burgundians under their king, Gundicarius, were defeated by, and obtained terms of peace from, the Romans under Aëtius†.

Socrates‡, in an undated entry, says that the Burgundians made a successful attack on the Huns after the death of the Hunnish king Uptar. This may have been the immediate cause of the overwhelming defeat inflicted on the Burgundians by Attila shortly afterwards§.

* Olympiodorus Thebaeus, under year 412 (Latin transl.): "Jovinus apud Moguntiacum, Germaniae alterius urbem, studio Goaris Alani et Guntiarii Burgundionum praefecti, tyrannus creatus est."

† Paulus Diaconus (De episc. Metens.): "Eo igitur tempore...Attila rex Hunnorum omnibus belluis crudelior, habens multas barbaras nationes suo subjectas dominio, postquam Gundigarium, Burgundionum regem, sibi occurrentem protriverat."

‡ Socrates: "Exinde fidente animo adversus Hunnos progressi (Burgundiones) sunt: nec spes eos fefellit. Etenim rege Hunnorum, cui nomen erat Optar, prae nimia ciborum ingluvie nocte quadam suffocato, Burgundiones in Hunnos duce destitutos subito irruentes, paucique plurimos aggressi, victoriam reportarunt. Cum enim ipsi tria duntaxat hominum millia essent Hunnorum decem circiter millia interfecerunt."

§ Prosper of Aquitaine, under year 435: "Eodem tempore Gundicarium Burgundionum regem intra Gallias habitantem Aëtius bello obtinuit pacemque ei supplicanti dedit, qua non diu potitus est. Siquidem illum Hunni cum populo atque stirpe sua deleverunt."

Idatius, under year 435: "Burgundiones qui rebellaverant a Romanis duce Aëtio debellantur."

Some Burgundians seem to have fought on the Roman side under Aëtius in the great battle against Attila in 451 (cf. Jordanes, Ch. 36). The remnant of the people found their way south to the Rhone valley, where they formed a new kingdom. According to Prosper Tiro* they obtained Savoy in the year 443. For nearly a century the Burgundians managed to retain their independence in the face of constant struggles with the Franks and Ostrogoths, but in 534 they were finally defeated by the sons of Chlodovech (Clovis) and their territory became incorporated with the kingdom of the Franks.

THE BURGUNDIANS IN SAGA.

In addition to the historical evidence which has just been quoted, we have access to abundant information regarding the Burgundians in the mhg. *Nibelungenlied* and in the O.N. poems and sagas. The subject of all of these alike is the destruction of the Burgundians at the hands of Attila, an event which offered plenty of scope for poetic and imaginative treatment. The story of the Burgundians was united in O.N., and afterwards in mhg., with the saga of the Völsungs, which celebrated the deeds of Sigurd (Germ. Siegfried) the hero and dragon-slayer of the North, a figure in many respects resembling Dietrich of Bern.

---

* Prosper Tiro, under year 436 : "Bellum contra Burgundionum gentem memorabile exarsit, quo universa gens cum rege per Aëtium deleta."

Idatius, under year 436 : "Burgundionum caesa viginti millia."

Prosper Tiro, under year 443 : "Sabaudia Burgundionum reliquiis datur cum indigenis dividenda."

It is beyond the limits of this essay to discuss the Scandinavian and German versions of the story of the Burgundians in their mutual relation. Quite possibly the groundwork of the story, which is the same in all accounts—namely, the luring of the Burgundians to the country of the Huns and the subsequent treachery of Attila—may be an historical account of the way in which the destruction of this people took place. We may, in any case, in view of the information contained in the works of various classical historians, accept the authority of the *Nibelungenlied* and of the O.N. records, that Gundaharius (Germ. Gunther, O.E. Guthhere) was leader of the Burgundians at the time of the catastrophe. Thus the historical references to the Burgundians up to the time of their incorporation with the Franks cover about four centuries. The first time that we hear of them they appear to have been situated in and around the basin of the river Oder, after which we find them migrating by slow stages across Europe, in a south-westerly direction, as far as Savoy, where they made their permanent home.

Our chief source of information regarding the kings of the Burgundians is the *Lex Burgundionum* compiled by the lawgiver King Gundobad at the end of the fifth century. We can also rely to a certain extent on the evidence of O.N. and mhg. literary records.

In the *Lex Burg.* the reference made by Gundobad to his ancestors is as follows :—

"Si quos apud regiae memoriae auctores nostros, id est Gibicam, Godomarem, Gislaharium, Gundaharium, patrem quoque nostrum, et patruum, liberos liberasve fuisse constiterit in eadem libertate permanent." All that we can gather from this as to the relationship

of these four kings is that Gebica was earlier than
the other three. In German saga literature Gunther
(Gundaharius) and Giselher (Gislaharius) are brothers,
and have a third brother Gernot : their father is
Dankwart.

In Scandinavian saga, Gjuki, king at Worms on the
Rhine, has three sons, Gunnar, Hǫgni (Germ. Hagen) and
Guttorm, but Guttorm is only a half-brother of the other
two. According to the Waltharius of Ekkehart, Gibicho,
" king of the Franks," has a son Gunther.

Thus all saga literature dealing with the Burgundians
agrees in representing three Burgundian princes, who
perhaps correspond to Gundaharius, Godomar, and Gislaharius, of the *Lex Burg.*, as brothers, and sons of a king
corresponding to Gebica of the *Lex Burg.* There is,
however, no historical confirmation of this.

Of these four kings mentioned in Gundobad's code,
the figure of Gundaharius is by far the most prominent.
Round him clusters the whole wealth of saga and story
commemorating the glorious deeds of the Burgundians
and their defeat by the Huns under Attila, through which
the reign of Gundaharius was brought to an untimely
end.

After founding their new kingdom in the Rhone
valley, the Burgundians were ruled by the aforementioned
Gundobad, the compiler of the *Lex Burg.*, who flourished
at the end of the fifth and beginning of the sixth
centuries. Gundobad was succeeded by Sigisbert and
afterwards by Gondomar. Under the latter prince the
Burgundians were finally defeated by the sons of Chlodovech, and Gondomar himself abandoned his kingdom
and fled to Italy.

The allusion to the *Vǫlsungasaga* contained in *Beowulf*, ll. 875–900*, may be mentioned at this point. The first part of the passage contains a reference to the exploits of Sigemund, and to Sigemund's nephew Fitela; Sigemund is called *Wälses eafera* (l. 897), which clearly identifies him with Sigmund, the son of Vǫlsung, and Fitela with Sigmund's son and nephew Sinfjǫtli. The *Beowulf* passage proceeds to give an account of Sigemund's single-handed fight with a dragon: in all Scandinavian versions of the story, however, the hero of the dragon fight is not Sigmund, but his son Sigurð.

Sigurð is represented, in German and Scandinavian sources alike, as a king possessing territory in the Netherlands, but we find no references to either Sigmund or Sigurð in historical records, and there is a general tendency to regard their figures as mythical.

---

* Clark Hall's translation of the passage is as follows: "He related everything that he had heard men say of Sigemund, his deeds of valour, many untold things, the struggle of the Wälsing (C.H. son of Waels), his wanderings far and wide, the feuds and treacheries—things that the sons of men knew nothing of save Fitela who was with him, when he, the uncle, would tell something of such a matter to his nephew as they had always been friends in need in every struggle, and had felled with their swords large numbers of the race of monsters.

"There arose no little fame to Sigemund after his death-day, since he, hardy in battle, had killed the dragon, keeper of the hoard. Under the grey rock he, son of a prince, ventured the perilous deed alone,—Fitela was not with him.

"Yet it befell him that the sword pierced through the wondrous snake, so that it, the sterling blade, stuck in the rock—the dragon died a violent death. By valour had the warrior secured that he might enjoy the ring-hoard at his own will; the Wälsing (C.H. son of Waels) loaded a sea boat, bare the shining treasures into the bosom of the ship. Fire consumed the dragon.

"In deeds of bravery he was by far the most renowned of adventurers among the tribes of men, and thus he throve erewhile."

But, as has been pointed out by Mr Chadwick*, the traditions regarding Sigmund and his family cannot, on account of their great age, be lightly dismissed as mythical, although some elements in the story which is told of them—e.g. the fight with the dragon—are undoubtedly to be considered as such. In addition to the *Beowulf* reference, Sigmund and Sinfjǫtli occur also in two of the *Edda* Poems (*Helgakviður Hundingsbána*) which are entirely free from German influence, but here as in the *Beowulf* the name of Sigurð is not mentioned. In the *Beowulf*, as we have seen (cf. *sup.* Ch. II, p. 121), Sigmund is brought into relation with Heremod, a Danish prince, and in *Hyndlj.* the two names are again found side by side. The natural inference from all this is: (1) that the association of Sigmund with Heremod must date from a very early time, while English and Scandinavian traditions were still influencing one another, and (2) that the information contained in the *Beowulf* about Sigmund and Sinfjǫtli was therefore in all probability not due to late German influence, but was part of the body of tradition brought by our forefathers from their continental home. Although there is not conclusive proof of the actual existence of Sigmund and his family, the antiquity of the traditions concerning them gives them at least as valid a claim to historicity as any other characters of the Heroic Age : and since we have scarcely any knowledge of the course of events on the lower Rhine at the beginning of the fifth century, there is certainly not sufficient ground for doubting that such princes as Sigmund and Sigurð may actually have reigned there.

* *Op. cit.* p. 148 f.

(b) WALDERE SAGA.

I.   The only reference to the saga of Waldere in O.E. literature is contained in the epic fragment which bears his name.

The foreign authorities which contain evidence with regard to this saga may be classified according to the three distinct versions of the saga which exist.   They are as follows* :

1.   Alemannic version of the Waldere—or Walthari—saga which appears in

> (a) Ekkehart's *Waltharius*, ed. by V. Scheffel and A. Holder, Stuttgart, 1874; German transl. by H. Althof, Leipzig, 1896.

> (b) References in the *Nibelungenlied* and in *Biterolf*.

(This is the version which appears in the O.E. *Waldere*.)

2.   Frankish version of the saga which appears in

> (a) *Thiđrekssaga*.

> (b) M.H.G. fragments of "Walther und Hildegunde," *Z. f. d. A.*, Vol. II, pp. 216 ff.

(Reference in Austrian poem, "von dem übelen weibe," *Z. E.* No. XXVIII, 3.)

---

* For this classification, I am indebted to Symons' article "Die deutsche Heldensage" in Paul's *Grundriss*, Vol. III.

3. Polish version of the saga which appears in

    (*a*) Latin chronicle of Boguphalus (thirteenth century) *Chronicon Poloniae Sommersberg. script. rer. Siles.*, Vol. II, 37–39.

    (*b*) Polish chronicle (sixteenth century).

(Here the saga has received additions altogether foreign to it in its German form : this version need not therefore be discussed in the present connection.)

I. ALEMANNIC VERSION OF WALTHARI SAGA.

A.S. WALDERE.

The A.S. *Waldere* consists of two fragments of what was either a ballad on the Walthari saga, or an epic poem in the same style as the *Beowulf.* Fragment A is a speech made by Hildeguth, who incited her lover Waldere to battle, while Fragment B is a dialogue between Waldere and Guthhere.

The fragments translated into Modern English are as follows:

A. " ...incited him willingly. Assuredly the handi-work of Wêland fails no man who can wield Miming the hard one. Often in the battle there fell, bloodstained and wounded, one warrior after another. Champion of Attila ! Let not yet thy courage fail on this day, let not thy prowess decline !

" ...But the day is come when thou shalt assuredly do one of two, either shalt thou lose thy life, or thou shalt obtain lasting glory among men, son of Aelfhere ! By no means, my beloved, can I chide thee with words, that I have ever seen thee at the sword-play, through fear of any man, evade the combat, flee to the rampart and save thy life, although many enemies hewed thy shield with their bills. But thou didst ever seek further battle— didst pursue thy cause over the border (?)—therefore I feared thy destiny, that thou shouldst follow up the fight too bravely, the struggle with another man. Uphold thine honour by good deeds, while God's care is over thee ! Neither be thou anxious for thy sword ; to thee was the best of treasures given, for our help. With it thou shalt humble Gunther's pride, because he first began unright- eously to seek this combat. He refused the sword and treasures with many rings : now, deprived of both, he shall go from this battle to seek the ancient possession of which he is lord, or here first die, if he..."

B.   " ' ...a better (sword) except this one, which I too have kept hidden in secret in its scabbard (stone-chest). I know that Theodoric wished to send it to Widia, and also great treasure of jewels with the sword, and to adorn with gold many other things with it (?), he received the reward long due, because that he, the kinsman of Nithhad, the son of Wêland, Widia had delivered him from danger : he hastened forth over the territory of the giants.'   Waldere spoke, the mighty amongst warriors : he had in his hands the consolation of battle, the gem of fighting bills, he spoke in these words : ' What, thou didst even think, friend of the Burgundians, that the hand of Hagen should do battle with me, and disable me for battle on foot.   Take if thou dare, the hoary byrny, from the one weary in battle !   Here on my shoulders lies (stands) the legacy of Aelfhere good and well-arched(?), adorned with gold, an honourable apparel for the noble prince whose own hand defends the treasure of his life against his enemies : it will not desert me when evil faithless kinsmen again make the attack, meet me with swords as ye did. But he can grant the victory, who is prompt and wise of counsel towards all that is good; he who believes in his holy help, in the assistance of God, will find it to the full, if he (i.e. God) remembers his previous merits: then must the great men distribute riches, and rule their possession...."

The background of events underlying these two fragments is to be found in the Latin poem *Waltharius*, of the tenth century, written by the monk Ekkehart I of St Gallen.

The argument of the poem is shortly as follows:

Attila, the famous king of the Huns, whose home was in Pannonia, made an expedition against the Franks, and forced their king Gibicho* to render him tribute and hostages. Hagen was handed over by Gibicho as hostage, his own son Gunther being still too young. Hagen was of royal birth and of Trojan† origin, Troja being the fabulous home of the Franks.

Attila continued his victorious progress through the land of the Burgundians and through Aquitaine. From Heriricus (O.H.G. Hererîh), the king of the Burgundians, who reigned in Chalon-sur-Saône, he obtained as a hostage his daughter Hildegund, and from Aelfhere, king of Aquitaine, his son Walther (Waltharius). Walther and Hildegund although only children, were already betrothed to each other.

---

* This is, of course, a mistake: for as we have seen (cf. p. 215), Gibicho and Gunther (*Lex Burg.* Gebica, Gundabarius) were kings, not of the Franks, but of the Burgundians. Cf. also for older form of the saga, *Wald.* fragments where Guthhere is addressed as *Wine Burgenda*.

† Cf. *Nibelungenlied*, Hagen von Tronje; *Thiðrekss*. Hagen af Troja.

The hostages fared well at the court of the Hunnish king, and were treated by Attila as if they were his own children. When Hagen and Walther grew up, they excelled in all manner of knightly accomplishments; each of them was entrusted with a high military command, while Hildegund became chief maiden in the household of the queen.

But meanwhile Gibicho died, and was succeeded by Gunther, who refused to pay tribute to Attila; Hagen made this the opportunity to escape from the Hunnish court and to flee back to his own country. After Hagen's flight, Attila's queen was afraid that Walther might also attempt to escape, and advised her husband to marry him to a Hunnish maiden, in order that his interests and affections might be bound to the home of his adoption. The betrothal of Walther and Hildegund and their love for one another was not known at the Hunnish court.

But Walther was warned by Hildegund of Attila's design, and the two arranged a plan for escape, which they carried out successfully, taking with them a quantity of treasure. When their flight was discovered, Attila offered a large reward to anyone who would capture and bring back the fugitives, but Walther's strength was known and feared, and no one could be tempted to set off in pursuit of him. Walther and Hildegund therefore continued their journey unmolested, until they reached Worms, the capital of Gunther, king of the Franks, where their identity was discovered by means of some strange fish with which Walther paid the ferryman who rowed them over the Rhine. Gunther, guessing who the stranger was, at once determined to follow him in order to rob him of his treasure, although warned by Hagen (who knew the strength of Walther's arm) that he would repent having done so. But to these warnings Gunther turned a deaf ear, for he regarded this as nothing short of a miraculous opportunity offered him to regain the tribute money which Attila had, for so many years, extorted from the Franks. With twelve chosen warriors, of whom Hagen, much against his will, was one, Gunther accordingly gave chase, and overtook Walther and Hildegund in the Vosges (Vosagus) Mountains (O.H.G. Wâskenstein, Wâsgenstein), where they halted to rest. Walther, who was encamped in a strong position, was not daunted by the array of warriors which Gunther had brought out against him. He spoke words of cheer and comfort to his gentle companion, who was terrified at the sight of so many armed men, and boasted that he could overthrow with ease in single combat any of the twelve except Hagen, whom he feared on account of their long acquaintance with each other's methods of warfare.

Disregarding Hagen's final warning, Gunther then sent up one by one eight warriors, each of whom Walther killed. The position in which he was entrenched did not permit of his being attacked by more than one at a time. The remaining three warriors (for Hagen had sat apart the whole time, refusing to take any share in the fight), of whom Patafried, Hagen's nephew, was one, then attacked Walther with a trident: but they met with no better success than their predecessors, and were all slain. Thus, of all the Franks, only Gunther and Hagen were left alive.

After many entreaties, Hagen yielded to Gunther's request that he would fight with him against Walther.

His duty towards his king was the only consideration which weighed with Hagen and caused him to break the vows of brotherhood which he had sworn to Walther; nothing else, not even the duty of avenging his slain kinsman, would have made him take arms against the friend of his youth.

Gunther and Hagen determined to lure their enemy into open country before attacking him, and to effect this they made a ruse of flight and retired towards evening to a point some distance away.

After a night's rest, Walther and Hildegund continued their journey. No sooner, however, had they left the shelter of the rocks and got into the open, than Walther was fiercely attacked by Gunther and Hagen. Walther reproached Hagen with having broken his oath of friendship, but Hagen defended his action as the just revenge for the death of a kinsman—namely Patafried.

The struggle between the three was long and terrible. At last they could fight no longer, for Gunther had lost a leg, Hagen an eye, and Walther his right hand. The demands of honour having been thus satisfied, a reconciliation between the warriors took place, and Walther called on Hildegund, who in great fear had watched the battle from afar, to come and bind up their wounds. Then they made merry together over their injuries, and finally parted as friends and brothers.

The Franks returned to Worms, while Walther and Hildegund journeyed home to Aquitaine without mishap. There they were married, and reigned in prosperity for thirty years.

II.   FRANKISH VERSION OF WALTHARI SAGA.

Mhg. fragment of the Poem *Walther
und Hildegund* *.

At the point at which the fragment commences,
Walther and Hildegund had escaped from the Huns and
were on their way home to Langres†, where Walther's
father Alker (O.E. Aelfhere) was king.   They had been
guided across the Rhine by Volker, whom Gunther had
given them as an escort.   Walther had sent messengers
before him to Langres to announce his coming to his
father and mother.   When Alker and his queen heard
these tidings they rejoiced, and made great preparations
to receive their son and his bride.   The messengers who
brought the news of Walther's arrival also related how
he had escaped from the Huns, and had slain those of
them who came out in pursuit of him.

After these things, Alker sent heralds all through his
land to announce to his subjects that his son Walther was
to be married to Hildegund of Arragon.   The heralds rode
to Engelland, Navarre, and Kerlingen, and after much consideration Walther also sent an invitation to his wedding
to King Etzel.   The news of the marriage was brought
to King Gunther by Volker on his return from Langres.

THIÐREKSSAGA‡.

Chaps. 241–244.   King Attila reigned in Susat.   He
made an alliance with Erminrek, King of Pul (Apulia), and
exchanged hostages with him.   Attila sent to Erminrek his

* Publ. in *Z. f. d. A.* Vol. II, p. 216.

† Langres is however represented by the poet as in Spain, and
Walther is spoken of as "der Vogt von Spanige."

‡ German transl. by F. v. d. Hagen.   Cf. *sup.* p. 203.

nephew Osith, with twelve knights, while Erminrek sent to
Attila his nephew Valtari of Vaskasteine with other twelve
knights.   Valtari was twelve years old when he came to
Attila's court, and he remained there until he was nine-
teen.   After he had been there a year, Attila received as
a hostage Hildegunn, the daughter of the Greek Earl Ilias.
Valtari and Hildegunn fell in love with each other, without the knowledge of Attila, and one day, while Attila and
all his court were feasting, they conferred in secret and determined to escape.   The next morning they fled, taking
much of Attila's treasure with them.

When Attila discovered the trick that had been played
upon him, he despatched twelve warriors, amongst whom
was Högni, the son of Alldrian, in pursuit of the fugitives.
Valtari and Hildegunn were quickly overtaken, but Valtari
fought with and killed eleven of the twelve warriors, Högni
being the sole survivor.   The two sat down together to a
meal of swine's flesh, after which they fought a second
time : but Valtari put out Högni's eye by hurling at him
the backbone of the swine which they had eaten, whereupon the latter turned and fled back to Attila.

Valtari and Hildegunn, however, continued their journey to the court of Erminrek, where they were well received.
They afterwards became reconciled to Attila by sending
him rich gifts.

III.   COMPARISON OF DIFFERENT AUTHORITIES
DEALING WITH WALTHARI SAGA.

It is not necessary for our purpose to enter upon a
detailed comparison of the different versions of the Walthari saga given above ; the story is essentially the same

in all its versions with regard to the main facts, namely, Walther's life as a hostage at the court of the Hunnish king Attila, his successful escape with Hildegund, a fellow-hostage, and their adventurous journey to the home of Walther's parents, at the end of which they were married. Peculiar to the Alemannic version of the saga is Walther's encounter with Gunther and his warriors, and to the Frankish version, the pursuit of Walther by the Huns, and his subsequent reconciliation to Attila. As in its representation of Gunther (Guthhere) as king of the Burgundians, so also in its description of Hildegund's (Hildeguth's) character, does the O.E. *Waldere* without doubt preserve an older tradition than Ekkehart's *Waltharius*. In the latter authority she is portrayed as a timid, shrinking maiden, terrified at the sight of fighting and of blood, and fearful for the safety of her beloved. This picture of Hildegund is clearly tinged by the medieval monastic ideal of feminine character: that of the O.E. *Waldere* bears a much more genuine and ancient imprint, for here Hildegund (Hildeguth) is the direct descendant of the Valkyries, a bold and warlike maiden, jubilating in her hero's lofty courage, and counting death but a little thing as compared with the gaining of enduring reputation in battle.

IV. HISTORICAL VALUE OF THE WALTHARI SAGA.

The story of Walther and Hildegund seems to bear the impress of a genuine historical narrative*, and there is no reason to doubt that the events which it relates

* Heinzel has showed clearly (*Wiener S. B.* cxvii, 2) that the works of the historian Priscus supply plentiful parallels from Hunnish history during the reign of Attila to all the events described in the story.

really took place. The most interesting question in connection with the saga, and one which has not as yet been
satisfactorily solved, is that of the identity of Walther
himself. Who and what was he ?

In all accounts of the story of Walther his name is
associated with the Wâskenstein, or Vosges Mountains,
which appears to have been the scene of his single-handed
victory over Gunther and his warriors. According to
the mhg. *Walther and Hildegund*, Walther's home was
Langres in Haute-Marne, which lies in the N.E. of
France, and is separated from Worms and the Rhine
valley (through which Walther's journey led him) only
by the Vosges Mountains. The Waltharius of Ekkehart,
on the other hand, represents Walther as a prince of
Aquitaine, and therefore presumably a Visigothic hero.
But it is very improbable that anyone coming from
Pannonia, the seat of the Huns in southern Austria-
Hungary, to Aquitaine would travel viâ the middle Rhine
and the Vosges Mountains; Langres would be a far more
fitting conclusion to such a journey. Moreover, it is
possible that the idea of assigning to Walther a home
in Aquitaine may have first arisen through verbal confusion. In a Wessobrunner codex of the eighth century
we find *Wascôno lant* = Aquitania, and it is not improbable that this form underwent confusion with Waskenstein
= Vosagus or Vosges Mountains, although the two are
quite independent. On the whole, the existing evidence
seems to point to the conclusion that Walther was not a
Visigoth. We have therefore to consider the alternative
possibilities with regard to his home and nationality.

The events of the Walthari saga belong to the first half
of the fifth century, and in all probability to some date

previous to 437, in which year Gunther, king of the Burgundians, who is an important figure in the story of Walther, was defeated and slain by the Huns.

It is evident that Walther was not a Burgundian, else he would not have been engaged in hostilities with Gunther and Hagen. It is also improbable that he belonged to the Franks, whose conquest of and settlement in Gaul did not take place until the end of the fifth century*. The most probable alternative appears on the whole to be that Walther belonged to one of the tribes of the Vandili or Suevi, who began their great southerly migration from the banks of the Rhine about the year 406 A.D.†—a movement which ended only when they had passed over the Pyrenees. Some of the stragglers amongst the emigrants may still have been in N.E.

---

* In this connection, however, I am indebted to Mr H. M. Chadwick for a suggestion, well worthy of consideration, with regard to Walther's origin. Although the conquest of Gaul by the Franks was not accomplished until the end of the sixth century, as early as the end of the third century there appear to have been some Frankish settlements on the west side of the Vosges Mts, in the neighbourhood of Langres (cf. Zeuss, *Die Deutschen und die Nachbarstämme*, pp. 336, 582–84). Zeuss quotes Eumenius, who, writing to Constantius, says: "ita nunc per victorias tuas, Constanti Caesar invicte, quidquid infrequens Ambiano et Bellovaco et Tricasino solo, Lingonicoque restabat, barbaro cultore revirescit." These bands of Franks—Chamavi and Attuarii— had been transplanted by Constantius from the lands round the mouth of the Rhine.

Now in Ekkehart's *Waltharius*, Gunther is called King of the Franks, while Hildegund is referred to as a Burgundian princess. At a later date both Langres and Chalon-sur-Saône were in the province of Burgundy, while Worms and the surrounding districts had passed into the hands of the Franks. It seems just possible that the names Frank and Burgundian in the story may have become transposed, and that whereas Gunther was in reality a Burgundian, Hildegund—and Walther her husband—were in reality Franks.

† Cf. Zeuss, *Die Deutschen und die Nachbarstämme*, pp. 449 ff.

Gaul (Langres) as late as 435, which may be taken as the approximate date of Walther's flight from the Huns, and the subsequent settlement in Spain of the main body of the Vandili and Suevi may account for the representation of Walther as a Spaniard in later (especially mhg.*) authorities.

Several scholars (Müllenhoff, Scherer, Symons, &c.) have laid great weight on a supposed connection between the Walthari saga and the " mythical " (?) Hilde saga (cf. Ch. VI, pp. 190 ff.). The discussion of this point really lies outside the scope of the present work, but it may be said, that although the later versions of the Walthari saga possibly reflect in some measure, and may have taken over certain features of the Hilde saga, the oldest version, viz. that of Ekkehart's *Waltharius* and the O.E. *Waldere,* contains nothing in common with it beyond the identity of one name—Hagen—and the fact that in both sagas the hero fights with the warrior bearing this name. It is true that the heroines of the two sagas bear the names Hilde and Hildegund respectively, but on this no conclusions can be based, owing to the extreme frequency of the name Hilde—and derivatives of it—in early Teutonic literature. Nor can any weight be attached to the occurrence of a story of abduction in both sagas. Quite apart from the consideration that abduction was in these times more often than not the only possible way of obtaining a bride, the underlying circumstances are totally different in the two cases. Finally, there is by no means sufficient ground to at once dismiss the Hilde saga as mythical ; for, except in one respect, viz. the never-ending fight between

---

* In the *Nibelungenlied, Biterolf*, &c. Walther is frequently referred to as " Walther von Spanje " or " der Vogt von Spanje."

the two kings, the story, as has been shown (cf. Ch. VI, p. 201) may very well represent an historical episode. Certainly the only reference of any length which is made to the subject in O.E. literature, viz. *Deor*, lines 35 ff., is almost crudely matter-of-fact, and one which it is only possible to conceive as a reminiscence of actual personal experience.

CHAPTER VIII

THE ERMANRIC SAGA.

THE O.E. heroic poems contain various scattered references to the great Ostrogothic king Ermanric and to the saga which bears his name. It is beyond the scope of this book to treat the Ermanric saga in detail (cf. Jiriczek, *D. H. S.*, Vol. I, pp. 55–118); the points which here fall under discussion are:—

- (*a*) The historical significance of the figure of Ermanric: cf. *Deor*, ll. 20 ff.; *Wids.*, ll. 7 ff., l. 18, ll. 88 ff.
- (*b*) The catalogue of Ermanric's heroes: cf. *Wids.*, ll. 109–130.
- (*c*) The story of Hama and the Brosingamene: cf. *Beo.*, ll. 1197–1207.

(*a*) ERMANRIC.

I. ERMANRIC IN O.E. LITERATURE.

Beowulf, ll. 1197–1201.

> "Naenigne ic under swegle sêlran hŷrde
> hordmâththum haeletha, syththan Hâma aetwaeg
> tô þaere byrhtan byrig Brosinga mene,
> sigle and sincfaet, searo-nithas fleah
> Eormenrices*."

* "I have never heard of a finer jewel in the possession of men under the sky, since Hama brought to the bright castle the Brosingamene, necklace and casket, and escaped from the treacherous hostility of Ermanric."

Deor, 20 ff.

> " We geascodan Eormanrîces
> wylfenne gethôht : âhte wîde folc
> Gotena rîces ; thaet waes grim cyning.
> saet secg monig sorgum gebunden,
> thaet thaes cynerices ofercumen waere*."

Widsith, ll. **7 ff.,** ll. **88 ff.**

> "...He...
> Hrêthcyninges hâm gesôhte
> eastan of Ongle Eormanrîces,
> wrathes waerlogan."

l. 18 :

> " Eormanrîc (weold) Gotum."

ll. 88 ff., more detailed reference to Ermanric saga :

> " And ic waes mid Eormanrîce ealle thrage,
> thaer me Gotena cyning gode dohte,
> se me beág forgeaf burgwarena fruma," &c.

ll. 109—130, list of Ermanric's champions.

Waldere B. l. 4, for Wudga (Widia).

II. Chief Foreign References to the Ermanric Saga.

Historical.
>   Ammianus Marcellinus.

Semi-Historical.
>   Jordanes.

Legendary.
>   Scandinavian. Saxo.
>   (Older)   Poetic *Edda* ; *Hamđis-mál.*
>   Prose *Edda* ; *Skáldsk.*
>   *Vǫlss.*

* " We heard of Ermanric's wolf-like disposition : his sovereignty in the kingdom of the Goths was wide extended. He was a grim king. Many men sat there overwhelmed by anxiety, expecting trouble, and they wished with all their heart that his rule was at an end."

Scandinavian. *Þiðss.*

German. Mhg. poems, e.g. *Dfl.*, *Bit.*, *Alp.*, *Nib.*
Deutsches Heldenbuch [5 Bde. Berlin, 1866–73].
Anhang zum Heldenbuch, pp. 111–126.
Deutsches Heldenbuch [ed. v. d. Hagen. Leipzig, 1855].
Quedlinburg Annals [Pertz, *Mon. Germ. Scrip.*, III, 32].

AMMIANUS MARCELLINUS.

The evidence of Ammianus regarding Ermanric is of a strictly contemporary nature and is the earliest reference to this king that we possess.

Ammianus (Ch. XXXI, 3, 1*) relates that the Huns, having completely subjugated the Alani, whom they compelled to enter into alliance with them, fell upon the dominions of Ermanric, a king whose mighty deeds had caused him to become known and feared throughout many lands. This sudden attack of the Huns took Ermanric by surprise, and, after a fruitless attempt at resistance, he committed suicide in order to escape the fate which threatened him from his enemies.

JORÐANES.

Jordanes (*Get.* Ch. XIV, 82*), quoting an earlier historian Ablabius, says that a part of the people living on the coast of the Pontus were called Ostrogothae, but whether this was from the name of their prince, Ostrogotha, or on account of their easterly situation, was unknown : the rest of the same people were called Vesegothae (Visigoths) on account of their westerly situation.

---

* This passage is quoted in full at the end of the chapter. Cf. p. 255.

According to Jordanes (*Get.* Ch. XXIII*) Hermanaricus succeeded a king named Geberich, and conquered a large number of nations, many of whom lived in the south of Russia. He then conquered the Heruli, after which he turned his arms against the Venthi (Slavs) and the Aisti, whom he also conquered. In his reign the Gothic kingdom was invaded by the Huns.

Jordanes differs from Ammianus in his account of Ermanric's death. The story which he tells (cf. Ch. XXIV) is shortly this. Ermanric had caused to be trampled under wild horses a woman named Suanihilda of the tribe of the Rosomonen. The reason for this crime was that Suanihilda's husband had decamped from Ermanric's court "in a fraudulent manner." Sarus and Ammius, the brothers of Suanihilda, avenged their sister's death by a murderous attack on Ermanric. As the result of the wounds which they inflicted, the king was seized by a fatal disease. The malady was aggravated by his despair at the approach of the invading Hunnish armies, and he died soon afterwards.

Scandinavian authorities—notably *Hamðis-mál*, Saxo, *Skáldsk.* and *Vǫlss.*—tell a story which obviously stands in close relation to the account given by Jordanes.

HAMÐIS-MÁL.

Hamðis-mál (contained in the older *Edda*) is the oldest Scandinavian authority which contains the story of Swanhild and Ermanric; but the poem in its present form is incomplete, the first part (which dealt with the

* See note on p. 234.

murder of Swanhild) having been lost. The events related
in the poem as it stands are as follows :—

The stern-hearted Guðrún stirred up her sons Hamði
and Sǫrli to avenge the death of their sister Swanhild,
who had been trodden to death by horses at the order of
Jǫrmunrek (Ermanric). They agreed to go on this quest
rather reluctantly, for they foresaw that they should not
return from it alive. Guðrún brought out from her
storehouse weapons, and armour which made the wearers
invulnerable, and these she gave her sons for their expedition. As the two rode out they met their half-brother
Erp, who offered to ride with them to Jǫrmunrek's court;
but Hamði and Sǫrli despised this offer and slew Erp
there. Then they rode on, and came in course of time
to Jǫrmunrek's castle, where the king sat within feasting,
surrounded by his court. They dashed in, and attacking
Jǫrmunrek, cut off his hands and feet; whereupon the
whole company of the Goths set upon Hamði and Sǫrli,
but could do them no hurt with spear or sword because
of their magic coats of mail which their mother Guðrún
had given them. Finally however Jǫrmunrek, who was
still alive, gave orders to his men to stone Hamði and
Sǫrli, and thus they were both killed. Their death is
represented as partially the consequence of their murder
of Erp, whose assistance would have enabled them to kill
Jǫrmunrek outright at the first attack.

SAXO, Bk VIII, pp. 278–281.

Jarmericus (Ermanric) was king of Denmark : he was
advised by a treacherous counsellor Bicco to put to death
his wife Suanihilda (Swanhild) and his son Broderus (by

another marriage) on account of their alleged guilty
relations. Broderus was condemned to be hung, but the
punishment was a farce and he escaped almost unhurt.
Suanihilda was trampled underfoot by horses and killed.
Her brothers the Hellespontines came with an army to
avenge her death, and succeeded in killing Jarmericus.
They were assisted by Guthruna, a sorceress. Broderus
succeeded his father as king.

VǪLSUNGASAGA.

(Ch. XL). Jǫrmunrek was the name of a mighty king
of that time, and he had a son named Randver. Now
Jǫrmunrek was desirous of wooing Swanhild, the daughter
of Guðrún by Sigurð, and he sent his counsellor Bikki
and his son Randver to ask the hand of the maiden from
King Jónak her guardian and the husband of Guðrún.
They were successful in their quest and returned bringing
Swanhild with them; but on the way back to Jǫrmunrek's
court, Bikki urged Randver to make love to Swanhild,
saying that in age and beauty she was a far fitter mate
for him than for his father.

Randver fell into the trap which had been laid for
him, whereupon, on their arrival home, Bikki accused
him of guilt to Jǫrmunrek. Jǫrmunrek, as punishment
for their misdeeds, sentenced Randver to be hung and
Swanhild to be trampled to death by wild horses, but
afterwards, when it was too late, he repented bitterly of
having put to death his only son.

Swanhild's death was avenged by her stepbrothers,
Hamði, Sǫrli, and Erp, the sons of Guðrún and Jónak.
These three, urged on by their mother, set out for

Jǫrmunrek's court : on the way strife arose between them, and Hamði and Sǫrli killed Erp. Then the two survivors went on till they came to the abode of King Jǫrmunrek, whom they at once attacked. Hamði cut off his hands and Sǫrli his feet. But because Erp, who should have cut off his head, was not there, they failed in their purpose, and were themselves slain by Jǫrmunrek's men.

The story as contained in *Skáldsk.* Ch. XLII corresponds exactly to that of the *Vǫlss.* with the exception that in this case the murder of Swanhild was a sudden and spontaneous idea on the part of Jǫrmunrek and apparently took place some time after the death of Randver. One day, as he came back from hunting, Jǫrmunrek found Swanhild sitting in a wood, and gave orders that she should be trampled under his horses' feet.

In the *Quedlinburg Annals*, under the reign of Anastasius (491–578 A.D.), there is the following entry : " Ermanrici regis Gothorum a fratribus Hemido et Serilo et Adaccero quorum patrem interfecerat amputatis manibus et pedibus turpiter uti dignus erat occisio."

III. COMPARISON OF EVIDENCE REGARDING ERMANRIC.

All sources agree in representing Ermanric as a man of fierce and cruel disposition, but, as we have seen, the account given by Ammianus of his death varies considerably from that of Jordanes and later authorities. The story as told in the Norse sagas, in Saxo, and in the *Quedlinburg Annals* was probably in the first instance derived from the same source as the account given by

Jordanes, this being in all likelihood some ancient Gothic tradition. But the authority of Jordanes, who has notoriously mingled a great deal of legend with historical fact, is far less reliable than that of Ammianus, a contemporary historian, the truth of whose account there seems no reasonable cause to doubt. For the suicide of Ermanric we find a parallel in a custom of the Heruli*, who when they became too old to wield their weapons voluntarily gave themselves up to be killed by their friends.

The account of Ammianus is however by no means incompatible with the story told by Jordanes in which Ermanric is not killed but only wounded in the attack of Sarus and Ammius.

There are some points in the Swanhild story which vary in the different versions. According to Jordanes, Swanhild (Suanilta) was a woman of the Rosomonen (an unknown tribe): she was murdered by Ermanric, in revenge for the treacherous flight of her husband, who had formerly been in the king's service.

In Saxo, *Skáldsk.* and *Vǫlss.*, on the other hand, Swanhild (Suanihilda) is the wife of Jǫrmunrek (Ermanric) and her death is the result of her real or alleged guilt with Randver (Saxo, Broderus) Jǫrmunrek's son. In the Norse sagas, and in the *Quedlinburg Annals,* a third brother has been added to the Sarus and Ammius of Jordanes. In the sagas the names of the three are Hamdi, Sǫrli and Erp (*Ann. Quedl.,* Hemidus, Serilus, Adaccerus), Saxo however is the only authority according to which the brothers were successful in actually killing King Ermanric.

* Cf. Procop. *Goth.* II, 14.

In Old Norse the Ermanric saga has been linked to the saga of the Nibelungen, Swanhild and her brothers being represented as the children of Guðrún, who was in turn the wife of Sigurð, Atli, and Jónak. In Saxo Guthrun appears as a sorceress but is not in any way related to Swanhild and her brothers.

There is nothing in the evidence which we have considered which conflicts in any way with what is said of Ermanric (Eormenric) in the O.E. poems *Widsith* and *Deor* : both poems agree with all other accounts in representing him as ferocious, cruel, and utterly untrustworthy in his dealings. He is "the savage truce breaker" (*Wids.* l. 9), "the grim king holding many in bondage" (*Deor*, l. 23 f.).

(b)   ERMANRIC'S "INNWEORUD."

From the person of Ermanric we pass on to the list of his warriors—"innweorud"—enumerated by *Widsith* in ll. 109–130. Some of these names are known to us from other sources—some cannot be traced at all. *Hethca* and *Beadeca* are unknown ; the names which occur next are those of the Herelingas ; *Emercan sohte ic and Fridlan*. From other authorities (mhg. poems*, Lat. chronicles of eleventh and twelfth centuries, Norse saga) we know that the Herelingas were the brothers Emerca and Fridla (mhg. Imbreke and Fritila) to whom tradition (*Dfl., Gen. Vip.,* &c.) sometimes adds a third, Herlip. The Herelingas or Harlunge—to use the more common mhg. form of the name—are everywhere represented as the nephews of Ermanric. They some-

---

* Cf. *Dietrich's Flucht, Biterolf, Wolfdietrich, &c.*

times appear as the sons of Diether. Their legendary home in the mhg. poems* is Breisach in the Breisgau, and they have a devoted foster-father in the faithful Eckehart, who has become one of the most popular figures of German legend. The Harlunge were murdered by their uncle Ermanric, on account of their great treasure, which he afterwards seized. In late authorities (e.g. *Thđs.*, cf. Ch. 257) the motive of Ermanric in killing his nephews has been altered : he executes vengeance on the Harlunge on account of their dishonourable intentions with regard to the ladies of his court and in particular the queen.

According to Saxo, who is doubtless referring to this same legend, the sons of Jarmericus' sister made an attempt on their uncle's throne but at Bicco's prompting he captured and hanged them.

East-Gota, Becca, etc.

We have the evidence of Jordanes (*Get.* XIV, 82) that in the time of the Emperor Philip a prince of that name (Jordanes, Ostrogotha) ruled over the Goths, who inhabited a tract of land on the shores of the Pontus. As *Widsith* in many cases mentions, side by side, names of rulers who are separated from one another in actual time, by years and even by centuries, it is quite possible that Ostrogotha may have reigned as prince of the Goths previous to Ermanric, and that he was not in reality one of his *innweorud.*

The name of Ostrogotha appears in Jordanes' genealogy of the kings of the Goths†: he is represented as the

---

* Cf. Grimm, *Deutsche Heldensage.*
† Cf. list of genealogies in Appendix II.

father of Hunuin, in agreement with *Wids.* l. 114, where East-Gota is called *frôdne and gôdne faeder Unwénes.*

Of Secca nothing is known.

Becca we may assume to be identical with Scand. Bikki (Saxo, Bicco), the evil counsellor who stands like a dark shadow behind Ermanric's throne, urging him on to the ruin of all his best friends.

The character corresponding to Becca-Bikki appears in mhg. as Sibeche or Sibich, and in the *Thđs.* as Sifka, and this name is mentioned by the *Widsith* poet (Sifecan) in the next line (l. 116) to that in which Becca occurs. The fact that in *Widsith*, which is our earliest authority regarding this matter, the two names are kept distinct and evidently denote different persons, may perhaps be evidence that there were originally two evil counsellors who stood behind Ermanric's throne, and that these, owing to their similarity of character, were later contracted into one, who appears either as Bikki-Becca or as Sibich-Sifka. But cf. below under *Sifecan* (p. 246).

Our chief authorities for the character of Becca are the *Thđs.* (Chs. 276–283), Saxo (Bk VIII, 279–287), and *H. B. Anhang,* and to a less extent, the prose *Edda* and *Vǫlss.*

According to the *Thđs.* and *H. B. Anhang,* Ermanric, having insulted Sibiche's (*Thđs.* Sifka's) wife during his absence from home, made Sibiche thereby his sworn enemy. Saxo, on the other hand, relates that Bicco (Sibiche) was the son of a king hostile to Jarmericus (Ermanric), and that his brothers had been killed by Jarmericus in battle: Bicco afterwards joined the service of Jarmericus in order to compass his revenge for his slain kinsfolk. From the time Sibiche-Bicco entered

Ermanric's service all accounts agree in representing him as the very evil genius of his master, though in the O.N. sources (*Edda* and *Vǫlss.*) there is no suggestion of his having been actuated by motives of revenge for past wrongs. According to these records, Bikki's chief triumph consisted in accomplishing the ruin of the king's wife Swanhild and his son Randver (Saxo, Broderus). Through his counsels he first helped to bring about a guilty connection between them, and afterwards betrayed them both to Ermanric. According to Saxo the accusation was altogether false, and the punishment of Broderus was only one in show; but according to Snorri (*Skáldsk.*) Randver was really guilty of misconduct with Swanhild, and was hanged at the instigation of Bikki, while all accounts agree in the story of the death of Swanhild.

According to Saxo and *H. B. Anh.* it was Bikki or Sibiche who instigated Ermanric to hang his nephews the Harlunge in order to obtain their treasure.

In the *Thᵭs.* it is also through the machinations of Sifka (Becca) that the destruction of Ermanric's three sons, Friedrich, Reginbald, Samson, is effected. In this authority, the story of Swanhild's death is entirely omitted, although it is curious to note that the death of Samson, Ermanric's youngest son, took place in a similar way; he was trampled under foot by his father's horse as a punishment for a supposed insult to the daughter of Sifka. It looks as if some confusion had taken place here, and this is quite possible, as the *Thᵭs.* is late in date, and gives the legends in many cases in a distorted form.

According to the *Thᵭs.*, Chs. 322 ff., it was through the evil counsel of Sifka that Ermanric was plunged

16—2

into war with his nephew Dietrich (O.E. Theodric), and when Dietrich returned from his exile, he defeated and slew Sifka in a great battle outside Rome.

Seafola may correspond to the Saben of German legend. In *Bit.* l. 10,995 we are told that Sabene was the son of Sibich. In the mhg. poem of *Wolfdietrich unt Saben*, Saben appears as the false counsellor in a rôle exactly analogous to that of Sibich in the Ermanric saga, and although his ancestry is not given, it seems probable that he was the *Sibichensuon* of *Biterolf* l. 10,995, who inherited his father's characteristics.

THEODRIC.

This has usually been interpreted as a reference to the historical Theodoric the Great, the Ostrogothic king of Italy (493–526), who is known in legend and folklore as Dietrich of Bern, where he ranks as the first of all knights.

The sagas of Dietrich of Bern and of Ermanric are inextricably entangled with each other, although the two men are in actual time more than a century apart. Dietrich appears in the saga as the nephew of Ermanric. He was exiled from Italy by his uncle and took refuge at the court of the Huns*. After repeated contests with Ermanric, in which he was, according to H.G. tradition, always victorious, and yet was always obliged to return to the Huns, Dietrich finally regained his inheritance after an exile of thirty years.

In addition to this pseudo-historical account of Theodoric there are countless stories and fairy tales

---

* Cf. *Deor*, ll. 18 f.

which deal with his victorious encounters with giants, dwarfs and dragons, and which have gradually accumulated round his figure, causing him to become the greatest hero of German legend.

It is difficult to account for the persistent confusion of historical facts with which we are confronted in the Dietrich and Ermanric sagas. There is no apparent reason why the personality of Theodoric, which, far from being vague and shadowy, dominated the age in which he lived, should be made subservient to that of Ermanric, who was certainly not a greater man and about whom far less is known.

A suggestion has been made which is worthy of consideration that there may have been two Theodorics*, the earlier of whom flourished in the fourth century as a vassal of King Ermanric, while the latter was the historical Theodoric the Great, who ruled over the Ostrogothic kingdom in Italy from 493–526.

The existence of such a character as this earlier Theodoric would do much to explain away the chronological displacement of Theodoric in the sagas: for it is quite conceivable that the deeds of the earlier Theodoric should have become transferred to his more famous successor and that a confusion thus arose, which ended in the total assimilation of the less to the greater, and the substitution of the great Theodoric for his forgotten predecessor.

* I am indebted for this suggestion to Mr H. M. Chadwick.

HEATHORIC AND SIFECAN, HLITHE AND INCGENTHEOW, ETC.

Sifeca(n) is capable of a twofold interpretation. We have seen (p. 242) that the name is the same as the Sifka of *Thđs.* and the Sibich(e) of the mhg. poems, and that it is used in these authorities to denote an evil counsellor of King Ermanric, who appears in Scand. literature as Bikki or Bicco, and in *Wids.* as Becca. According to this explanation, Sifeca may then denote one of Ermanric's ministers, whose character strongly resembled that of Becca.

Another explanation has however been put forward by Binz*. He interprets the whole line as a reference to four characters of the *Hervararsaga*. According to Binz, Heathoric is to be identified with King Heidrek of the above-mentioned saga, Sifeca with Sifka, his mistress, and Hliđe, Incgentheow with Hloð and Angantyr, his two sons.

Although there is a good deal to be said for this explanation, it can hardly be accepted as conclusive, since the names (with the exception of Sifeca, which we have seen to be susceptible of a totally different interpretation), are by no means so much alike in the two cases as to justify the assumption of a reference by the *Widsith* poet to the *Hervararsaga*.

Binz has further attempted to identify Wyrmhere with Ormar of the *Hervararsaga*, but this seems improbable.

Rumstein appears to be identical with the Jarl Rimstein of the *Thđs.*, who was a disobedient vassal of Ermanric. Ermanric besieged the castle of Jarl

* *P. B. B.* 20, 207.

Rimstein with a large army, and defeated him in battle; the Jarl himself fell in the fight, by the hand of Witig (cf. *Thđs*. Chs. 126 & 127).

To the identity of Gislhere we have no clue, for it seems quite impossible that he should have any connection with the Gislaharius of the *Lex Burgundionum*.

Freotheric seems to refer to Ermanric's son who was put to death by his father, probably through the misrepresentations of Ermanric's evil counsellor, Sibich-Becca. In most authorities, Freotheric (Frederic) is represented as Ermanric's only son*, but in the *Thđs*. the one son has been expanded into three—Friedrich, Reginbald, Samson.

An extract may here be quoted from the *Quedlinburg Annals* as it bears upon the fate both of Ermanric's son Frederic and on that of his nephews the Harlunge—Imbreike and Fritila:—

Annales Quedlinburgenses. Martianus, 450–457. "Eo tempore Ermanricus super omnes Gothos regnavit astutior in dolo, largior in dono: qui post mortem Friderici unici filii sui, sua perpetrata voluntate, patrueles suos Embricam et Fritlam patibulo suspendit, Theodricum similiter patruelem suum instimulante Odoacro patruele suo de Verona pulsum apud Attilam exulare coegit."

WUDGA AND HAMA.

We almost always find the names of Wudga and Hama coupled as those of companions-in-arms. That they were well known in almost every place to which

---

* Cf. *Ann. Quedl. Dfl.* 1. 2455. Heinr. v. München's *Chron.* 1. 295.

the Ermanric and Dietrich sagas spread, is shown by the frequency of the references and the countless adventures attributed to them.   They are famous alike in the *Thđs.* and in all mhg. poems and chronicles, and they were the most dreaded amongst the warriors of Dietrich and Ermanric.

But the characters Wudga and Hama or—to use the names in the more usual German form—Witig and Heime, are not altogether easily explained.   A curious fact about them is that they are represented as being alternately in the service of Dietrich and Ermanric.   At first the vassals of Dietrich, they not only appear to desert their master, but even become actively hostile to him in the course of the great struggle between Dietrich and his uncle Ermanric.   Witig, especially, comes into prominence in this connection : he was a knight unsurpassed in strength and prowess by all save Dietrich : he was at first the devoted servant of Dietrich, but afterwards turned with equal fierceness against him, and became the leader of Ermanric's armies, and was finally slain by Dietrich. As one might anticipate, much more than a mere suspicion of treachery attaches to the names of Witig and Heime in many sources, and they are often quoted as the type of disloyal and treacherous vassals.   It is, however, important to note the different view taken in the *Thđs.*, especially with regard to Witig, who is here represented as the ideal knight, strong, brave, gentle and incapable of a mean or dishonourable action.   No breath of treachery sullies his character.   It was not by any overt act on his part that he became the vassal of Ermanric, but purely owing to the circumstance of his marriage with Ermanric's ward, the mother of the Harlunge brothers.   As Ermanric's vassal, Witig was then bound, although sorely against the grain, to lead the forces of his master against those of his old master Dietrich.

The *Thds.* represented Heime as a good knight, but of a fierce and cruel disposition : he does not play such an important part in the saga as Witig. In his old age Heime re-entered the service of Dietrich (*Thds.*, Chs. 17 ff., 79 ff., 189 ff., 332 ff., 429 ff.).

It is a strange circumstance in the history of the careers of Witig and Heime, that in these days, when loyalty and fidelity to the over-lord were held so dear, two warriors, possessed of almost every knightly virtue, should be found constantly transferring their allegiance from one great monarch to another who was his deadly foe.

There must be some underlying facts which are unknown to us, to account for this. No certain explanation can we give of these puzzling relations, but a natural suggestion is that in the unusual relations of Witig and Heime to Ermanric and Dietrich we have further grounds for the theory hazarded above, that there were two Dietrichs (Theodorics), and that the one who played such an important part in the Ermanric saga did not originally represent Theodoric the Great, but an earlier Theodoric, the vassal of Ermanric. If this were so, the apparent inconsistency and treachery of Witig and Heime would instantly vanish : for as knights of Dietrich they would also owe allegiance to Ermanric, who was Dietrich's over-lord, and in the case of Dietrich's defection from his master, their first duty would still be to support Ermanric.

In saga literature Witig is usually represented as the son of the smith Wêland (G. Wieland): this union is probably of Low German origin. In Saxo and in the older *Edda*, Witig and Heime do not appear at all.

Witig has been identified with a Gothic hero, Vidigoia, who is twice mentioned by Jordanes. In *Get.*, Ch. v, Vidigoia is spoken of as one of the heroes whose deeds are celebrated by the people in song: in Ch. xxxiv as a great Gothic warrior who was treacherously slain by the Sarmatians*.

It is possible that in the sagas, the Sarmatians may have been replaced by the Huns, whose name was a more familiar one, but in any case we need not hesitate to identify the Wudga (mhg. Witege) represented as fighting for Ermanric against the Huns in *Widsith* and *Rab.* with the historical Vidigoia, the celebrated figure of Gothic tradition †.

(c) Brosinga Mene.

There still remains for consideration the obscure allusion in *Beowulf* ll. 1197–1201, where we are told that Hama stole and escaped with *Brosingamene*, which apparently was the property of Ermanric. Discussion has raged round this passage without arriving at any very definite conclusion. We may shortly examine the evidence of other authorities which throw any light on the story.

The *Thðs.* (Ch. 435 ff.) contains a long account of a theft perpetrated by Heime in a monastery belonging to Ermanric, where he had formerly been in orders. Heime

---

* "Vidigoia Gothorum fortissimus Sarmatum dolo occubuit."

† In *Dfl.*, *Rab.* and *H. B. Anhang*, Witege is named side by side with Witegouwe, "his brother," both being represented as the sons of Wieland. This is clearly a case in which two forms of the same name have been mistaken for two distinct names.

stole a great deal of treasure in gold and silver on behalf
of his master Dietrich, to whom he had returned after
quitting Ermanric's service. A curious parallel to this
story occurs in the end of the prose *Vǫlss.* where Heimir,
the foster-father of Brunhild, is forced to fly from his
country with Aslaug, the daughter of Sigurđ and Brunhild.
Heimir made a great harp which was hollow, into which
he put the child Aslaug with much gold and silver; he
then set out on his journey in the disguise of a wandering
minstrel.

Although the occurrence of this story in the *Vǫlss.*
may be a mere coincidence, yet the evidence of the *Thđs.*
alone is sufficient to prove that there was in the original
saga some well substantiated story of a theft committed
by Heime on the property of Ermanric. The question as
to what the *Brosingamene* which *Beo.* reports Hama to
have stolen actually was, is however more difficult. In
Norse mythology the necklace of the Goddess Freyja was
called the *Brisingamen.* At the instigation of Odin, Loki
stole the necklace from Freyja : it was however restored
to her by Heimdall.

It need not be doubted that *Brosingamene* is either
a corruption or another form of *Brisingamen*; but we do
not know what the meaning and significance of the word
is, whether there was only one or more than one *Brisinga-*
men, whether, in short, it is a generic term or the name
of some specific object. It cannot therefore be proved
that the *Brisingamen* of Norse mythology is identical
with the *Brosingamene* which Heime (Hama) is reported
to have stolen from Ermanric. This is, however, assumed
by Müllenhoff in his interpretation*, the chief points of

* *Z. f. d. A.* Vol. xxx, pp. 217 ff, "Frija und der Halsband Mythus."

which are (1) that by connecting Brisinga with Breisach, the traditional home of the Harlunge, the *Brosingamene* which was stolen by Heime is identified with the treasure, for the sake of which the Harlunge were murdered by Ermanric*; and (2) that the Harlunge themselves are interpreted as mythical beings, to wit, the twin Dioskuri or Aryan Açvina, the gods of the morning.

As matters stand, the identification of the treasure of the Harlunge with the *Brosingamene* is mere conjecture, nor is there, in the story, anything to indicate that the figures of the two brothers are of less historical value than that of Ermanric himself: it is difficult to see what ground there is for the idea that they should be regarded . as mythical characters.

The chief objection to Müllenhoff's explanation is, however, that it is based on an assumption which we have seen to be unwarranted, viz. that the *Brosingamene* of Ermanric was the same as the *Brisingamen* of the Goddess Freyja.

It is of course possible that the *Brosingamene* was originally an attribute of the gods, which was afterwards transferred to mortals, a process for which parallel cases might be cited : but even if this were known to be the case, there would be no justification whatsoever for connecting myth and historical tradition any further.

---

* According to the *Thđs*. the father of the Harlunge was called Áki Örlungatrausti—this character is to be identified with the Getreue Ecke-hart of German legend who is everywhere referred to as the guardian of the Harlunge brothers (*Dfl.*, *Rab.*, *Alp.*, &c.). It is in this connection perhaps worth while noting that according to the story of *Vǫlss.* cited above, Heimir in the course of his wanderings fell in with a peasant named Aki, by whom he was murdered for the sake of the treasure which he carried.

A document of St Gallen of the year 786* contains an entry according to which a certain Heimo and his daughter Suanilta made gifts of money to several monasteries.

The fact that these names Heimo (Heime) and Suanilta (Swanhild) are here linked together has given rise to the suggestion by Müllenhoff, that Heime, who, according to *Beo.* ll. 1197 ff. stole the *Brosingamene*—apparently consisting of treasure—from Ermanric, was the husband of Swanhild, referred to by Jordanes in the words *pro mariti frandulento discessu.* There is not at present enough evidence to confirm this hypothesis; except for this allusion, we have no ground for connecting Heime and Swanhild. The one feature common to Heime and to the husband of Swanhild is that they both robbed Ermanric (this appears to be the best interpretation of *frandulento discessu*), and it is highly probable that Ermanric in the course of his reign was robbed by many others besides Heime.

IV. HISTORICAL BACKGROUND UNDERLYING THE ERMANRIC SAGA.

The Ermanric saga regarded from an historical standpoint is valuable in its possibilities rather than in its certainties. We cannot affirm with absolute assurance more than what is already well-known historical fact, namely, that a powerful king named Ermanric ruled over

---

* *Urkundenbuch der Abtei St Gallen*, ed. Wartmann, 1863, Vol. I, 110: "Ego Heimone et filia ejus Svanailta aque tradamus et transfundimus ad monasterium sancti Gallone, qui est constructus in pago Harbonensi, ubi ejus sacrus corpus requiescit."

the Goths during the middle years of the fourth century,
and that his death took place simultaneously with the
first attack made on his dominions by the Hunnish
forces.

All references in literature to Ermanric go to confirm
the evidence of history that he was a monarch of great
power and vast dominions. His jurisdiction appears to
have extended as far as the shores of the Baltic* at the
part where the Vistula enters it, and he was known and
feared amongst Northern peoples as the mighty king
Jǫrmunrek. Ermanric is a familiar figure in Scandinavian literature from the earliest times, and the fact that
he was known by the *Widsith* poet is perhaps better
proof than any other of his widespread fame at a very
early date.

There is no reason to doubt that the stories of Swanhild, of Heime's theft, and of the Harlunge brothers are
founded on historical fact, though we are not in a position
to say definitely that such is the case. The only parts of
these stories which may be regarded as spurious are those
in which the number of characters occurring in any given
connection in an early authority has been added to in the
later accounts of the same story. Thus it is very improbable that Swanhild had in reality more than two brothers,
that the Harlunge were originally more than two in
number, or that Ermanric had more than one son.

---

* This is implied rather than actually stated. Jordanes says that
Ermanric ruled over the Aisti, who lived according to King Alfred
eastwards from the mouth of the Vistula to Ermanric's court. The
visit of Ealhild, a princess of the Myrgringas, of which an account is
given in *Wids.* ll. 5 ff., may have been a case of the giving of hostages,
in which case Ermanric's jurisdiction extended perhaps as far north as a
tribe whose territory bordered on Angel.

With regard to the catalogue of Ermanric's *innweorud* which is given by the *Widsith* poet, it is difficult to say anything definitely.

It is, however, more probable than not that all the names are those of historical characters, whom the poet had heard spoken of in connection with Ermanric, although they do not all appear to have been contemporaries of that king.

NOTE TO CHAPTER VIII.

The following are the most important of the extracts from Jordanes, Ammianus and the *Quedlinburg Annals* bearing on the Ermanric saga.

Ammianus (Ch. XXXI, 3, 1). " Igitur Hunni pervasis Alanorum regionibus, quos Gruthungis confines Tanaitas consuetudo nominavit, interfectisque multis et spoliatis, reliquos sibi concordandi fide pacta junxerunt eisque adjunctis confidentius Ermanrichi late patentes et uberes pagos repentino impetu perruperunt bellicosissimi Regis et per multa variaque fortiter facta vicinis nationibus formidati."

Jordanes (*Get.* Ch. XIV, 82). "Nunc autem ad id, unde digressum primus, redeamus doceamusque, quomodo ordo gentis, unde agimus, cursus sui metam explevit. Ablabius enim storicus refert, quia ibi super limbum Ponti, ubi eos diximus in Scythia commanere, ibi pars eorum qui orientalem plagam tenebat, eisque praeerat Ostrogotha, utrum ab ipsius nomine, an a loco, id est orientales dicti sunt Ostrogothae, residui vero Vesegothae, id est a parte occidua."

(*Get.* Ch. XXIII ff.) " Nam Gothorum rege Geberich rebus excedente humanis post temporis aliquod Hermanaricus nobilissimus Amalorum, multas et bellicosissimas arctoas gentes perdomuit suisque parere legibus fecit. Quem merito nonnulli Alexandro magno comparavere majores...et gentem Herulorum quibus praeerat Alaricus, magna ex parte trucidatam reliquam suae subigeret ditioni."

(Ch. xxiv) "Post autem non longi temporis intervallum, ut refert Orosius, Hunnorum gens omni ferocitate atrocior exarsit in Gothos. Hermanaricus, rex Gothorum licet, multarum gentium extiterat triumphator, de Hunnorum tamen adventu dum cogitat Rosomonorum gens infida, quae tunc inter alias illi famulatum exhibebat, tali eum nanciscitur occasione decipere. Dum enim quandam mulierem Sunilda (Sunielh, Sunihil) nomine ex gente memorata pro mariti fraudulento discessu rex furore commotus equis ferocibus illigatam incitatisque cursibus per diversa divelli praecipisset, fratres ejus Sarus et Ammius, germanae obitum vindicantes, Hermanarici latus ferro petierunt : quo vulnere saucius aegram vitam corporis imbecillitate contraxit. Quam adversam ejus valitudinem captans Balamber rex Hunnorum in Ostrogothorum partem movit procinctum, a quorum societate iam Vesegothae quadam inter se intentione sejuncti habebantur. Inter haec Hermanaricus tam vulneris dolorem, quam etiam incursiones Hunnorum non ferens grandaevus et plenus dierum centesimo decimo anno vitae suae defunctus est."

Quedlinburg Annals (Anastasius, 491–518). "Amulung Theoderic dicitur : proavus suus Amul vocabatur qui Gothorum potissimus censebatur, et iste fuit Thideric de Berne de quo cantabant rustice olim. Theodericus Attilae regis auxilio in regnum Gothorum reductus suum patruelem Odeacrum in Ravenna civitate expugnatum interveniente Attila ne occideretur exilio deportatum paucis villis juxta confluentiam Albiae et Salae fluminum donavit."

CONCLUSION

AN attempt has been made in the foregoing chapters to estimate the amount of historical truth contained in the O.E. heroic poems. Emphasis has been laid on the reliability of the evidence of the poems, derived from their great antiquity, i.e. it is of the nature of contemporary testimony and therefore was less likely to be corrupted than later accounts of the same events. When, in addition, we find this evidence confirmed by independent authorities of later date and different nationality, we are further justified in the belief that the tradition in question is based on historical truth. This we have found almost uniformly to be the case: there is scarcely a single episode of the poems which is not confirmed by the testimony of later Scandinavian or German records. Only in the case of one or two isolated references, and of some personal and tribal names contained in the catalogue of the Widsith poet, does all other evidence fail us.

Of course, the coincidence of English and Scandinavian evidence with regard to any tradition is not a conclusive proof of its historical value but must be followed up by a thorough investigation of the nature of the tradition in question and the possible influence that mythology and folk-lore may have had in its development. A general

survey of the poems conducted on these lines has shown
that with the exceptions of the Sceaf myth, some names
in the Widsith catalogue, and the further possible exception
of the Wêland saga, we have found good ground for believing
that the traditions contained in the O.E. epic poems are
all based on historical fact. In some cases the weight of
evidence in favour of the historicity of tradition has been
so overwhelming as to exclude the possibility of doubt,
as for example Offa's duel by the river Eider, and the
successful campaign which Eadgils-Aðils, with the assistance of Beowulf-Bǫðvar, waged against Onela. In other
cases it has been found necessary to have recourse to
a more indirect method of reasoning. In the absence of
actual proof, the accumulation of evidence often tends
strongly towards the probability that a tradition is
historical. Where, at the same time, the possibility of
a mythical background can be eliminated it may be
assumed with comparative certainty that the events
related are based on actual occurrences.

With regard to *Widsith*, which is little more than
a catalogue of names and facts, no one denies that this
is so. The same cannot be said of the view generally
held with regard to the *Beowulf*. There seems, however,
little doubt that much more stress should be laid on the
historical importance of this poem also than has usually
been the case. The supposed mythical elements which it
contains have received undue prominence. Such elements
may, probably do, exist, but they are accretions which
with care may be separated from the main thread of the
events. Surely the coincidence of evidence in different
authorities, both in the case of *Beowulf* and in that of the
other narratives considered, is too remarkable for any

sober-minded critic to regard it merely as a series of fortuitous coincidences.

Respect for the O.E. heroic poems considered in the light of historical documents increases, the more fully they are studied without preconceived determination to find in them mere myth or allegorical types. They are store-houses of valuable information concerning the doings, customs, and beliefs of ancient Teutonic peoples*. Not-withstanding the obscurity arising in certain instances from the fragmentary form in which some of the poems have been preserved, we may go a step further and say that the primary interest of these poems, which were originally designed for the amusement and entertainment of our warlike ancestors, now lies in their relation to the history of the far-away times which gave them birth.

* A consideration of the last two points would fall under the head of sociology rather than that of history, unless the latter term received its Spencerian interpretation.

APPENDIX I

Myrgingas. Cf. Ch. IV on Offa Episode.

Hrêthcyning, i.e. Ermanric. Cf. Ch. VIII on Ermanric saga. A.S. hrêð = glory or renown.

Hwala. The only other known occurrence of the name *Hwala* is in MSS. B and C of the A.S. Chr. under the year 855, where very far back in the genealogies we find the names *Itermon Hathraing, Hathra Hwalaing, Hwala Bedwiging, Bedwig Sceafing, id est filius Noe.*

It has been suggested that *Eaforum Ecgwelan* (cf. *Beo.* l. 1710) may contain a reference to the same person.

Alexandreas = Alexander the Great of Greece.

Aetla weold Hunum. . The Huns were an Asiatic race. They appeared in Europe in the middle of the fourth century, moving westwards from the Ural Mountains with irresistible strength and great ferocity. The Huns were of Tartar origin, and came originally from a home in N.E. Asia. About the year 374 A.D. they crossed the rivers Volga and Don, and fell upon the kingdom of the Goths. During the first half of the fifth century the Huns were led by the great Attila, under whom they swept across Europe, penetrating even to Gaul, and inspiring universal terror through the cruelty of their deeds.

Between 445 and 450, Attila ravaged the Eastern Empire between the Euxine and the Adriatic, and in 450 he invaded Gaul. His forces were estimated at about half a million. Attila was defeated by the combined forces of Romans and Franks, after which he turned southwards with a view to marching on Rome. But he died in 453, and, deprived of their great leader, the Hunnish armies quickly became disorganized. The Huns dispersed and disappeared as suddenly as they had come, having, in their whirlwind course, changed the whole face of Europe. The probability is that they were to some extent assimilated by the Teutons among whom they settled, and that they became to all intents and purposes Teutonic.

Eormanric (weold) Gotum. Cf. Ch. VIII on Ermanric saga.

Becca (weold) Baningum. Cf. *Wids.* l. 115, *Seccan sohte ic and Beccan.* Becca probably belongs to the East Gothic cycle, cf. therefore Ch. VIII on Ermanric saga. Nothing is known of the Baningas.

Burgendum (weold) Gifica. Cf. Ch. VII on the Burgundians.

Casere weold Creacum. *Casere* is of course merely the word "Caesar," i.e. Emperor. The representation of the Emperor as ruling the Greeks and not the Romans points to the conception in the poet's mind of the Empire as centred in Constantinople. From the year 476–800 A.D. there was only one Emperor in the Roman Empire and his seat of government was in Constantinople.

Caelic (weold) Finnum. Caelic is otherwise unknown.

Finnas, like O.N. Finnar, may be a generic name embracing both Lapps and Finns. In O.E. references it usually denotes the Lapps, as for example in Orosius, *Voyages of Ohthere and Wulfstan.* By the Scridefinnas of Procopius (*Goth.* II, 15), who are mentioned in *Wids.* l. 29, the Lapps are also evidently meant.

Hagena (weold) Holmrygum. Cf. Ch. vi on Deor.

Heoden (weold) Glommum. Cf. Ch. vi on Deor.

Witta weold Swaefum. In Bede's genealogy (*Hist. Eccles.* i, 15), Vitta is the name of the grandfather of Hengest, who in 449 invaded Kent along with Horsa. According to Sweet's genealogy, dating from circa 872, Vitta is the father of Hengest.

Wids., l. 44, mentions the Swaefe as conterminous with the Engli. They were probably a northern band of the Suevi, who in early times were known as the people of the Elbe. We find mention of a people called the North Suevi in continental documents (cf. also Ch. iv).

Wada (weold) Haelsingum. In the *Thđs.* Vađe is a giant, the son of King Wilkinus. He is married to a mermaid and their son is the famous smith Wêland.

In the *Gudrun* Wate is a fierce sea-king who reigns in Sturmen or Sturmland. His figure recalls to some extent that of the God Neptune.

The stem *Haelsing-* is found helping to form compounds in a number of northern names, e.g. Helsingaland, Helsingfors, &c. These names might quite well be originally due to the existence of a tribe, Helsingas or Haelsingas, although nothing is known directly of such a tribe.

Meaca (weold) Myrgingum. Meaca is otherwise unknown.

Marchealf (weold) Hundingum. Marchealf is otherwise unknown.

Nothing is known of a tribe called the Hundings. In the *Vǫlsungasaga* and in Saxo we hear of a King Hunding, who was slain by Helgi Hundingsbani: according to the *Edda*, Helgi Hundingsbani was the son of Sigmund the Vǫlsung, but Saxo has confused him with Helgi the son of Halfdan, king of Denmark, who lived much later and was quite a different person.

As the authority of *Widsith* is much older than that of Saxo, we seem to have here a case of the contraction of a tribe or nation into a single man. The same thing has apparently taken place in the case of Heathobeardan and Hothbroddus (cf. Ch. II, p. 105).

Theodric weold Froncum.

Theuderic was the eldest of the four sons of Chlodovech (Clovis), the great king of the Franks, who first gave shape to the Frankish Empire. When Chlodovech died, his realms were divided according to an ancient Teutonic custom, amongst his four sons, Theuderic, Chlodomer, Childebert, and Chlotar. Theuderic, who reigned from 511–533, received as his portion the former kingdom of the Ripparian Franks, which lay along the river Rhine from Köln (Cologne) as far south as Basel (Bâle), as well as some territory lying to the east in the valley of the Main. It was in the early years of Theuderic's reign that Chochilaicus, a "Danish" pirate king, made a raid on the Lower Rhine. He was defeated and slain by Theuderic's son Theudebert. In 531 Theuderic, with the help of his brother Chlotar, conquered Thuringia and made it a tributary state. He died in 533.

In the *Quedlinburg Annals*, under the year 532 A.D., we find the following entry, in the reign of Hugo Theodoricus under the Emperor Justinian (527–65):

"Eodem anno Hugo Theodericus rex Chlodovec regis filius ex concubina natus cum patri successisset in regnum ad electionem suam Irminfridum regem Thuringorum honorifice invitavit. Hugo Theodericus iste dicitur, id est Francus, quia olim omnes Franci Hugones vocabantur a suo quodam duce Hugone."

This passage is interesting for two reasons. In the first place, we learn from it that the Franks were originally called "Hugones," which forms an instructive parallel to *Beowulf,*

l. 2913, where in speaking of Hygelac's fatal expedition, the poet says :

> " Waes sió wrôht scepen
> heard with *Hugas*, syththan Hygelâc cwom
> faran flot-herge on Fresna land,
> thaer hyne Hetware hilde gehnaegdon,
> elne ge-eodon mid ofer-maegene,
> thaet se byrn-wîga bûgan sceolde,
> feóll on fêthan*."

Secondly, it appears from this passage that King Theuderic was commonly known as Hugo Theodericus. Theuderic was an illegitimate son of King Chlodovech, and after his father's death he quarrelled with his three brothers about the partition of the kingdom. These historical events seem to find an echo in the Hug- and Wolfdietrichsaga, and attempts have been made to identify episodes in Theuderic's career with parts of this saga. The figure of Theuderic corresponds, however, not to that of Hugdietrich, but to that of his son Wolf-dietrich.

Thyle (weold) Rondingum. Both names are otherwise unknown.

Breoca (weold) Brondingum. The only other reference to Breoca is *Beo.* ll. 505 ff. (where the name occurs as Breca) and especially in l. 520, where the country which he governed is referred to as the land of the Brondings. Beowulf was reported to have had a nine days' swimming match with Breca on the open sea.

Billing (weold) Wernum. Billing is otherwise unknown.

---

* " The strife with the Hugas became sharp, after Hygelac came with his fleet to the land of the Frisians, where the Hetware vanquished him in battle, (and) bravely achieved by their superior numbers that the armed warrior should yield, should fall amongst his warriors."

The Werni are clearly the same as the Varini mentioned by Tacitus (*Germ*. Ch. 40), who unfortunately gives no clear indication as to their position, though we may infer from him that they lived near the sea and south of the Elbe.

Ptolemy places the tribes Ouirouinoi and Teutonoaroi approximately in Holstein-Lauenburg, and the Auerpoi and Teutones approximately in Mecklenburg*. These two pairs of names seem to be doublets. It is possible that the Warni are mentioned in a corrupt form by Pliny (*Nat. Hist.* IV, 99 †) where they, together with the Goths and Burgundians, are classed as the Vandili, who constituted the north-easterly division of the five divisions into which Pliny divides the Germani †. " On the whole," says Mr Chadwick (*op. cit.* p. 200), " the evidence such as it is distinctly favours the idea that the Varini belonged to the eastern or Baltic half of Germany." Mention is also found of the Warni in later times. According to Procopius (i.e. 550 A.D.) *Goth.* II, 14 (cf. Ch. II, p. 62), the Heruli passed through the territory of the Warni on their way north, before reaching the Danoi, and he says in another passage (v, 14) that the Warni were separated from the Franks only by the Rhine. Their territory lay apparently near the coast, for they were attacked by the Angloi from over the sea (*Goth.* IV, 20). Perhaps a branch of the Warni had settled in Holland, but since Procopius' knowledge of the geography of Northern Europe was but vague, some mistake may have taken place here. We read in Fredegarius (*Chron.* Ch. 15) that the Warni rebelled against the Franks in 596, but where they lived at this time is not stated. Detached bands of Warni are found in Italy and Spain at different times during the sixth century, and the last time they are mentioned is in the heading of a Code called " Lex Angliorum et Werinorum, hoc est Thuringorum," which dates from early in the ninth century. The

* Ptolemy, *Geographia,* II, 11. 9.

† Cf. Ch. VII, p. 211.

most probable view is that this code belongs to part of the old Thuringian kingdom, which was situated in Central Germany round the basin of the Elbe, and hence it is likely that some part of the Warni had settled there. It may be noted that from the time of Tacitus downwards, the names of Angli and Warni have frequently been found in close interconnection *.

Oswine (weold) Eowum.   Oswine is otherwise unknown.

Eowum seems to be the same word as Auiones, a tribe mentioned by Tacitus (*Germ.* XL), and included among the seven which worshipped the Goddess Nerthus. The name may mean "Islanders": we do not find it used elsewhere as a tribal name. The island of Öland, it may also be noticed, is called by King Alfred Eowland.

Ytum (weold) Gefwulf.   Gefwulf is otherwise unknown.

Ytum may be the same word as A.S. Eotan, O.N. Jótar, Eng. Jutes, which is the name used by Danish historians for the inhabitants of Jutland. Two forms appear in English corresponding to O.N. Jótar, viz. (a) *Eota* or *Eotena*, (b) *Yte* or *Ytena*.

Y of *Yte* would correspond to *Ie* and give *Jete*, a W.S. form with Umlaut (cf. also p. 183).

Fin Folcwalding (weold) Fresna cynne.   Cf. Ch. v on Finn saga.

Sigehere lengest Sae-denum weold.   For Sigehere and the Danes cf. Ch. II.

Hnaef (weold) Hocingum.   Cf. Ch. v on Finn saga.

Helm (weold) Wulfingum.   Helm is otherwise unknown. In *Beowulf*, and in various Scandinavian poems, references to his tribe occur.

* Cf. Chadwick, *op. cit.* pp. 108 ff., 198 ff.

In *Beowulf* they are called Wylfingas, in Scandinavian references Ylvingar; in Scandinavian literature they are sometimes identified with the Vǫlssungar.

Wald (weold) Woingum. Both names are otherwise unknown.

Wod (weold) Thyringum. Wod is otherwise unknown.

The Thuringas were an important nation up to the beginning of the sixth century, and occupied territories around and northwards of the basin of the Saale, and bordering on the Franks. Their kingdom was destroyed by the Frankish king Theuderic in 531 A.D.

Saeferth (weold) Sycgum. These names recall the *Sigeferhth Secgena leod* mentioned in Finn (cf. Ch. v on Finn saga).

Saeferth's name occurs in a genealogy of East Saxon kings contained in Sweet, *O. E. T.* p. 179, while much higher up in the same genealogy we find the name Gesecg. Now one of the ancestors of the West Saxon kings, as contained in the genealogy of the A.S. Chronicle under the year 855, is named Gewis, and Bede (*Hist. Eccles.* III, 7, &c.) repeatedly speaks of the West Saxons as Gewissae or Gewissi, by which name, as he says, they were formerly called. On the analogy of the forms Gewissae and Gewis it seems permissible to reason that *Secgena* (Sycgan) may have been formed in a similar way from Gesecg, and may thus have been at one time no other than a dynastic name for the East Saxons.

Sweom (weold) Ongentheow. Cf. Ch. III on Swedish traditions.

Sceafthere (weold) Ymbrum. Sceafthere is otherwise unknown.

The forms *Ymbrum* and *Sycgum* suggest the possibility that *y* may have taken the place of an earlier *e*. If this is so, the Embrum may have been the inhabitants either of the

Pagus Ambria—now Ammerland—on the borders of Olden-burg and West Hanover, or of the island Amrum (formerly Amberum), and there may be some historical connection be-tween these two places. In Nennius' account of the North-umbrian kings, the Northumbrians are twice spoken of as *Saxones Ambronum*, which is glossed "i.e. Eald Saxonum*."

As the Northumbrian English could not possibly be iden-tified with the Ambrones it is clear that some mistake has taken place here; the existence of the gloss is, however, evidence that the Old Saxons, or some part of them, were called Ambrones.

Possibly the word Ambrones in Nennius was originally merely a scribal error for Umbrones = Northumbrians.

Sceafa (weold) Longbeardum. History knows no Lombardian prince of this name. For Longbeardas see below.

Hun (weold) Haetwerum. Hun is otherwise unknown. The Haetweri are mentioned in *Beo.* l. 2363 and l. 2916, as Hetwari. In alliance with the Franks and Frisians they defeated Hygelac. This tribe is clearly the same as the Chattuarii who are mentioned in connection with the same events in the *Gesta Francorum*, Ch. XIX (cf. p. 43).

The name survives in the Pagus Hattuariensis between the Zuyder Zee and the Rhine, the first mention of which dates from the beginning of the Christian era (Velleius).

Offa weold Ongle. Cf. Ch. IV on the Offa Episode.

Alewih weold Denum. Cf. Ch. II, especially pp. 118 ff. *Widsith*, ll. 70-75:

"I have also been in Italy with Aelfwine—so far as my knowledge goes he, the son of Eadwine, had of all mankind the readiest hand for the acquisition of praise, the most un-grudging heart for distributing rings, i.e. shining bracelets."

Aelfwine (Alboin) the son of Eadwine (Audoin) was an historical king of the Lombards. In the first half of the

* Nennius, Sec. 63, MS. K.

sixth century the Lombards, whose territory lay on the middle
Danube, were neighbours and bitter enemies of the Gepidae,
who had remained in the Hungarian plains when the rest of
the Gothic people moved west to Spain and Italy. In 567,
the Lombards, assisted by the Tartars and Avars, put an end
to the struggle by almost exterminating the Gepidae : this
took place under the leadership of Alboin the son of Audoin.
The next year, 568, Alboin put into effect a long-cherished
scheme for the invasion of Italy. In 552, while the old king
Audoin was still alive, the Lombards had provided horses
with a contingent of 5,000 men for his invasion of Italy.
This perhaps first gave rise in Alboin's mind to the idea of
himself invading Italy, an idea which received fresh impetus
after he had seen the beauties and the fertility of that land.
At that time an independent Lombard invasion was out of
the question, as the Lombards were still fully occupied with
the Gepidae, and their king Audoin was an old man. In 568
the way at length seemed open, and Alboin, leaving his kingdom, under certain conditions, to his allies, the Avars, crossed
the Alps in the summer, with the whole Lombard nation, and
took possession of the plains of North Italy, which, owing to
previous wars and pestilence, were then in a state of desertion.
Very little opposition was offered to Alboin's advance : only
in places such as Padua, Verona, Pavia, which contained an
imperial garrison, was there organised resistance.

The Lombards spread themselves over the whole valley
of the Po. They became divided into West and East Lombards. Many scattered portions of other tribes joined Alboin,
such as Saxons, Suabians, Bulgarians, and Slavs. At last
Pavia, the last stronghold, fell, and was chosen by Alboin as
the capital of Lombardy.

Alboin was murdered in 572 at the instigation of his wife,
the daughter of Cunimund, king of the Gepidae, whom Alboin
had slain.

APPENDIX II

English Genealogies.

West Saxon Genealogy.

(This genealogy makes no claim to completeness, being designed to deal only with names which have occurred in the consideration of the O.E. poems.)

W.S. Genealogy in A. S. Chronicle under year 855.

> Sceaf.   id est filius Noe.
> Bedwig.
> Hwala.
> Hrathra.
> Itermon.
> Heremod.
> Sceldwea.
> Beaw.
> Taetwa.
> Geat.
> Godwulf (Nennius, Folcbald or Folcpald).
> Finn.
> Frithewulf.
> Frealaf.
> Woden.
> Baldaeg.
> Brand.
> Frithogar.
> Freawine.
> Wig.
> etc. etc.

The genealogy as given by William of Malmesbury and Aethelweard varies slightly from that in the A. S. Chr.

William of Malmesbury.

Noae.	
Strephius.	
Bedwegius.	
Gwala.	
Hadra.	
Stermonius.	
Heremodius.	Aethelweard.
Sceaf.	Sceaf.
Sceldius.	Scyld.
Beowius.	Beo.
Tetius.	Tetwa.
etc. etc.	etc. etc.

The non-W.S. genealogies, i.e. a group consisting of a text printed by Sweet—Cotton MS. Vespasian B. 6 fol. 108 ff. (811—814 A.D.)—*Historia Britonum*, a chronicle under year 547, probably of northern source, and several later texts (Corpus, 183), all place Geat at the head of the genealogy. Only in the A. S. Chr. under year 855, in Aethelweard and in the texts derived from these, are the genealogies carried back to Sceaf. The last mentioned authorities date from about the end of the tenth century.

Mercian Genealogy in A. S. Chr. under year 755.

Woden.	Woden.
Wihtlaeg.	Wihtlaeg.
Waermund.	Waermund.
Offa.	Offa.
Angeltheow.	Angeltheow.
Eomaer.	Eomaer.
Icel.	Icel.

Cnebba.
Cynewald.
Creoda.
Pybba.
Eawa.
Osmod.
Eanwulf.
Thingferth.
Offa.

Cnebba.
Cynewald.
Creoda.
Pybba.
Penda.

Danish Genealogies.

Sven Aagesen.	Saxo.
Skiǫld.	Humblus I.
Frothi.	Dan I.
Haldan.	Humblus II.
Helge.	Lothar.
Rolf Kraki.	Sciold.
Rǿkil.	Gram.
Frothi hinn frøkni.	Hading.
Wermundus.	Frotho I.
Uffi.	Haldanus I. Roe I.
Dan Elatus.	Helgo. Roe II.
Frothi senex.	Hrolvus crace.
Fridlevus.	Hotherus.
Frothi largus.	Roricus Slyngebond (ringslinger).
Ingild.	Wiglecus.
Olavus.	Waermundus.
	Uffo.
	Dan timidus.
	Huglecus.
	Frotho vegetus II.
	Dan III.
	Fridlevus celer I.

Frotho legislator III.
Fridlevus II.
Frotho largus IV.
Ingellus.
Olavus.
Frotho V.
Haldan II.

Langfeðyatal.
Oden.
Skiǫldr his son.
Friðleifr his son.
Fridefrode his son.
Havarr his son.
Frode his son.
Varmundr his son.
Olafr his son.
Danr.
Frode his son.
Fridleifr.
Frode his son.
Ingjaldr his son.
Halfdan—brother.
Helgi oc Hroar, sons.
Rolfr Kraki Helgi's son.
Hraerekr Ingiald's son.

Gothic Genealogy.

Genealogy of Gothic kings given by Jordanes, *Get.*
Ch. xiv.

Gapt.
Ulmul.
Augis.
Amal.

Isarna.
Ostrogotha.
Hunuin.
Athal.
Athiulf.
(H)ermenaricus.
Wultuulf brother of Hermenaricus.
Valaravans.
Vinitharius.
Vandalarius.
Theudemer.
Theodericus.

Icelandic Genealogy.

Flateyjarbók, i, p. 27.

GENEALOGY A.

Fródi.
Vermundr enn vitri.
Ólafr enn lítillati.
Danr enn mikillati.
Fródi enn frithsami.

GENEALOGY B.

Fródi.
Hans son Vémundr enn vitri.
Hans dóttir Ólof.
Hon var módir Fróða ens frithsama.

BIBLIOGRAPHY

I. GENERAL WORKS OF REFERENCE

A. M. Chadwick. *The Origin of the English Nation.* Cambridge. 1907.

J. J. Conybeare. *Illustrations of Anglo-Saxon Poetry.* London. 1826.

W. Golther. *Die deutsche Heldensage.* Dresden. 1894.

J. Grimm. *Deutsche Mythologie.* Göttingen. 1835.

W. Grimm. *Deutsche Heldensage.* Göttingen. 1829. 3rd ed. Steig, Gütersloh. 1889.

N. F. S. Grundtvig. *Udsigt over den nordiske oldtids heroiske digtning.* 1867.

O. L. Jiriczek. *Die deutsche Heldensage.* Strassburg. 1898. Transl. (*Northern Hero Legends*) M. Bentinck Smith. London. 1902.

F. Jonsson. *Old Norske Litteraturs Historie.* Copenhagen. 1894–1902.

W. P. Ker. *Epic and Romance.* London. 1897.

R. Kögel. *Geschichte der deutschen Litteratur,* vol. I, Part I. Strassburg. 1894.

G. Körting. *Grundriss der Geschichte der englischen Litteratur.* Münster i. W. 1887.

H. Möller. *Das altenglische Volksepos.* Kiel. 1883.

Mone. *Untersuchungen zur Geschichte der teutschen Heldensage* 1886.

K. Müllenhoff. *Zur Kritik des ags. Volksepos. ZfdA.* 1859, vol. XI, pp. 272 ff.

—— *Zeugnisse und Excurse zur deutschen Heldensage,* in *ZfdA.* 1865. Vol. XII, pp. 253—386.

A. Olrik. *Danmarks Heltedigtning.* Copenhagen. 1903.

H. Paul. *Grundriss der germanischen Philologie.* Strassburg. 1891– .

Raszmann. *Die deutsche Heldensage und die Heimat.* 1857–8.

L. Uhland. *Zur deutschen Heldensage,* in Pfeiffer's *Germania.* Vol. II, pp. 344 ff. 1857.

—— *Schriften zur Geschichte der Dichtung und Sage.* 1866–70.

K. Weinhold. *Die Riesen des germanischen Mythus. Wien. S. B.* XXVI, 253 ff.

J. C. Zeuss. *Die Deutschen und die Nachbarstämme.* Munich. 1837.

II. WORKS ON THE OLD ENGLISH HEROIC POEMS

Text of all the poems in C. W. M. Grein's *Bibliothek der angelsächsischen Poesie.* Göttingen. 1857. 2nd ed. R. P. Wülcker. Cassel. 1881–3.

The *Beowulf.* (Editions in chronological order.)

G. J. Thorkelin. *De Danorum Rebus Gestis Secul.,* vols. III, IV. Copenhagen. 1815.

J. M. Kemble. *The Anglo-Saxon Poems of Beowulf, the Traveller's Song, and the Battle of Finnsburh.* London. 1833. 2nd ed. 1835.

B. Thorpe. *The Anglo-Saxon Poems of Beowulf, the Scôp or Gleeman's Tale, and the Fight at Finnsburg.* Oxford. 1855.

S. Grundtvig. *Beowulf's Beorh.* Copenhagen. 1861.

M. Heyne. Text with complete Glossary. Paderborn. 1863.

T. Arnold. *Beowulf—a heroic poem of the VIIIth century* (text and translation). London. 1876.

J. A. Harrison and R. Sharp. *Beowulf, with text and glossary on the basis of M. Heyne's text.* Boston, U.S.A. 1882. 4th ed. 1895.

A. Holder. *Beowulf. Text and Glossary.* Freiburg im Breisgau. 1884.

A. J. Wyatt. *Beowulf, with text, index of proper names and glossary.* 1894.

M. Trautmann. *Beowulf.* Bonn. 1904.

F. Holthausen. *Beowulf.* Heidelberg. 1906.

English translations of the *Beowulf* by

J. M. Kemble. London. 1837.

B. Thorpe⎱
T. Arnold⎰ in eds. quoted above.

H. W. Lumsden. In *Modern Rhymes*. London. 1881.

J. Zupitza. Facsimile of the entire *Beowulf* MS. E.E.T.S., London. 1882.

J. M. Garnett. *Beowulf and the Fight at Finnsburg translated into verse*. Boston, U.S.A. 1882.

J. Earle. *The Deeds of Beowulf done into modern prose, with Introduction and Notes*. Oxford. 1892.

J. Leslie Hall. (Poetical translation.) Boston, U.S.A. 1892.

W. Morris and A. J. Wyatt. *The Tale of Beowulf* (in archaic verse). Kelmscott Press, 1895. London. 1898.

J. R. Clark Hall. *Beowulf and the Fight at Finnsburg, in Modern English Prose*. London. 1901.

C. B. Tinker. *The Translations of Beowulf—a Critical Bibliography*. New York. 1903.

C. G. Child. New York. 1904.

Beowulf. Works Explanatory and Illustrative.

T. Arnold. *Notes on Beowulf.* 1898.

G. Binz. *PBB.* vol. xx, pp. 141 ff. *Sceaf und seine Nachkommen.*

R. C. Boer. *Arkiv f. nord. Fil.* vol. xv, pp. 19—88.

L. Botkine. *Beowulf, Analyse hist. et géogr.* Paris. 1876.

K. Bouterwek. *Das Beowulfslied. Germ.* vol. I, pp. 385—418. 1856.
—— *Zur Kritik des Blds.* in *ZfdA.* vol. XI, pp. 59—113.

A. Brandl. *Der gegenwärtige Stand der Beowulfforschung. Arch.* vol. CVIII, pp. 152 ff.

S. Bugge. *PBB.* vol. XII, pp. 1—112, 370—5. *Ark. f. nord. Fil.* vol. I, pp. 1 ff. *ZPH.* vol. VIII, pp. 287—9 ; vol. IV, p. 192.

H. Dederich. *Hist. und Geogr. Studien zum ags. Beowulfsliede.* Köln. 1877.

F. Detter. *Über die Heathobeardan im Beowulf. Verhandl. d. Wien. Phil. Vers.* 1893. pp. 404 ff.

L. Ettmüller. *Beowulf—Einleitung.* Zurich. 1840.
—— *Carmen de Beovulfi Gautarum regis rebus gestis.* Zurich. 1875.

H. Gering. *Der Beowulf und die isländische Grettissage. Anglia.* Vol. III, pp. 74 ff.

C. W. M. Grein. *Die historischen Verhältnisse des Beowulfliedes* in *Ebert's Jahrbuch für romanische und englische Litteratur,* vol. IV, pp. 260—285.

J. Grimm. *Über das Verbrennen der Leichen. Abh. d. Berl. Akad.* 1849. pp. 191 ff. (*Kl. Schr.* vol. II, pp. 221 ff.); *ZfdA.* vol. III, p. 151.

N. F. S. Grundtvig. *Bjowulfs Drape.* Copenhagen. 1820.

A. Heusler. *Zur Skjöldungen Dichtung. ZfdA.* vol. XLVIII, p. 57.

—— Review of Olrik's *Danmarks Heltedigtning. AfdA.* vol. XXX, p. 26.

M. Heyne. *Die Halle Heorot.* Paderborn. 1864.

J. M. Kemble. *Über die Stammtafel der Westsachsen.* Munich. 1836.

Fr. Klaeber. *Hrothulf. M. L. N.* vol. XX, pp. 9 ff.

F. Kluge. *Beowulf und die Hrolfssage. Eng. St.* vol. XXII, p. 144. *PBB.* vol. IX, pp. 187 ff.

R. Kögel. *Der Name Beowulf. ZfdA.* vol. XXXVII, pp. 268 ff.

A. Köhler. *Die Einleitung des Beowulfs und die beiden Episoden von Heremod. ZPH.* vol. II, pp. 305 ff.

Th. Krüger. *Zum Beowulfliede.* Bromberg. 1884.

—— *Über den Ursprung und die Entwickelung des Beowulfliedes.* Archiv, vol. LXXI, pp. 129 ff.

—— *Geschichte der Beowulf Kritik.* (Cf. Wülcker's *Grundriss,* p. 675.)

L. Laistner. *Nebelsagen.* Stuttgart. 1879.

H. Leo. *Beowulf.* Halle. 1839.

F. Moorman. *The Interpretation of Nature in English Poetry.* (*Q. F.* 95.) Strassburg. 1903.

K. Müllenhoff. *Beowulf.* Berlin. 1889.

—— *Sceaf und seine Nachkommen*⎰ *ZfdA.* vol. VII, pp. 410 ff.
—— *Der Mythus von Beowulf* ⎱

—— *Die innere Geschichte des Beowulfs. ZfdA.* vol. XIV, p. 242.

G. Neckel. *Studien uber Frothi. ZfdA.* vol. XLVIII, pp. 163 ff.

A. Olrik. *Kilderne til Sakses Oldhistorie,* vol. II. Copenhagen. 1894.

F. York Powell. *Recent Beowulf Literature. Academy,* Nos. 648—654. Oct. 4th and Nov. 15th, 1884.

E. Rickert. *The Old English Offa Sage*. *Mod. Philol.* vol. II, pp. 29 ff., 321 ff.

G. Sarrazin. *Beowulf Studien*. Berlin. 1888.

—— *Die Beowulfsage in Dänemark*. *Anglia*, vol. IX, pp. 195 ff.

—— *Beowa und Böthvar, ib.* vol. IX, pp. 200 ff.

—— *Neue Beowulf-Studien*. *Eng. St.* vol. XVI, pp. 79 ff., XXXIII, pp. 221 ff., XXXV, p. 10.

—— *Rolf Krake und sein Vetter*. *Eng. St.* vol. XXIV, p. 144.

—— *Die Hirschhalle*. *Angl.* vol. XIX, pp. 368 ff.

—— *Der Schauplatz des B.-lieds und die Heimat des Dichters*. *PBB.* vol. XI, pp. 159 ff.

—— *Altnordisches in Beowulf*. *PBB.* vol. XI, pp. 528 ff.

M. Schultze. *Altheidnisches in der ags. Poesie, speziell im Beowulfsliede*. Berlin. 1877.

E. Sievers. *Berichte der kgl. sächs. Gesellschaft der Wissenschaften*, vol. XLVII, pp. 175—192.

—— *Zur Rythmik des germ. Alliterationsverses*. *PBB.* vol. X, pp. 209—451 ff.

—— *Zu Beowulf*. *PBB.* vol. IX, pp. 135 ff., 370, vol. XVII, p. 2.

—— *Die Heimat des Beowulfdichters*. *PBB.* vol. XI, pp. 354 ff.

W. W. Skeat. *The Name Beowulf*. *Acad.* 1877, vol. I, p. 163. *Journal of Phil.*, July, 1886.

K. Stjerna. *Vendel och Vendelkråka*. *Arkiv f. nord. Fil.* N. R. XVII, pp. 71 ff.

H. Suchier. *Über die Sage von Offa und Thrytho*. *PBB.* vol. IV, pp. 500 ff.

B. ten Brink. *Beowulf (Q. F.* 62). Strassburg. 1888.

The Finn Fragment in addition to those mentioned above.

G. Binz. *PBB.* vol. XX, pp. 179—186.

R. C. Boer. *ZfdA.* vol. XLVII, pp. 125—160.

S. Bugge. *PBB.* vol. XII, pp. 20—37.

L. Ettmüller. *Beowulf*. Zurich. 1840. pp. 35—39.

C. W. M. Grein. *Ebert's Jahrbuch*, vol. IV, pp. 269—271.

G. Hickes. *Linguarum Septentrionalium Thesaurus*. Oxford. 1705.

M. H. Jellinek. *PBB.* vol. XV, pp. 428—431.

R. Kögel. *Op. cit.* pp. 163—167.

280   BIBLIOGRAPHY

H. Möller. *Op. cit.* pp. 46—102.

K. Müllenhoff. *ZfdA.* vol. XI, pp. 281—3.

M. Rieger. *ZfdA.* vol. XVIII, pp. 9—13.

H. Schilling. *M. L. N.* vol. I, pp. 178—183, II, 291—9, VI, 178 ff., VII, 231 ff.

Swiggett. *M. L. N.* vol. XX, pp. 169—171.

B. ten Brink. In Paul's *Grdr.* vol. I, pp. 445—-450.

M. Trautmann. *B. B. z. A.* vol. VIII, pp. 1—64.

Widsith.

For editions, see under *Beowulf* (Kemble, Thorpe, also in Conybeare, *Illustrations of Anglo-Saxon Poetry*).

G. Binz. *PBB.* vol. XX, pp. 141—223.

K. Bojunga. *PBB.* vol. XVI, pp. 545—548.

L. Ettmüller. *Scôpes Widsith,* p. 11. Pub. 1839.

F. Gummere. *M. L. N.* vol. IV, pp. 418—423.

H. Möller. *Op. cit.* pp. 1—39.

K. Müllenhoff. *Nordalbingische Studien,* vol. I, pp. 148, 165. In *Beowulf,* 1889.

—— *ZfdA.* vol. XI, pp. 275—294, and *Nachtrag in Bibl. der ags. Poesie,* vol. I, p. 401.

B. ten Brink. In Paul's *Grdr.* vol. II, pp. 538—545.

Deor.

English Translations by

Conybeare. *Op. cit.*

Morley. *English Writers,* vol. I, Part 1, p. 278 f.

Sweet. In Warton's *Hist. of Engl. Poetry,* 4th ed. vol. II, pp. 8—13. And in *Atlantic Monthly,* vol. LXVII, p. 287 (Feb. 1891).

Depping et Fr. Michel. *Véland le forgeron.* 1833.

F. Detter. *Arkiv f. nord. Fil.* vol. III, pp. 309 ff.

J. Golther. *Germ.* vol. XXXIII, p. 449.

R. Heinzel. *Über die Ostgermanische Heldensage* (*Wien. S. B.* 119). Vienna. 1889.

O. Jiriczek. *Die Deutsche Heldensage,* pp. 1—54.

Klee. *Zur Hildesage.* Leipzig. 1873.

Kuhn. *Sagen aus Westfalen,* vol. I, p. 42 f.

E. H. Meyer. *AfdA.* vol. XIII, pp. 23 ff.

—— *Indogermanische Mythen,* vol. II, pp. 678 ff.

K. Meyer. *Germania,* vol. XIV, pp. 283 ff.

—— *Die Dietrichsage in ihrer geschichtlichen Entwickelung.* Basel.
1868.

K. Müllenhoff. *ZfdA.* vol. XI, pp. 272—5, VII, 530 f., XII, 261.

M. Rieger. *Germania,* vol. III, p. 176.

J. W. Tupper. *M. L. N.* vol. X, pp. 125—7.

Waldere.

H. Althof. *Das Waltharilied übersetzt und erläutert.* Leipzig.
1896.

S. Bugge. *Til de oldengelske digte om Beowulf og Waldere. ZPH.*
vol. VIII, pp. 40, 287.

P. J. Cosijn. *De Waldere Fragmenten.* Arnstedt. 1895. *Akad.
der Wiss. Letterkunde.* 3rd Reeks, Deel XII.

F. Dieter. *Anglia,* vol. X, pp. 227—234, XI, 159—170.

J. Grimm. *ZfdA.* vol. V, p. 2.

—— *Lateinische Gedichte des X^{en} und XI^{en} Jahrhunderts,* pp. 101 ff.
Göttingen. 1838.

Heinzel. *Über die Walthari Sage. Wien. S. B.,* CXVII, II. 1888.

R. Kögel. *Op. cit.* vol. I, Part 1, pp. 235 ff., I, 2, 278 ff.

M. D. Learned. *The Sage of Walther of Aquitaine.* Baltimore.
1892.

K. Müllenhoff. *ZfdA.* vol. X, pp. 163 ff., XII, 264 ff., XXX, 255 ff.

Victor Scheffel und Alfred Holder. *Waltharius. Ein lateinisches
Gedicht des X^{en} Jahrhunderts.* Stuttgart. 1874.

Scherer. *Der Wasgenstein in der Sage. Kl. Schr.* Vol. I, pp. 543 ff.
1874.

B. Sijmons. In Paul's *Grdr.* vol. III, pp. 703—709.

G. Stephens. *Two Leaves of King Waldere's Lay.* London. 1860.

M. Trautmann. *B. B. z. A.* vol. XI, pp. 133—138.

Other Works useful for Reference.

Ammianus Marcellinus. *Historical Works* (translation from Latin
by C. D. Yonge in Bohn's Classical Library. London. 1862).

Anglo-Saxon Chronicle. Ed. by John Earle and Charles Plummer.
Oxford. 1892.

Corpus Poeticum Boreale. G. Vigfusson and F. York Powell. Oxford. 1883.

Deutsches Heldenbuch. 5 Bde. Berlin. 1866—73.

—— Fr. von der Hagen. Leipzig. 1855.

Diutiska. Denkmäler deutscher Sprache u. Litteratur. G. Graff. Stuttgart und Tübingen. 1826—9.

Edda (The Older). *Edda Saemundar.* Ed. Th. Möbius. Leipzig. 1860.

—— *Saemundar Eddahins Fróda.* Ed. S. Bugge. Christiania. 1867.

—— *Edda-lieder.* Altnordische Gedichte heroischen und mythischen Inhalts. Ed. F. Jonsson. Halle. 1888—90.

—— *Die Lieder der Edda.* Herausgegeben u. erklärt von B. Sijmons. Halle. 1906.

Edda (The Younger). *Edda Snorra Sturlasonar.* Th. Jonsson. Copenhagen. 1875.

—— *Die prosaische Edda* im Auszuge, nebst *Vǫlsungasaga* und *Nornagestspáttr.* Ed. G. Wilken. Paderborn. 1883.

Flateyjarbók. 3 Bde. Ed. C. R. Unger. Christiania. 1868.

Fragmenta Historicorum Graecorum. Ed. K. Müller. Paris. 1841—52.

Gudrun. Ein mhd. Gedicht. Ed. B. Sijmons. Halle. 1883. In Paul's *Altdeutsche Textbibliothek.* Ed. E. Martin. Halle. 1883.

—— *A mediaeval epic.* Transl. M. P. Nichols. Boston, U.S.A. 1899.

Gudrun and Other Stories from the epics of the Middle Ages (containing also the stories of Hilde, Beowulf, Roland, Walther and Hildegund). John Gibb. London. 1881.

Jordanes (Jornandes), sixth century. *De origine actibusque Getarum.*

J. Langebek. *Scriptores Rerum Danicarum medii aevi.* 8 vols. Hafniae. 1772—1834.

Matthew Paris. *Historia Major.* Ed. W. Watts. London. 1640.

J. P. Migne. *Patrologiae cursus completus.* Series I, vols. 1—79, Paris, 1844—61. Series II, vols. 80—217, Paris, 1844—61. Series Graeca. Paris. 1857.

Nibelungenlied. Der Nibelunge Not und die Klage. Ed. K. Lachmann. Berlin. 1851.

—— *The Fall of the Niblungs.* Transl. M. Armour, in Everyman's Library. London. 1908.

Oldest English Texts. H. Sweet. E.E.T.S. 83. London. 1885.

G. H. Pertz. *Monumenta Germaniae Historica.* Hanover. 1826.

Pliny (The Elder). *Natural History.*

Procopius. *De bello Gothico.*

Ptolemy. *Geographia.* Ed. K. Muller. Paris. 1883—1901.

Recueil des historiens des Gaules. Ed. M. Bouquet. Paris. 1739.

Rerum Anglicorum Scriptores. Ed. Sir Henry Savile. London. 1596. Frankfort. 1601.

Rolls Series. *The Chronicles and Memorials of Great Britain and Ireland during the Middle Ages, published by authority of Her Majesty's Treasury, and under the direction of the Master of the Rolls.* London. 1858- .

Saga. *Fornaldar Sǫgur Nordrlanda.* Ed. C. C. Rafn. Copenhagen. 1829.

—— *Grettissage Ásmundarsonar.* Ed. R. C. Boer in *Altnordische Sagabibliothek.* Halle. 1900.

—— *The Story of Grettir the Strong.* Transl. from Icelandic by E. M. and W. Morris. London. 1900.

—— *Saga Thithriks konugs af Bern.* Ed. C. R. Unger. Christiania. 1853.

—— *Wilkinasage* (i.e. *Thiðrekssaga*) *und Niflungasaga.* Transl. F. v. d. Hagen. *Altdeutsche u. Altnordische Heldensagen.* Breslau. 1872.

——- *Heimskringla.* Ed. C. R. Unger. Christiania. 1868.

—— *Norégs Konunga Sǫgur.* Ed. F. Jonsson. Copenhagen. 1893—1900.

Saxo Grammaticus. *Saxoni Grammatici Gesta Danorum.* Ed. A. Holder. Strassburg. 1886.

—— *Saxo.* Books I—IX. Transl. into English by O. Elton. David Nutt. London. 1894.

Tacitus. *Germania.*

Translations of Anglo-Saxon Poetry. A. S. Cook and C. B. Tinker. Boston, U.S.A. 1902.

For EU product safety concerns, contact us at Calle de José Abascal, 56–1°,
28003 Madrid, Spain or eugpsr@cambridge.org.

 www.ingramcontent.com/pod-product-compliance
Ingram Content Group UK Ltd.
Pitfield, Milton Keynes, MK11 3LW, UK
UKHW012330130625
459647UK00009B/175